# Joining Forces

# Joining Forces

## Making One Plus One Equal Three in Mergers, Acquisitions, and Alliances

Mitchell Lee Marks

Philip H. Mirvis

Jossey-Bass Publishers • San Francisco

Substantial discounts on bulk quantities of Jossey-Bass books are available to corporations, professional associations, and other organizations. For details and discount information, contact the special sales department at Jossey-Bass Inc., Publishers (415) 433-1740; Fax (800) 605-2665.

For sales outside the United States, please contact your local Simon & Schuster International Office.

Jossey-Bass Web address: http://www.josseybass.com

TCF Manufactured in the United States of America on Lyons Falls Turin Book. This paper is acid-free and 100 percent totally chlorine-free.

**Library of Congress Cataloging-in-Publication Data**

Marks, Mitchell Lee.
 Joining forces : making one plus one equal three in mergers, acquisitions, and alliances / Mitchell Lee Marks, Philip H. Mirvis.
 — 1st ed.
   p.   cm. — (The Jossey-Bass business & management series)
 Includes index.
 ISBN 0-7879-0350-7 (alk. paper)
 1. Consolidation and merger of corporations.   2. Consolidation and merger of corporations—United States.   3. Strategic alliances (Business)   4. Strategic alliances—United States.
 I. Mirvis, Philip H., 1951–     .   II. Title.   III. Series.
 HD2746.5.M288    1998                                    97-33872

FIRST EDITION
*HB Printing*   10 9 8 7 6 5 4 3 2 1

The Jossey-Bass
Business & Management Series

# Contents

# Preface

Look at the business section in any newspaper and you will see the feverish pace at which mergers, acquisitions, and alliances are occurring. One day found three announcements of unions between major companies: Hewlett-Packard and Netscape Communications formed a strategic alliance to share technology and product development; Phillips Petroleum and Conoco reported plans to merge their gasoline refining and marketing operations; and AT&T and Unisource agreed to combine their European operations to create a telecommunications and multimedia giant to compete with rival alliances already taking shape.

And this was a relatively slow day for combinations! On August 26, 1996, twenty-five acquisitions were announced. The fifteen transactions whose terms were reported had a total value of $19.1 billion, but two months later, British Telecom's $22 billion bid to acquire MCI Communications eclipsed the value of all fifteen combined (which itself was then surpassed by WorldCom's $33 billion offer).

So far in the 1990s, thirty thousand mergers and acquisitions have been consummated in the United States, at a total cost in excess of $1.5 trillion dollars. This exceeds the pace of merger activity in the 1980s, when an estimated 25 percent of the U.S. workforce was affected.[1] Worldwide, the volume of merger and acquisition activity in 1996 added up to $1 trillion. A survey of twelve thousand managers, spanning twenty-five countries on six continents, found that 45 percent of companies employing more than a thousand people had been involved in a merger, acquisition, or divestiture between 1989 and 1991.[2] As for strategic alliances, precise figures regarding frequency are not easily calculated, as many of these ventures are not publicly announced. Booz Allen estimates that twenty-five thousand alliances formed in 1995.[3] And a recent survey of seven hundred CEOs of start-up and fast-growing companies found that nearly 90 percent had begun forming alliances. It's easy to conclude that acquisitions and alliances have become an integral part of corporate strategy.

Not only do acquisitions and alliances occur with greater frequency, but they affect entire industries. The health care, financial services, grocery, and chemical industries are being reshaped through combinations. Traditional boundaries separating telecommunications, computing technology, and entertainment are blurring as key players converge through acquisitions and alliances. These industrywide consolidations expose people to constant change in their work lives. As two hospitals were merging, their parent company itself agreed to combine with another health care holding company. Still attempting to recover from the fallout of their merger, hospital managers and employees described themselves as "shell shocked" at the pace and scope of changes coming their way.

## What This Book Is About

This book is concerned with a specific breed of merger, acquisition, or alliance: the type that attempts to build some strength or capacity greater than that present in the partners as independent organizations. Getting one plus one to equal three calls for sound strategy and a careful management process to guide identification and attainment of true and productive synergy. Opportunistic deals, combinations made purely for cost-cutting reasons, or acquisitions meant more to satisfy a CEO's ego than to enact a cogent business strategy are not likely to enhance the partners' abilities to achieve their desired business and financial results. Slamming two organizations together and eliminating redundancies may achieve one-time-only cost savings, but does the organization reap sustainable gains in ability to compete over the long haul?

Consider that hospital merger. If the primary aim is to reduce an oversupply of hospital beds, how has the merger helped the organization's ability to compete? In this case, the CEO set out to create a new and better way to deliver affordable health care services in her community. Each partner maintained general services but focused its energies on diagnosing and treating distinct ailments and clientele, to minimize duplication of expensive technology and services. The combined hospital emerged as the "health care provider of choice" in the community. Accomplishing this required clear and intelligent strategy in the choice of partners; a thoughtful and careful process for identifying each hospital's areas of specialization and dealing with all of the professional egos; and sensitivity to the human, organizational, and cultural dynamics involved.

The message is that if you're doing a deal, do it right. Be thoughtful in planning the combination, be ready for the multitude of integration problems that inevitably arise, be prepared for the drain on resources and distractions from performance, and be sensitive to the breadth and depth of human emotions triggered as previously separate organizations come together. Combining two into one is an extremely difficult task. Just doing a deal doesn't make it work; nor does a sensible strategy ensure operational success. Robert Allen of AT&T had a good idea in acquiring NCR, but he couldn't make it work; and AT&T's alliance with Olivetti, a match seemingly made in heaven, ended up hellish in divorce.

Mismanaged combinations have negative—not merely neutral—effects on organizations and their people. In 1991, Borland International paid $440 million for Ashton-Tate, then the dominant supplier of personal computer database software. Borland was intent on doing the deal, and due diligence did not reveal that Ashton-Tate had started to fall behind in its customer commitments. As product delays continued, Borland's inability to integrate the acquisition swiftly sank it. Borland went on to report huge losses for four straight years.

Human and cultural dynamics encumber every combination. Few deals made more sense on paper than the 1993 merger of Price Club and Costco Wholesale to create Price/Costco Inc.— making it the second largest operator of warehouse clubs after Wal-Mart's Sam's Club. The economies promised by the two companies coming together were compelling. But the real estate developers running Price and the dyed-in-the wool retailers heading Costco never hit it off. Rather than attempt to work together, Costco executives left en masse less than a year into the marriage. Even alliances that do not involve the full integration of partners can end up in bad blood. Viacom and MCA brought their alliance differences to court to settle a conflict over their USA Network partnership before MCA's parent company, Seagrams, bought out Viacom's stake.

Memories of previously mismanaged combinations linger to color people's views of current ones. As Wells Fargo gained the upper hand in a bidding war for First Interstate Bank, top talent from the target bolted without giving Wells a chance to declare its intentions. These executives vividly recalled what newspapers referred to as the "brutal" way that Wells handled the human side of its takeover of Crocker Bank years earlier. Even when good intentions are presumed, experienced managers find that communications in a combination consume two or three times as much time as for an independent initiative.[4]

## What This Book Offers

Corporate leaders in a combination need to focus on sending the right message and on spending their time doing the right things. Operations managers need tools and an organizing structure that helps them identify and realize the synergies promised. Employees need to understand why the combination is happening and how they can contribute meaningfully to its success. This book offers guidance to each of these groups, in three areas:

1. Insight into just how difficult these events are to manage and how much impact they have on organizations, people, cultures, business performance, and customers
2. Understanding of the resources required to manage combinations well
3. Knowledge of what it takes to make a combination yield something more than is present prior to joining forces

The book is organized in five parts. The first chapters look at the merger, acquisition, and alliance process overall. Chapter One reviews the factors driving combination activity today, the specific reasons companies combine, the outcomes, and how value is created, plus principles of change management that apply to almost every deal. Chapter Two details the dynamics that set mergers, acquisitions, and alliances on the right or wrong course.

The core of the book is the process for extracting value from a combination. Part Two highlights what has to be managed in the precombination phase to achieve success. Chapter Three describes precombination planning and cultural due diligence practices that bring strategy to life in selecting a partner and determining the desired degree of integration. Chapter Four then looks at the emotional side of dealings and offers methods for preparing people psychologically for the ensuing combination.

Part Three examines the combination phase, with Chapter Five discussing top management's leadership role. Chapter Six reviews the work of transition teams in studying and developing opportunities for value creation. Chapter Seven describes ways to engage the overall workforce in the combination process, minimize the stress and uncertainty that envelop them, and maximize their understanding of and support for the combination. Chapter Eight takes a deeper look at the sources and symptoms of culture clash in combinations and the requirements for building a new culture to support the objectives of the combined organization.

Part Four focuses on the postcombination phase. Chapter Nine describes how to integrate structures, policies, and practices and reinforce the desired culture. Chapter Ten examines how to help employees adapt to postcombination realities and how to build effective work teams.

Part Five summarizes the combination process. Chapter Eleven discusses methods for tracking its progress and creating opportunities to learn from current practices in order to manage future ones more effectively. Chapter Twelve reviews lessons and best practices of successful combination management.

This book is for people who lead, manage, supervise, work in, study, or advise organizations engaged in mergers, acquisitions, and alliances. It shows leaders what it takes to distinguish successful combinations from typical ones, to yield genuine gain. The book helps managers and supervisors use the transition process as an opportunity to identify and implement new and better ways of approaching work, as well as understand how to contend with the dual tasks of contributing to the combination while running the ongoing business. For all employees, the book raises awareness of the varied emotions people experience and how a combination impacts culture and accustomed ways of doing things. Importantly, it helps individuals understand and act upon what they *do* control (and accept what they *do not*) during the transition from precombination to postcombination. For those studying or consulting to organizations engaged in mergers, acquisitions, or alliances, the book offers a methodology for contending with the downside of a combination while mining the upside. It draws upon behavioral science, management, and organizational theory to complement the authors' practical experience gained over many years.

## A New Age of Mergers, Acquisitions, and Alliances

Our earlier volume, *Managing the Merger,* presented then-current theory and research about the human side of corporate combinations in the 1980s. We chronicled our ten-year study of Graphic Controls Corporation, a manufacturer of recording charts and medical instruments, and the trials of its chief executive, William M. E. Clarkson, as the firm struggled to retain control over homegrown business practices and a familylike corporate culture following a "white knight" acquisition by media giant Times Mirror. Since then, a new generation of management has repurchased the company through a leveraged buyout. In that book, we also documented W. Michael Blumenthal's leadership in merging Burroughs and Sperry to form Unisys. The combination went great guns for its first two years—aided by a carefully managed integration program—but thereafter foundered in the continuing shakeout of the mainframe computing industry. IBM, you will recall, lost over $50 billion in market value during this period and shed nearly two hundred thousand jobs.

The 1990s are, as they say, a whole new ballgame. Hostile takeovers are less in vogue and most deals are being planned and executed by corporate managers, rather than arbitrageurs or money men doing the financing with junk bonds. More often than not, companies are now looking to buy or partner with another firm to create long-term value, not merely to sell off assets or make a short-run killing. Indeed, *Joining Forces* concentrates on the value-creating combinations wherein partners aim to grow their business rather than just cut costs and consolidate.

Recent years have also witnessed new forms of combination. Most firms have abandoned notions of creating value through conglomeration, where they own a mix of unrelated businesses and manage them like a portfolio of assets. Today the strategic emphasis is to build on core competencies and "stick to the knitting,"

through industry-related mergers and acquisitions. To be successful, these combinations require careful alignment of product lines,
distribution channels, and, often, full-scale joining of the two companies' engineering, manufacturing, sales, and services areas. Additionally, companies try to gain new technologies and prospect
new markets by creating strategic alliances and joint ventures. In
these combinations, firms codesign or comarket products and services and often have executives from the two sides comanage the
venture. Timeworn analogies of marriage and warfare do not apply
to these deals. Alliance partners often have to learn to *both* cooperate *and* compete with one another.

Combinations of core competencies, as well as joint ventures
and alliances, put responsibility for leading and managing integration deeper down into companies. Although the CEO and the
board of directors typically study and sign off on the selection of a
partner and oversee the dealings, the drive to create real value is
led by the heads of business units and functions, along with their
management teams and frontline staff. For a merger or acquisition
to pay off, leadership has to fully and successfully integrate partners all through the ranks and to manage the often conflicting political and commercial forces surrounding an alliance or joint
venture.

Over the past several years, scholars have firmed up and tested
the theories advanced in our earlier book. Moreover, combination
managers have developed many best practices worthy of emulation. This book refers to theory but emphasizes practice; hopefully, it also provides a sensible roster of do's and don'ts. Mitchell
Lee Marks takes the lead in this edition, speaking to managers at
all levels who face the most complex and challenging job of their
careers.

The contents of this book come from our own experience as
consultants and researchers engaged in combinations. We worked
together in the case of Graphic Controls and Times Mirror, and in
the creation of Unisys. Marks has assisted in many prominent combinations, including Chemical Bank and Manufacturers Hanover;
Lockheed Martin; Matsushita and MCA; Pfizer Animal Health and
SmithKline Beecham; Molson Breweries and Carling O'Keefe; and
Abitibi-Price and Stone-Consolidated. In addition to cases described
in the earlier volume, Mirvis has worked with the combinations of

Hewlett Packard and Apollo; IBM and Lotus; Hexcel, Ciba, and Hercules; Boeing, Rockwell, and McDonnell Douglas; and the alliance between Ameritech and GE Information Systems. Both authors have also assisted in several other smaller deals.

With experience in more than fifty combinations over the last fifteen years, we have had the opportunity to work with many gifted and insightful colleagues in studying and facilitating the combination process. They have greatly influenced the ideas in this book. We are especially indebted to Peter Lawton for his ideas and friendship. Additionally, we very much appreciate the excellent work of Cedric Crocker, Byron Schneider, JoAnne Skinner, Judith Hibbard, Nathalie Mainland-Smith, Cheryl Greenway, Julianna Gustafson, and their colleagues at Jossey-Bass, as well as Tom Finnegan and Duane Cramer.

San Francisco, California                    MITCHELL LEE MARKS
Sandy Spring, Maryland                       PHILIP H. MIRVIS
October 1997

# The Authors

MITCHELL LEE MARKS is a management consultant based in San Francisco. His areas of expertise include CEO coaching, senior team development, organizational effectiveness, management development, human resource management, corporate culture, and strategic planning and implementation of organizational change. He works extensively with firms planning and implementing mergers, restructurings, and other transitions. He is recognized internationally for developing innovative approaches to achieving desired business results during transition.

Marks earned his B.A. degree in psychology at the University of California, Santa Cruz, and M.A. and Ph.D. in organizational psychology from the University of Michigan. Previously, he was national practice group leader in human resources management for William M. Mercer, Inc., and senior director at the Delta Consulting Group. He was founding director of the doctoral program in organizational psychology at the California School of Professional Psychology in Los Angeles and served on the faculties of the University of California, Irvine and California State University. He has lectured at the Harvard Business School and Smithsonian Institution and has presented to business, academic, and professional groups. He is the author of *From Turmoil to Triumph* and coauthor of *Managing the Merger,* along with numerous articles in management and scholarly journals. Marks's work has been reported in *The Wall Street Journal, Fortune, U.S. News & World Report, Business Week, The New York Times, The Washington Post,* and *Sports Illustrated,* as well as on the *MacNeil Lehrer News Hour, NBC Nightly News, CNBC,* and other television programs.

PHILIP H. MIRVIS is an organizational researcher and consultant based in Sandy Spring, Maryland. He is also a professor in the Graduate School of Business Administration of the University of

Michigan, where he teaches via distance learning, and visiting professor of strategic and international management at the London Business School. His research concerns human behavior in organizations and focuses on the changing character of the workforce and workplaces. He consults with organizations and communities internationally.

Mirvis received his B.A. from Yale University in administrative science and M.A. and Ph.D. degrees from the University of Michigan in organizational psychology. He has been with the Center for Applied Social Science, Boston University, and the Survey Research Center, Institute for Social Research, University of Michigan; he is also board cochair of the Foundation for Community Encouragement. He has published widely for academic and professional audiences; edited, authored, or coauthored several books, including *Failures in Organization Development and Change, The Cynical Americans* (Jossey-Bass, 1989), *Building the Competitive Workforce,* and, with Marks, *Managing the Merger.* Mirvis has lectured in China, India, and Japan and to faculties at leading universities in the United States and Canada.

# Joining Forces

# Part One

# Synergy in Mergers, Acquisitions, and Alliances

## Chapter One

# The Elusive Equation

One plus one equals three. Billions of dollars and millions of jobs hinge on fulfilling this equation and the hope that a combination of two organizations can produce something more than the sum of the parts. Whether it's called synergy, leverage, or efficiency, the prospect of creating value through a combination is touted vigorously in boardrooms and executive suites where top managers and their financial, legal, and strategic advisers conjure up and put together deals.

The concept is alluring: combine the strengths of two organizations to achieve strategic and financial objectives that neither side can accomplish as easily or affordably on its own. The reality, however, is woeful: more than three-quarters of corporate combinations fail to attain projected business results. In fact, most produce higher-than-expected costs and lower-than-acceptable returns. Meanwhile, executive time and operating capital are diverted from internal growth; morale, productivity, and quality often plummet; talented crew members jump ship; and customers go elsewhere. In the great majority of combinations, one plus one yields less than two.

Why do they fare so badly?

Price is a factor. If you pay too much to buy a company or join a partner, the resulting debt load requires massive cost cutting; that prevents companies from investing in ways needed to make a combination pay off. A study of several hundred deals in the first half of the 1990s by *Business Week* and Mercer Management Consulting concluded that inadequate due diligence and lack of a compelling strategy thwarted even combinations that were sensibly financed.[1] Our own research finds that corporate politics and clashing cultures are factors, too. As executives compete for top appointments and clout, as functions do battle over procedures and turf, and as employees angle for better opportunities (or simply to keep their jobs), even well-intentioned pledges of camaraderie and fair play give way to self-promotion and flank protection.

Of course, planning makes a difference—for better or worse. Bankers, lawyers, and industry consultants can certainly help executives gauge whom to partner with or buy, how much to spend, how to structure the transaction, and where to position end products or services in the marketplace. But when it comes to sorting out who gets which jobs, deciding whose methods and systems to use, and actually shaping a combined company culture that will create value, plans don't make or break the combination. It is fundamentally up to the two managements to make their deal work.

From the outset, let us face squarely the reality that most mergers, acquisitions, and alliances have costs. Stress levels can be acute, and workloads exhausting; former colleagues may be fired and careers derailed; corporate cultures often clash; new structures may not align; and selected systems might fail to mesh. These are the typical, predictable, and troubling trials people face when they join in a combination. Managers have to work their way through myriad traumas and tribulations to achieve a "postcombination" organization that is more competitive, efficient, and effective than its prior components. As one senior executive we worked with put it, "Buying is fun; merging is hell."

But the upside is enormous. A recent *Fortune* article, "Why CEOs Are Learning to Love Mergers," says it plainly: competing in a global economy takes scale and scope. This is what's behind the megamergers of the 1990s and many of the strategic alliances. On a more incremental basis, there is the matter of growth: many small high-tech businesses need capital to grow, and more-established firms need these start-ups to grow their top line—hence the record number of acquisitions in high tech and other growth fields. And there is the matter of leveraging competencies and technologies. Industry is giving birth to "cooperative competition," whereby companies may compete with one another in some arenas but do a joint venture in others. In many instances, such ventures are but a first step toward eventual acquisition by one or another partner, or they may result in a spin-off business that is then sold to another firm. In either case, what better way to prospect in a new market area, gain some know-how, and make some money?

This book shows how to make one plus one equal three. Our focus here is not on financing deals, the legal ins-and-outs, or corporate strategy per se, but on the flesh-and-blood factors that make combinations succeed. Using principles and practices derived from successful cases, we describe why and how executives have joined forces successfully. We also select some unsuccessful cases, as these can be instructive and humbling. The companies we profile achieved their strategic and financial objectives by building *productive capacity:* searching for and locking in better ways of doing business. They were led by executives who took care to understand the vagaries of putting companies together; were willing to unite two groups of managers to plan for and build their new organization; and were sensitive to the human, organizational, and cultural issues that had to be addressed along the way. Most important, these executives wanted to grow their businesses and create added value for their shareholders, customers, employees, and themselves.

## Productive Combination

*Productive combination* results when organizations join forces in a manner that genuinely enhances the capacity of the postcombination organization to achieve its desired strategic and financial objectives. To get one plus one to equal three, a combination must yield more than synergies based on economy of scale and elimination of redundancy. Although financial synergies can contribute significant savings, one-time gains do not leave the organization in a position to maintain a competitive edge in the long run. Neither does a focus on cost cutting tap the full potential of a combination. One study found that in 90 percent of all combinations, initiatives associated with generating revenue drove more value than any other action.[2] Increasing revenue 1 percent has five times greater impact on the bottom line than decreasing operating expenses 1 percent. Yet managers in most combinations spend the bulk of their time searching for ways to reduce operating expenses.

Productive combinations, by contrast, build some capacity or asset that either was not present prior to the combination or was present and is now more fully utilized. This equates to using an acquisition or alliance to promote organizational change. Although many of the practices of executives and companies we have worked with fit under the umbrella of change management, we have found that lessons from generic change management texts do not neatly apply to the specific challenges posed by combinations; nor do they take account of the intellectual and emotional demands that senior executives encounter. Managing change in a combination begins with asking why companies merge, acquire, or form an alliance. This constructs the basis of what has to be planned and prepared for, and then what has to be done, to create value through a combination.

## Reasons for Combining Forces

Many factors prompt executives to acquire or forge alliances with another organization. Perhaps a combination can help a company pursue a strategy that would otherwise be too costly, risky, or technologically advanced to achieve independently. Other times, deals are opportunistic, as when a troubled competitor seeks a savior or when a bidding war ensues after a firm is put into play. Still other times, acquisitions or alliances can be defensive moves to protect market share in a declining or consolidating industry.

The overarching reason for combining with another organization is that the union promotes attainment of strategic goals more quickly and inexpensively than if the company acts on its own. In this era of intense and turbulent change, with rapid technological advance and ever-increasing globalization, combinations also enable organizations to gain flexibility, leverage competencies, share resources, and create opportunities that otherwise are inconceivable.

### Product/Service Diversification

An acquisition or alliance swiftly expands product or service offerings without taking the time or risking the capital required for internal development. Horizontal integration (joining related product or service lines) drives many acquisitions. As an example, Honeywell's acquisition of Lippke Control Systems, the paper-quality sensor division of Ahlstrom in Germany, expanded the buyer's portfolio of products and gave it access to a new $1 billion market.

### Vertical Integration

A company may choose to acquire a supplier to ensure predictability in availability or cost of raw materials, or acquire a distributor to provide a new channel for products or services. In the classic example, a baked goods company acquires a flour miller to control costs and ensure supply of required raw material (backwards integration) or buys a trucking company or chain of retail shops to assure itself of distribution and markets (forward integration). Walt Disney Company's acquisition of Capital Cities/ABC guaranteed a distribution channel for its television programs and film library. A Disney alliance with the city of New York and other corporations redeveloping Manhattan's 42nd Street lines up theaters for Disney's live Broadway productions.

## Globalization

In many instances, acquisitions and alliances propel companies onto the global playing field. American-based Hexcel's merger with the fibers division of Ciba-Geigy doubled its European market share in the composite materials business and gave it a stronger presence in Asia. Cross-border alliances offer firms a wider geographic reach into diverse global markets and allow customized approaches to local markets and individual customers. Sometimes, an alliance with a local company is the only way to enter a country where regulation does not permit wholly owned subsidiaries. This is true in developing countries, especially China, but also when foreign firms want to do business in the United States. Wishing to put global weight on a medium-sized European airline, the leadership of KLM faced U.S. rules prohibiting more than 20 percent ownership of an American carrier. Instead, it entered into a marketing and operating alliance with Northwest Airlines.

## Risk Sharing

A strategic alliance allows a company to undertake activities—ranging from new product introductions to new technology creation—too costly and risky to pursue on its own. As an example, oil companies today form alliances for large and risky exploration projects, in marked contrast to the fierce competition that prevails among their independent marketing operations. More broadly, industry research consortia allow a number of companies to carry out basic research that is beyond the resources of any one of them.

## Access to Technology and Other Resources

Combinations also offer convenient access to specialized resources. An industry alliance allows firms to establish links with a multitude of groups: competitors, suppliers, distributors, customers, and universities. Tapping outside resources allows a firm to build competitive strength by immediately adding knowledge or a specialized competence—with lower capital investment than if the firm develops it alone or acquires it. Concurrent with its acquisition of Ahlstrom's control systems division, for instance, Honeywell formed an alliance with Ahlstrom to automate their paper machines because the German partner recognized that its control expertise had dropped a generation behind the state of the art. Ahlstrom still makes the machines, but Honeywell makes the controls. This is a classic win-win alliance: Ahlstrom gets upgraded technology and Honeywell gets direct access to Ahlstrom's customers.

## Operational Flexibility

A series of acquisitions can give a company a portfolio of assets to deploy in exploring new technologies or attracting new customers. America Online, for instance, acquired an Internet browser manufacturer to gain market share against its rivals. Unfortunately, the company attracted far more customers than could be served reliably and found itself with an unsatisfied and litigious clientele. An alliance also allows an organization to commit limited resources to a business opportunity without requiring a major disruption to ongoing activities. When the consulting arm of Deloitte and Touche sought to bolster its change management consulting business, for instance, leadership realized there was insufficient staff to concurrently work on projects and develop change management consultation. So D & T formed an alliance with a boutique consulting firm to develop the processes and tools for its practice.

## Innovation and Learning

Combinations can also spark innovation by bringing technologies and people together in creating new products and services. IBM's purchase of Lotus depends on achieving such synergies between the two companies' "intellectual capital." In theory, combinations can also facilitate organizational learning through sharing expertise, competencies, and best practices between partners. In practice, interestingly, studies of U.S.-Japanese joint ventures find that although the American side strives for short-run financial returns, their Japanese partners focus on bringing technical and marketing know-how back into the parent company.

## Consolidation

Of course, cost cutting and efficiency are major factors behind many deals. Industrywide consolidation, for instance, drives many deals in health care, utilities, financial services, and the media. As an example, the shrinking military budget has prompted consolidation in the defense industry through such combinations as Lockheed Martin and Northrop Grumman. But cost-cutting motives aside, successful companies take advantage of industry consolidations to grow their top-line sales. PacifiCare's rapid acquisition of health maintenance organizations in the western United States gave it entry into new markets. And Boeing's purchase of a portion of Rockwell, followed by a merger with McDonnell Douglas, tripled its defense business and put it on a par with the other consolidating defense contractors.

## Resource Sharing

Greater economies of scale sometimes enhance organizational effectiveness through better use of resources. This is seen in alliances among health care organizations that share diagnostic and other high-tech equipment requiring large expenditures, and in industry partnerships such as IGA that pool the buying power of small grocers.

## Combination Forms

Organizations can link together in many forms of legal combinations, ranging from a relatively informal network to outright absorption of one entity by another. The forms of combination vary by the depth of commitment and level of investment between the organizations joining forces (Figure 1.1). At the lower end of the continuum is the relatively simple relationship of organization A *licensing* a product, service, or trademark to organization B. Next, a *strategic alliance* is a cooperative effort by two or more entities in pursuit of their own strategic objectives. A *joint venture* goes further, by establishing a complete and separate formal organization with its own structure, governance, workforce, procedures, policies, and culture—while the predecessor companies still exist. At the far end of the continuum are mergers and acquisitions. A *merger* usually involves full combination of two previously separate organizations into a third (new) entity. An *acquisition* typically is the purchase of one organization for incorporation into the new parent firm.

Important differences distinguish these forms. Financial investment and risk increase along the continuum in Figure 1.1, but so does the control held by the lead company. Concurrently, the impact on the target company or lesser partner grows, as do the requirements for integration. The pain of separation swells in moving from a partnership or joint venture to a merger or acquisition. If, for whatever reason, a combination does not live up to its expectations (or if the needs and desires of either party change), then the formal bonds of a merger or acquisition are much more difficult to undo than are the relatively tentative and loose arrangements of an alliance or joint venture.

In an alliance or joint venture, you do not own the other company, nor do you unilaterally control decision making. So key questions need answers: Where is the authority? the power? the influence? Merger implies cooperation, but what may be announced as a merger is rarely perceived as being a combination of equals by the members of at least one of the partnering organizations. People from one side are likely to feel a sense of superiority and greater entitlement, while those from the other side may see themselves in a relatively weak position and fear a perceived threat to themselves and their way of doing things.

Thus, these forms of strategic combination differ in psychological terms as well as legal and financial. A strategic alliance

**Figure 1.1. Types of Strategic Combination.**

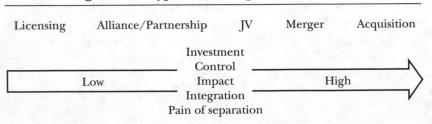

involves commitment and sharing of resources including money, technology, and people, but it is defined by temporary business relationships among autonomous partners. An acquisition is a more dramatic and substantial commitment, entailing complete union of the previously independent partners.

Psychologists Sue Cartwright and Cary Cooper use the metaphor of marriage in describing varying types of organizational combinations.[3] They liken an alliance to two people living together; the partnering individuals or organizations are content to accept each other as they are and maintain their independence. Rather than wishing to impose change or compromise, the partners see the relationship as essentially supportive, with differences and idiosyncracies tolerated and frequently seen as desirable and beneficial to long-term continuance of the association.

In a traditional marriage (in business as with people), one partner assumes dominance—although there may be considerable denial and debate as to which partner perceives that role as being rightfully theirs. Any differences in managerial style and culture identified early in the courtship are likely to be regarded as novel and may even enhance the attractiveness of the marriage partner. However, once the contract is legalized, the dominant partner moves to impose its values and beliefs and make the other more like itself. In conventional organizational marriages—let's call them acquisitions—the acquirer or dominant partner assumes the responsibilities of redesigning the acquired organization and displacing its culture as quickly as possible. It runs into difficulties such as resistance to change when its values and beliefs are not accepted by the target company.

What Cartwright and Cooper call a "modern marriage" is the rarest form of organizational marriage. But it's the type most likely to result in a productive combination, with synergies between partners that create something that cannot be realized independently. The essence of this modern organizational marriage is shared learning: the partners are stronger and more successful together than if they continue to operate separately. Differences in organizational procedures or cultures are seen as potentially adding value to the partnership and are respected and built upon as their partnership unfolds.

Historically, executives have preferred acquisitions over alliances to be in clear control. To be sure, they are very different organizational forms. Alliances involve forming relationships between individuals or organizations that retain substantial independence, in contrast to one side's dominance (at least in the legal domain) over another in an acquisition. Relative to acquisitions, alliances feature less-hierarchical structures, more collaborative cultures, and somewhat equitable distributions of power and authority among the alliance's principal participants. Alliances frequently are formed to produce a specific product or service rather than to affect the overall operations of an organization; they are not company-focused. They frequently involve several different organizations that may, in other settings, actually compete against one another in a specific market. The members of alliances are primarily concerned with improving the quality of the product or service they provide, better serving their mutual customers, and findings ways in which together they can gain a greater share in their mutual market or broaden the scope of the market for which they sometimes compete.[4]

Increasingly, alliances are favored as new business realities make them more advantageous. As we noted, in attractive new foreign markets laws may preclude the possibility of a merger or acquisition. An unstable political situation, unpredictable currency exchange, or unfamiliarity with the country's business environment could make an acquisition too risky. Or the most desirable partner may be open to alliance but not to acquisition.

## Combination Outcomes

Given the many reasons for combination activity and the frequency of combinations in business today, one might guess that mergers, acquisitions, and alliances are prudent, even intelligent, actions that propel organizations to attain their strategic and financial goals. The sad reality, however, is that most acquisitions and alliances fail to produce desired results. Numerous studies confirm that as few as 15 percent achieve their financial objectives.[5] We conclude from these studies that although there are many factors that support acquisition and alliance activity, most organizational combinations fail. Mergers, acquisitions, and alliances do not perform nearly as well as their initial analyses and projections indicate.[6]

To give some flavor to these statistics on success and failure, it is useful to classify combinations based on their value-creation outcomes. Figure 1.2 displays outcomes ranging from unmitigated disasters, through combinations that represent more or less the sum of their constituent parts, to those achieving "breakthrough" synergies.

## Disasters

Disasters result when top talent exits, culture clashes are left unchecked, information technology (IT) systems don't talk to one another, and the combination's planning and implementation are guided by political rather than productive objectives. But it is also the outcome whenever unrealistic expectations are set by overly optimistic precombination analyses. The financial analysts who run the numbers and the strategic planners who derive the rationale think they have isolated the drivers that will most rapidly create shareholder value. Oftentimes, however, the hoped-for synergies and sources of cost reduction are overestimated and the anticipated transition management costs (measured in both time and money) are underestimated. The result is a calamity so intense that, in one-half of all combinations, the acquisition is subsequently divested or the alliance canceled, as in the following case.

> Kmart acquired seven specialty retailers in the early 1990s. In addition to being a financial drain, the acquisitions distracted executive focus from the company's core discount business, and Kmart lost more ground to Wal-Mart Stores. In 1993, Kmart was forced to sell its specialty stores when analysts predicted the company would go into bankruptcy.

**Figure 1.2.  Combination Outcomes.**

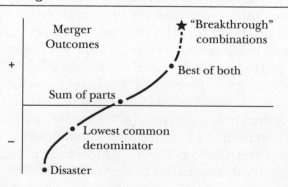

## Lowest Common Denominator

Less dire, yet still substantially disappointing to those with greater expectations, are combinations characterized by *lowest common denominator* thinking. Frequently, trade-offs compromise the quality of decision making and deter achieving anything near the potential of the deal. These trade-offs often center on the desire for expediency trampling over careful transition management; the barest acceptable solution is chosen and rationalized by the objective of "getting on with things." In one consumer products industry combination, for example, entire levels of management were alternated between the two companies: senior vice presidents came from company A, VPs from company B, managers from A, directors from B, and so on. Clearly, excellent performers were let go simply because they had the misfortune of being on the wrong side for their level. Another lowest common denominator combination is First Chicago's 1995 acquisition of NBD Corporation. Here, a meager rationale—some banking industry observers suggest the merger was motivated by First Chicago's fear of being swallowed up by NationsBank—and disparate corporate cultures (a freewheeling money center institution and a conservative middle-market lender) resulted in contention and a series of trade-off decisions on how to put the companies together. While not true disasters, lowest common denominator combinations still fail to make one plus one equal two.

## The Sum of the Parts

Here, one and one do equal two. That result may be fine for some organizations, but the combination still misses the opportunity for creating something more than the predecessor organizations can accomplish on their own. The thinking that guides combination planning and implementation is not downright stupid, but it lacks the vision and motivation required for people to reach for the best possible organization. Frequently, a manager gets the nod to run a function and is given free reign to build the unit as she pleases. More likely than not, this results in the tendency to go with what she knows and replicate the precombination function in the post-combination organization. The dynamics of the postcombination organization (both internal and external) may not be the same as those of the precombination organization, and what worked well previously may not be the best solution for the new organization. When Bank of America swallowed up Security Pacific in 1992, it gained market share and cut $1.2 billion in costs. But BofA also had to write down $5 billion in assets and take merger-related charges of $449 million; together, the amount was more than Security Pacific's net worth. BofA digested its large competitor, but by and large it did not gain any long-term competitive muscle from all the added calories.

## The Best of Both

In these cases, serious thought goes into considering which partner's way of doing things better fits the postcombination organization. Perhaps one side has recently installed a state-of-the-art IT system, while the other has world-class human resource practices. Don't confuse this with the immature tit-for-tat of "you got this so I'm getting that" decision making that characterizes the planning process in many combinations. Rather, choosing the best of both requires careful analysis and deliberation about which side's ways fit best with the vision and values that are to guide the postcombination organization. For one plus one to equal more than two, time and care have to be taken to articulate the requirements for the postcombination organization, guide a planning process that succeeds in letting the best rise to the top, and counter personal agendas and politics with a regard for the overall organizational good.

Chemical Bank's 1991 merger with Manufacturers Hanover achieved $750 million in cost savings—yet it propelled the combined bank into a market leadership position in several key businesses. In what leaders dubbed a merger of equals, there were nevertheless sharp differences in the firms' business practices, management styles, and corporate values as stated by executives themselves:

| Cultural Area | Chemical Bank | Manufacturers Hanover |
|---|---|---|
| Business practices | Process-driven | Market-driven |
| | Protocol | Rough around the edges |
| | "Clients" | "Customers" |
| | Decentralized | Centralized |
| | "Carrot" HR practices | "Stick" HR practices |
| | Liberal benefits | Less vacation |

| Behaviors | Avoid conflict | Thrive on conflict |
|---|---|---|
| | Individualistic | Team spirited |
| | Polite | Direct |
| | Thoughtful, slow acting | Quick acting |
| | | |
| Values | Collaborative | Authoritarian |
| | Princetonian gentlemen | Irish street fighters |
| | High integrity | Low integrity |
| | Unwilling to give up | Ready to compromise |

To capitalize on Manny Hanny's strengths, the new Chemical Bank applied its market-driven orientation and centralized business approach to retail banking. In the case of higher-end services and the middle markets, by contrast, the former Chemical's more decentralized organization and process-driven approach prevailed. Ultimately, balance between the two sides would predominate in staffing decisions. Even though the combined bank's top leadership would bring "Princetonian gentlemen" and "Irish street fighters" together in a governing council to set strategy, the two groups would run their sides of the business somewhat independently.

## Breakthrough Combinations

For the full value to be developed in a combination, it may be necessary to consider options other than those currently in use at the partner companies. Breakthrough combinations stretch both partners to think outside of the box and look beyond their existing models of organization, and portfolios of products and markets, to achieve novel and ultimately winning results. These are the rarest of combinations, but also the most productive. In the merger of Twentieth Century Companies (now named American Century Companies) and Benham International, for example, leadership leveraged existing products to develop a whole new line of investment vehicles and used the combination as a means to build a new brand identity in the highly competitive mutual fund marketplace. Whereas the firms separately were perceived as niche players and limited service providers, the combined company emerged as a comparative powerhouse. On a broader basis, General Electric has given new life to the conglomerate form by its model of "integrated diversity," in which different parts of the organization generate

cash versus growth and yet continuously share personnel, resources, and best practices with one another.

## Putting Companies Together to Create Value

What produces productive combinations that create greater-than-
expected value? Why do so many combinations result in lowest-
common-denominator organizations or, worse, actually destroy
value? It's necessary to have a sound and sensible reason for joining forces; then comes the matter of putting the companies together effectively. Figure 1.3 arrays the twin ingredients of strategy
and implementation into a simple 2 x 2 matrix that emphasizes
their joint importance to success. As to the relative importance of
the axes, research studies repeatedly find that in unsuccessful combinations shortcomings in implementation are the more prominent and potent factor.

What are the key tasks during implementation? They include
refining a winning strategy for the combination, aligning the new
organization behind it, building a culture to support it, and getting people to deliver desired results. In even the best-conceived
combinations, creating meaningful synergies is demanding and
chancy. We hear frequent complaints that power and politics intrude on every decision and subvert attempts to create value.

**Figure 1.3.  The Role of Strategy and Implementation
in Combination Results.**

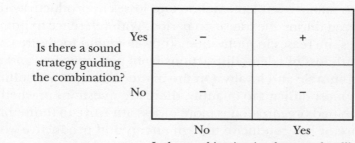

Is there a sound strategy guiding the combination?

Yes    −    +

No    −    −

No    Yes

Is the combination implemented well?

## Gain Versus Pain

At the most basic, human level, a value-creating combination can be conceived as a positive ratio of the gain that is realized versus the pain that is experienced by joining the organizations:

*GAINS*
Financial returns and profitability
Aligned organizational structure
New approaches to conducting work
Motivated and capable talent
Desired culture
Cost savings

---

*PAINS*
Expenses and drain on profitability
Time and resources required to manage transition
Reduced work productivity and quality
Unintended consequences for employee attitudes and behaviors
Culture clash
Customer concerns

In purely financial terms, this is the ratio of returns to expenses; in the metric of value creation, it is the extent to which business profitably grows. As for building productive capacity, gains stem from aligning organizational structures with winning strategies and developing new methods to do business that draw on the best of both partners—or prove to be altogether superior to what the companies originally had to offer. The future value of these gains has to be weighed against present-day time and resources required to manage implementation and losses in productivity that are suffered during the transition period. With reference to human resources, increases in motivation, know-how, and focus are compared with loss of talent, distractions from performance, and declines in morale and loyalty. On the matter of corporate culture, which is most difficult to quantify, there are questions of whether the combined organization is more or less attractive to future hires and more or less conducive to high energy and productive work. Finally, it is important to calibrate whether cost savings have been achieved at the expense of market penetration, and if current and prospective customers are more or less attracted to what the combining companies have to offer. A true value-creating combination requires managing above and below the line of this ratio: finding ways to maximize the gain *and* ways to minimize the pain.

Productive combination can be realized by building upon the best from both organizations, by breakthrough changes, or by some combination of the two. It is much more psychologically taxing to adapt to transformational change than to incremental change. Yet choosing from the best of both partners also implies change from the status quo and adaptation to new ways of doing things. Even when one side dominates, the other side must contend with abandoning their practices, systems, and orientations; this, too, necessitates psychological adaptation. Given the inevitable pain of psychological loss, why not realize some gain in building a postcombination organization that is more than the sum of the parts?

## Conceptual and Practical Underpinnings of Productive Combination

There is no one best way to manage a merger, acquisition, or alliance. Personalities, products, and procedures vary considerably from one combination to another, making a one-size-fits-all prescription for achieving productive results ill-advised. The objectives in one deal may call for expedient implementation, another a more cautious approach. Nevertheless, there are some principles of combination management that apply in almost every case.

To begin, productive combination builds on one of the simplest yet most helpful models of organization change: the three steps of *unfreezing, changing,* and *refreezing* introduced by social psychologist Kurt Lewin.[7] Suppose that your target for change is not an organization or an individual, but an ice cube. If you want to convert the cube to a cylinder, you can proceed in one of two ways. The first is to use a hammer and chisel; with the right skill, you can transform the ice cube into the shape of a cylinder. But there's a clear cost to this approach: you lose a good amount of ice as the cube is chiseled. The alternative is to unfreeze the ice cube, change its mold to that of a cylinder, and refreeze it. Unless you're clumsy in pouring unfrozen water from one mold to the other, or the new mold has a hole, you gain the desired cylinder with no loss of volume.

With organizations, then, the first step in the process of desired change is to unfreeze present behaviors or attitudes. The unfreezing event might be the decision to enter into a strategic alliance or acquire a target organization. The logic is that an organization, like a person, is reluctant to abandon old habits and accustomed ways. As companies combine the status quo is upset, for employees and for the two organizations. This engages both personal and organizational defense mechanisms that collectively contribute to resistance to change. Leaders of combinations can best counter this resistance by laying out a compelling rationale for joining forces and working with their colleagues to face the reality ahead collectively. We term this *strategic and emotional preparation*.

The second step is changing the organization from its original behavior or perception to a new one. This means articulating and developing the desired change. Once the combining partners are unfrozen, the new mold might take the form of strengthening the customer service culture, making a leaner or less hierarchical organizational structure, deploying new work processes, or selecting people with the skills and capabilities required to achieve new objectives. Recognize, however, that top executives, business and functional managers, and everyday employees have to create this new mold and manage the possible spillage. To do so requires their collective involvement in value creation and thoughtful handling of the change process.

The third step, refreezing, is to establish processes that reinforce and lock the desired behaviors or perceptions into the organization. This could be through financial incentives that reinforce desired behaviors, information systems to transport data across units of an organization, or changes in policies and procedures to support the new organization. Refreezing completes implementation and results in what Lewin characterized as a new level of "equilibria." Alas, few companies can savor such a steady state, as new opportunities and problems, and new deals and combination prospects, beckon. Perhaps a better analogy is to a muscle. Muscles that are well exercised and fit are ready when you need them. In this regard, Larry Bossidy, CEO of Allied-Signal, argues that no one is better prepared to handle complex change than a company that has managed it successfully in the past.

Although the unfreezing-changing-refreezing model is simple to report, it is much more difficult to actually implement. First of all, today's realities of downsizing, dead-ended careers, and changing psychological work contracts prompt many people to cling to what they have. Organizational change and transition do not occur in a vacuum. People's experience of previous organizational change—whether personal or vicarious—sets a context within which they assess the current change. Given the miserable track record of acquisition and alliance activity historically, it is no wonder that people feel threatened and insecure when they learn of an imminent combination involving their organization. They cannot hear all the supposed organizational benefits if they fear losing their perks, status, or employment.

Even guided by sound strategy and carefully designed implementation, it is incredibly difficult to manage mergers, acquisitions, and alliances. The vast scope of change, the huge number of decisions to be made, and the myriad human reactions to change and transition entangle the combination process and encumber the realization of strategic synergies. Our observations in more than fifty combinations have yielded some timeless truisms of productive combination, born of the practical experiences of organizations and their people as they attempt to combine their operations:

1. *People have to let go of the old before they can accept the new.* As psychologist Harry Levinson points out, "all change is loss."[8] In a combination, people lose identification with their former organization and colleagues who retire early, leave voluntarily, or are laid off. Even the seeming winners have to cope with uncertainty and loss of familiar methods and routines. In almost every successful combination we have worked with or observed, management has taken steps to help people let go of the past through activities as varied as grieving meetings, rap sessions, and ritual burials of memorabilia.

2. *The tendency is to look at the prospects of a combination as a glass half-empty, not half-full.* People focus first on all the possible ways in which a combination might adversely affect them and their work situation. Amid all the downsizing and free-agent job hopping in companies today, the natural reaction is to discount promises of a happy marriage and prepare oneself for an unpleasant divorce. Leaders of combining organizations have to contend with people who may be carrying "baggage" from previously mismanaged deals as well as disappointing or even disastrous restructurings, downsizings, reengineerings, and other so-called change initiatives. Straight talk and employee involvement in the combination process are the

best means to counter cynics and rekindle people's desires to be on a winning team.

3. *Combining productively is a nonlinear process.* Even the most successful combinations follow a course of two steps forward and one step backward. With so much to do and so much at stake, progress in the journey from precombination to postcombination inevitably produces some backtracking. Decisions have a way of coming undone, and changes in the business environment often necessitate midcourse corrections. This is one reason why we strongly favor bringing executives together en masse for periodic combination planning and review sessions, and why we think it prudent to develop methods for monitoring progress over time.

4. *You have to drive in two lanes at once.* Amid efforts to plan and implement desired organizational change in a combination, there is still a business to be run. Operations managers tend to forgo the details of combination management and instead focus on day-to-day business matters. Obviously, someone has to mind the store. This is why it is so important to create a transitional organization structure to plan and oversee the combination—and why effective executives insist that time and attention be focused on locating and realizing opportunities in the combination.

5. *You pay now or you pay later.* You pay now by taking the time to carefully consider combination options and making educated decisions that contribute to a productive combination. Or else you pay later by making quick-and-dirty decisions up front and living with the consequences down the road. In managing a combination, it is far better to do things right the first time than have to clean up after mistakes.

A combination can be a rare opportunity to influence organizational behavior and employee attitudes.[9] If the transition period is managed to take advantage of this opportunity, then people are more apt to settle into new behaviors in line with business objectives.

As a final note: expect to make mistakes. There are so many decisions to be made in combining previously independent organizations that even the best-planned and most carefully executed combinations have their miscues. Every action in managing a combination produces an unintended reaction. Consider the experience of a consumer products firm that sought to make a positive gesture by keeping a major product line housed in the facilities of an acquired competitor, which meant moving some of its own people to the location. Leadership's intention was to blur the line between who took over whom. But acquired staff regarded the newcomers as spies from the lead company. The transferred employees, in turn, felt they were the ones acquired because they had to adapt to the ways of the target location. Fortunately, executives from headquarters listened to complaints from both sides and spent time building positive relations before any major problems occurred. "This took face-to-face meetings between senior leadership and the people in the field and not just relying on conference calls or faxes," recalled the company's chief financial officer. "Otherwise, we could never have built the trust required or let individuals know how serious we were about building a unified team."

Executives learn that there is always a downside to any course of action in a combination. They accept this as part of what it takes to get one plus one to equal three. These leaders keep their sights set on the strategic opportunities, get their management teams and employees to embrace this vision and discern what matters in getting there, and manage everyone involved to maximize gain and minimize pain.

## Chapter Two

# Why Deals Go Sour

Mergers, acquisitions, and alliances involve more people and more organizations than ever before, as deals escalate in both financial size and strategic ambitions. Managing these events productively benefits from understanding trends in combination activity, both historical and current; looking closely at the combination process for clues as to why, despite popularity with executives, they perform so poorly in meeting business objectives; and recognizing the unintended human and organizational consequences mismanaged combinations generate.

## Combinations Historically and Today

Combinations have long been a factor in sculpting the business landscape. Five distinct waves of merger activity have influenced the shape of organizations and industries in the United States.

1. Beginning in the 1890s, the first wave witnessed thousands of horizontal mergers, which brought together companies in the same industry. Small and medium-sized companies combined to form such giants as United States Steel, Standard Oil of New Jersey, Du Pont, and General Electric.

2. Federal legislation in 1914 halted these industrial consolidations. Over time, however, court decisions gutted this legislation and a second wave of buying and selling surged from 1925 through 1931. Vertical combinations, in which a buyer acquired a major supplier or customer, predominated in this period, producing American Cyanamid, Radio Corporation of America, General Foods, and others.

The Great Depression and World War II slowed the frenzy, and stiff government action brought it to an end. The passage in 1950 of the Cellar-Kefauver amendment to the Clayton Antitrust Act gave government regulators the power to scrutinize mergers for competition-inhibiting or monopoly-creating potential. And scrutinize the government did: in 1962, for example, the U.S. Supreme Court ruled that Brown Shoe could not acquire G. R. Kinney because the combined operation would control 2.3 percent of existing shoe outlets and thereby lessen retail and wholesale competition.

3. The strong postwar economy of the mid–1950s led large corporations to seek new avenues of growth. With regulation and enforcement inhibiting deals within industries, motivation and money were redirected toward diversification. Conglomerate mergers (linking firms with different customers and technologies, often in different industries) defined the third merger wave. This wave swelled in the 1960s with the rise of inflation and the preeminence of portfolio models of corporate finance. Between 1961 and 1968, Litton Industries made 79 acquisitions, Gulf & Western made 67, and Teledyne, which had no assets in 1960, took over 125 firms.

4. In 1974, Mobil acquired Montgomery Ward (then part of Marcor) for $1.6 billion; a year later GE acquired Utah International for $1.9 billion. These events ushered in the fourth wave of combination activity—characterized by financially driven opportunistic deals—and fundamentally changed the scope of deal making in a variety of ways.
   - First, the size of combinations reached previously unimagined levels. The Marcor and Utah International acquisitions alone exceeded the billion dollars in assets acquired in all of Teledyne's and Litton Industries' deals between and 1961 and 1968. Blockbuster deals, such as Beecham Group's purchase of SmithKline Beckman and the Kohlberg Kravis Roberts takeover of RJR Nabisco, were routine headline grabbers in the business press in the 1980s.
   - Second, while some conglomerates rose out of obscurity in the 1960s, megamergers involved already well-known, successful firms such as GE and RCA, Time and Warner, and Philip Morris and General Foods. Many conservative,

old-school industry giants combined, causing the collapse of long-standing corporate cultures and threatening the security of millions of people who joined large companies in expectation of cradle-to-grave employment.

- Third, justice department officials in the Reagan and Bush administrations virtually eliminated the practice of contesting large combinations, responding instead to the call to establish organizations with the scope and size to compete globally (a practice retained during the Clinton administration).

- Finally, the fourth merger wave featured new players using new tactics in the contest for corporate control. Corporate raiders decried the self-indulgence of senior managers who enjoyed bloated salaries and handsome perks while allowing share prices to fall well below their potential value. The most opportunistic raiders then purchased those undervalued shares, pumped up prices through bidding wars, and got paid off in greenmail or by selling their shares at a premium to white knights. Others restructured firms, downsized staff, and sold off prime assets (breakup raiders) or simply took over control from incumbent management and whipped firms into shape (discipline raiders).

As the economy soured in the late 1980s—and public disdain for the greed of Wall Streeters and yuppie stockbrokers rose—unfriendly takeover attempts, corporate breakups, and other financially driven moves slowed. Junk bonds lost currency, and banks and other lenders did not have the risk capital available to finance deals. Before it ended, however, the fourth wave of combination activity radically transformed the corporate terrain. Some 250 of the firms on the 1980 Fortune 500 did not survive intact to the 1990 list.

5. The mid–1990s have seen a merger wave of tsunami proportions crash ashore. The U.S. economy is strong, and once again financing on a global scale is available. The scale of deals continues to climb as corporate giants combine with firms of similar size. Time Warner, for instance, has purchased Turner Broadcasting, and Disney now owns Capital Cities/ABC. Once again, corporate strategy is guiding transactions. Now strategists advise firms to build on the core competencies and stick

to known markets. More often than not, companies doing deals in the 1990s seek to do business together rather than merely boost share prices or create a portfolio of assets to reduce risk. Several other factors distinguish this current wave from its predecessors:

- *Full-scale combinations take many forms.* Although horizontal mergers (combining firms with the same products or in the same markets) are prominent, vertical mergers and acquisitions are also back in fashion. Introducing "value chain" analyses into corporate strategy has encouraged companies to gain control over the most valuable segments of their supply or distribution chains. There has also been an increase in "concentric" combinations wherein companies acquire firms primarily for a specialized capability, say, R&D or sales, align that portion with their core business, and absorb or "hive off" the rest.

- *Temporary combinations are on the rise.* The number of strategic alliances and joint ventures has increased manyfold in the 1990s. They allow firms to jointly capitalize on each other's capabilities without making a long-term commitment to one another. As noted in the previous chapter, these combinations also take numerous forms and serve diverse purposes.

- *Deals are made for growth.* Whatever form the combination takes, the emphasis today is on creating value through combination rather than shrinking your way to prosperity. Of course, sheer size can be a competitive advantage in many industries. By acquiring credit-card issuer First USA and its nationwide portfolio of sixteen million customers, Banc One gained a national platform in a key business. In stagnant industries, purchasing a competitor satisfies stakeholder desires for increased revenues and profits.

- *Globalization drives more deals.* As companies mature and bump up against national borders, the desire for growth propels them into new territories, access to which comes with acquiring or aligning with local companies. Prospering in certain industries today requires a global reach. Rupert Murdoch's acquisition and alliance spree in the media and entertainment industry took off in Australia and Europe before he set his sights on the U.S. market.

- *Entire industries are put into play.* Deregulation, social policies, and changing customer demands effect combination
  activity throughout whole industries. The Telecommunications Act of 1996 opened up the long-distance telephone
  business and spawned some of the biggest combinations
  ever, such as the $21 billion Nynex-Bell Atlantic merger
  and WorldCom's $14 billion acquisition of MFS Communi-
  cations. Removal of strict FCC regulations limiting station
  ownership prompted consolidation in the U.S. radio industry, including Westinghouse's purchase of Infinity
  Broadcasting, joining together the two largest players in
  the industry.
- *Human assets are more crucial to success than ever.* In the information age, the value of many firms lies in their intellectual capital. Witness the many high-tech combinations
  where the departure of key technologists from acquirees
  deflates hoped-for synergies. People with experience and
  know-how in the target companies are required to keep
  operations running. Yet today, employees aren't waiting
  around to see what's happening: they're packing their own
  parachutes and bailing out!

## Phases of a Combination

Even as more companies today base their decisions to combine on
a reasonable and defensible strategy, and have many more options
available on how to put their two organizations together, the
human factor takes on greater importance in determining failure
or success. We were involved in a study of combinations in banking and finance conducted by the Management Analysis Center; it
identified important differences between the "typical" and "successful" cases over the three stages of a combination:

| Phase | Typical Emphasis | Successful Emphasis |
|---|---|---|
| Precombination | Financial | Strategic |
| Combination | Political | Combination planning |
| Postcombination | Damage control | Combination management |

## The Precombination Phase

In the precombination phase, much of the emphasis in the typical
case is focused on financial implications. Buyers typically concen-

trate on the numbers: what the target is worth, what price premium to pay if any, what the tax implications may be, and how to structure the transaction. Executives entering an alliance who scope out the size of returns but neglect how they will be achieved also fit the typical scheme. The decision to do a deal is thus framed in terms of the combined balance sheet of the companies, projected cash flows, and hoped-for return on investment.

Two interrelated human factors add to this financial bias. First, in most instances members of the "buy team" come from financial positions or backgrounds. They bring a financial mind-set to the study of a partner, and their judgments about synergies are mostly informed by financial models and ratios. They often do not know very much about, say, engineering, manufacturing, or marketing; nor do they bring an experienced eye to assessing a partner's capabilities in these regards. Then there is a tendency for "hard" criteria to drive out "soft" matters in these cases: if the numbers look good, any doubts about, say, organizational or cultural differences tend to be scoffed at and dismissed.

*In the successful case,* by contrast, buyers bring a strategic mind-set to the deal. But there is more to this than overarching aim and intent. Successful buyers also have a clear definition of the specific synergies they seek in a combination and concentrate on testing them well before momentum builds and any negotiations commence. Here, too, human factors play a part. For instance, in successful cases members of the buy team come from technical and operational, as well as financial, positions. During the scouting phase, they dig deep into the operations and markets of a candidate when gauging its fit. "Acquisitions are too important to be left to our corporate development department," one experienced executive opined to us. "I get my management team involved early on to kick the tires and look under the hood before we consider buying another firm." Another put the distinction plainly, "Our M & A department gets paid to buy a company. I get paid to run one."

Sensible buyers consider carefully the risks and problems that might turn a strategically sound deal sour. This does not mean that financial analyses are neglected or that they are any less important to success. To the contrary, what puts combinations on the road to success is both an in-depth financial understanding of a proposed combination as well as a serious examination of what it will take to produce desired financial results. The result of this exercise is a road map to guide the combination and show how it will work. This serves important purposes. First, it guides more detailed precombination planning and subsequent decision making and action in putting the firms together. Second, it provides the basis for conveying the merits of the deal to diverse stakeholders. Finally, it gives otherwise skeptical managers and employees something substantive to consider in weighing their doubts and, in the best of cases, something tangible to hope for in the way of career opportunities and challenges.

### Problems in the Precombination Phase

The precombination phase encompasses strategy setting, scouting, partner evaluation and selection, and deal making. Obviously, the quality of work conducted in this phase has a substantial influence on the eventual results of a combination. Still, a Boston Consulting Group study found that during the precombination phase eight of ten companies did not even consider how the target company would be integrated into operations following acquisition.[1] In our experience, several other weak points afflict the typical acquisition and alliance program in the precombination phase:

- *Unclear business strategy.* To begin, some buyers are not sure what they want to do in the marketplace and tend to follow fashion in their industry when it comes to merging or aligning. This is particularly true in the case of industries where the market leaders make aggressive moves and followers either have to catch up or leave the game. The rapid-fire series of combinations in banking, telecommunications, entertainment, and the like exemplify this type, as do the myriad ventures and alliances in the automotive industry. More frequent are cases where a buyer has access to a mountain of cash but no means of growing internally; they roll the dice in their choice of investment and selection of a partner. Although the game can be exciting, it seldom yields any sustained payoff.
- *Weak core business.* At a manufacturing firm, a few acquisitions were made to shore up flagging core business lines. In one of them, however, a poorly managed business wholly integrated a small competitor that added scant value and sapped time and energy from addressing more fundamental problems in the business. In another case, a dying business line received "life support" from an acquiree in the form of new sales staff with

new customer contacts. As it turned out, however, the patient
was terminally ill with worn-out technology. Neither aggressive staff nor new customers could keep the business alive. Better to fix or close these failing businesses than try to revive
them with fresh blood. And the lessons are by no means limited to acquisitions; many alliances are formed after some
major problem or challenge has been identified that could
not be solved through the regular mechanisms of the existing
organization.[2]

- *Poor combination strategy.* At other times, the buyer has logic
  and experience in its favor but discovers that the strategic assumptions behind the combination are flawed. In 1988, for
  example, Kodak wanted to become a major player in the very
  profitable pharmaceutical segment producing ethical drugs.
  Kodak's Life Science division, an outgrowth of its chemical
  business, was developing compounds the company felt had
  good patentable value. However, the process of clinically testing, obtaining regulatory approval, and marketing new drugs
  is expensive and risky. Kodak sought to acquire a firm that had
  these capabilities. Accordingly, it paid a premium for Sterling
  Drug and justified doing so by trumpeting the synergies between Kodak's scientific skills and Sterling's market strengths.
  As it played out, Sterling proved to be only a modest force in
  the ethical drug segment and could not elevate Kodak to the
  status it sought in the pharmaceutical business. After five years
  of poor earnings, Kodak acknowledged its mistake and divested Sterling.

- *Pressure to do a deal.* Equally debilitating is when the basic rationale underlying the decision to look for an acquisition or
  alliance partner is not clear or when the fundamental criteria
  for selecting a target are not broadly understood. In some instances, corporate planners do not fully think through why
  they are acquiring a particular company and how that company fits specifically with their strategy. Literally, they set out to
  find a target when they were not clear why they want to join
  forces with it. Why would staff planners and executives buy
  something when they don't know what they're shopping for?
  At a diversified financial services firm we studied, corporate
  staff was charged by the company's executive committee to
  "formulate a growth strategy via acquisition" and "identify

targets that fit our criteria." The staffers figured that not bringing forward a recommended target would be seen as a failed
response to the executive committee. After all, wasn't it their
job to locate candidates? The fact that this committee had
never rejected an acquisition recommendation only reinforced the staffers' sense that they were doing the right thing
by bringing forward a candidate—any candidate—rather than
say they couldn't find one that fit the strategic criteria. Additionally, psychological factors contribute to the pressure to do
a deal. Few events in corporate life are more exhilarating than
making an acquisition. Searching for the right target, stalking
it, zeroing in, and then bagging it are considerably more exciting and energizing than the relatively mundane work of
pushing paper and running numbers back at headquarters.
Acquiring is winning: "we" get "them." It feels good to win, to
be on top, and corporate staffers in most firms get caught up
in the rush to do a deal.

- *Hurried due diligence.*  The rush lasts into the deal-making stage.
  As excitement over doing a deal escalates, staffers hurry due
  diligence. Certainly they look for major liabilities in the target,
  but they make inadequate effort at digging into the candidate
  to understand what is being purchased, how well it fits with
  the lead company's current businesses, and what potential pitfalls lie ahead. One corporate strategic planner likens her
  company's due-diligence process to her experience in conducting hiring interviews: "When I hear I'm getting a good
  candidate to interview, I make up my mind in the first two
  minutes whether I like the person and [then I] spend the rest
  of the hour confirming my first impression."

- *Overvalued targets and overestimated synergies, prospects, and returns.*  First impressions can prove costly in combinations. Insufficient due diligence can lead to overvaluation, resulting in
  paying too high a price for a merger partner or acquisition.
  Without a close look at the capabilities of a partner, it is easy to
  overestimate synergies and underestimate the costs and headaches involved in integrating businesses. In alliances as well as
  acquisitions, the momentum to do a deal hinders thorough assessment of the potential partner in areas such as core values
  that guide behavior on the job. Wishful thinking replaces the
  scrutiny needed to determine if the two parties can work well
  together.

## The Combination Phase

As the two sides come together, politics typically predominates. Oftentimes, it's pure power politics: the buyer decides how to put the two organizations together. USAir had a poor reservation system and woeful customer service, such that passengers deemed it "Useless Air." Its purchase of Piedmont Airlines gave access to a better system and cheerful staff. But whose reservation system was adopted in the first pass? Well, who bought whom?! Even when a buyer seeks to combine on the basis of operational synergies, power politics can intrude. Corporate staffers bring in their chart of accounts, reporting cycles, planning methodologies, and the like, imposing them on subsidiaries. No matter that these systems seldom enhance growth and often prove unworkable for the needs and business cycles of the acquired firm. Why do companies insist that subsidiaries conform to their bureaucracy? We term this *corporate staff hegemony.*

Political game playing runs rampant in many combinations. Individuals jockey for power and position; management teams fend off overtures for control from the other side by hiding information or playing dumb. In the typical situation, transition task forces are convened to recommend integration options, but personal empire building and conflictual group dynamics block the efforts to seek out and capture true synergy. Meanwhile, culture clash rears up as people focus on differences between the partners and fixate on which side wins what battles rather than join together in building a sense of a united team going forward.

*In successful combinations,* a planning emphasis prevails. There are still politicking and gambits for self-preservation, but much of the energy typically directed into gamesmanship is now more positively channeled into combination planning. Leadership clarifies the critical success factors to guide decision making and oversees the planning process to ensure that sources of synergy are realized. Managers and employees come together to discuss and debate combination options; if the process is well managed, high-quality combination decisions result.

Importantly, there is more than one flavor of combination planning. In some cases, it involves studying and recommending options for the organization. In other cases, when the form of organization is more or less predetermined, planning focuses on how to implement changes most effectively and with the least disruption to operations. Even if one side is clearly in the lead position, a joint planning process engages both partners and builds their operating and personal relationships.

### Problems in the Combination Phase

The optimism that energizes the decision to purchase a target or align with another firm carries into the combination phase in the form of high hopes and confident expectations. They are soon forgotten, however, as the grueling work of combination planning, the critical mass of personal stress and uncertainty, and the pervasive clash of cultures overwhelm people during the combination phase. Common problems besiege organizations and their people during this period, when the highs of doing a deal are replaced by the lows making the deal work:

- *Integration seen as a distraction from "real work."* As responsibility moves from corporate staffers to line executives, reality hits hard. Operating managers see inflated projections and don't know how to meet the numbers. These executives are usually busy running their current businesses, and their evaluations and rewards are based on the extent to which they meet the core business targets—not on how well the integration goes. They see integration as a distraction from getting products and services to customers. Thus, what on paper seems like a comprehensive and sophisticated integration program is in practice implemented rapidly and superficially.
- *Misunderstood value-added and critical success factors.* Operating managers who are handed acquisitions or an alliance frequently misunderstand the value-added potential of the target and ignore or downplay the critical success factors. Corporate strategists may develop a clever game plan, but it is those at the operational level who have to play the game. Many operations managers are less visionary and do not appreciate the strategic and political sensitivities in making the combination work. Rather than identify and mine sources of strategic synergy in integration planning, they take shortcuts that save time but result in lowest-common-denominator decisions. This works in the short run, as managers refocus their attention and energies on their "real work"; in the long run, however, it results in "dis-integration" of the partners and disappointing results.

- *Psychological effects denied or ignored.* In our experience, many companies fail to take account of the importance of human and cultural issues that influence success. How important are they? Look at the journal entries of one combination survivor, a woman progressing well up the ranks of middle management in a large pharmaceutical company being acquired:

> A huge cloud of uncertainty hangs over each employee. Officially, we still haven't been told a thing about the acquisition and must learn about it from the newspapers. The sleepless nights begin.

> Every day I have lunch with my friend G., a great guy with a good sense of humor and rock-solid values hard to find in industry. He will probably have to relocate out of state. This is ironic because the company just moved him here twenty months ago from halfway across the country. We will probably not see each other again.

> The company has been sold. It would be sick to suggest that this merger— which will result in the loss of thousands of jobs—is in the best interest of employees.

> My boss left last month. There's no one left to report to.

> I ran into B. today. He wasn't offered a job and is devastated. He is scared he may not be able to pay his kids' college tuition and may have to ask them to transfer to local schools. Any sense of joy I had at being on "Schindler's list" of employees who've got jobs with our new parent corporation has been wiped out by experiences like this.[3]

- *Culture clash denied or ignored.* It would be comforting if problems in the combination phase were limited to inept management. They aren't. In a British study of forty acquisitions, all companies conducted a detailed financial and legal audit of their intended target. Yet none made any attempt to audit the target's human resources to assess the talent they were acquiring or to identify cultural norms.[4] A survey of French and German managers involved in acquisitions and alliances found that technical issues were less instrumental in producing conflicts in work relationships than differences between the two countries in planning, authority, commitment, monitoring, and teamwork.[5] More than 50 percent of the sample reported that cultural differences gave rise to tensions. They also indicated that senior executives did not regard such differences as important.

### The Merger Syndrome

Several years ago, we identified the symptoms of the "merger syndrome" as a primary cause of the disappointing outcomes of otherwise well-conceived mergers and acquisitions.[6] The syndrome is triggered by the unavoidably unsettled conditions in the earliest days and months following the announcement of a deal; it encompasses stress reactions and development of crisis management in the companies involved. In one of our most striking discoveries, we found that the merger syndrome arises even when the partners have taken some care to devise a thoughtful integration designed to minimize upheaval and provide due consideration for its effects on people.

### Personal Reactions to Merger Stress

1. Personal preoccupation
2. Worst-case scenarios
3. Rumor-mongering
4. Distractions from job performance
5. Psychosomatic reactions

### Organizational Reactions to Merger Stress

1. Crisis management
2. Increased centralization (upward)
3. Decreased communication (downward)
4. War-room and combat mentality
5. Interpersonal and intergroup tension
6. Less insight, more groupthink

### Cultural Reactions to Merger Stress

1. Clash of cultures
2. We versus they
3. Superior versus inferior
4. Attack-and-defend
5. Win versus lose
6. Decisions by coercion, horse trading, and default

What creates the merger syndrome? For employees, it is a fusion of uncertainty and the likelihood of change, both favorable and unfavorable, that produces stress and ultimately affects perceptions and judgments, interpersonal relationships, and the dynamics of the combination itself. At the organizational level, the syndrome is manifested by increased centralization and lessened communication, leaving people in the dark about the combination and fueling rumors and insecurities. This often produces worst-case-scenario thinking that distracts employees from regular duties and causes them to obsess about the impact of the combination upon themselves and their work areas. All of this hampers integration, reduces productivity, and contributes to turnover of key people.

### Personal Signs of the Merger Syndrome

Signs of human stress are present in all combinations, even the friendliest and best-managed ones. The first symptom of the merger syndrome is heightened self-interest: people become preoccupied with what the combination means for themselves, their incomes, and their careers. They develop a story line about the implications, but it is a mix of fact and fantasy. No one has real answers—or if they do, the answers are apt to change. Not only do people become fixated on the combination, they tend to focus on the costs and ignore the gains. Soon after the combination is announced, the rumor mill starts and people trade on dire scenarios. At the headquarters of an acquired Fortune 500 company, rumors spread that three thousand people were to be laid off. Interestingly, only seventeen hundred were employed at the site! All of this adds up to distraction from job performance.

Combination stress takes its toll in people's psychological and physiological well-being. Reports of tension and conflict increase at the workplace and at home, because spouses and children worry about their fates and grow anxious, too. Rates of illness and absenteeism rise in workforces going through combinations. In the merger of two Fortune 100 firms we worked with, incidents of high blood pressure among employees doubled from 11 percent in the year preceding announcement of the combination to 22 percent afterward. Interviews with executives in the early stages of a combination are colored with reports of headaches, cold and flu symptoms, sleeplessness, and increased alcohol and drug usage. "I stopped smoking seventeen years ago," one manager told us, "and started again when the acquisition was announced."

Needless to say, these stress symptoms are present at all levels of the combining organizations. Many companies target their stress-management programs at hourly and clerical employees in hopes of reducing stress for the troops. What about the officers? They suffer from high levels of stress, and the consequences of their stress-impaired judgment reverberate through the organizations.

### Organizational Signs of the Merger Syndrome

To cope with the many tasks of combining, teams of executives in both the lead and target companies typically lurch into a crisis-management mode. The experience is stressful yet exhilarating; many liken themselves to generals in a war room. Decision making in these top groups can be crisp and decisive. However, because top managers are generally insulated during this period they often prepare self-defeating gambits. Top teams misestimate or wholly ignore the other side's priorities and counterstrategies; they cut themselves off from relevant information and isolate themselves from dissent. All of this is symptomatic of what psychologist Irving Janis terms *groupthink,* the result of accepting untested assumptions and striving for consensus without reality testing the possible consequences.[7] It feels good to executives to act as if they are taking their fate into their own hands and devising plans for surviving the crisis. However, crisis management only gives them the illusion that they're in control. In truth, they set themselves up for trouble.

While the executive teams are in their respective war rooms, people in one or both organizations are adrift. Decision-making powers become centralized and reporting relationships clog with tension and doubt. Priorities are unsettled; no one wants to make a false move. Meanwhile, downward communications tend to be formal and unsatisfactory. Official assurances that any changes will be handled smoothly and fairly ring hollow to a worried workforce. Everything seems to be up for grabs.

Down the line, managers isolate themselves from employees. Sometimes this is because they don't know what to tell employees. Many managers fantasize that talk about the combination only adds to people's stress—as if they think employees are in blissful ignorance, whistling while they work the day away. Go out and talk with the employees, however, and you quickly find that they regard no news as bad news: "What's management trying to hide from us? Something really bad must be going on if they're not talking to us."

Then, as they charge up to work together and integrate the businesses, executives from both sides jockey for position and fight for their budgets, projects, and power bases. Rather than cooperate, they attack and defend. Task force studies of how to integrate operations become mired in controversy. Clout and connections determine who runs what and what the combined functions will look like. Meanwhile employees update their scorecards, chart wins and losses, and begin to sort themselves out. This can send a corporate marriage off on a hellish honeymoon.

### Cultural Signs of the Merger Syndrome

All of this is exacerbated by the clash of cultures. By their very nature, combinations produce a we-versus-they relationship, with a natural tendency for people to exaggerate the differences rather than the similarities between the two companies.

What is noted first are differences in the ways the companies do business—maybe their relative emphasis on manufacturing versus marketing or their predominantly financial rather than technical orientation: "We have a major product review each month; they have a quarterly review."

Then differences are discerned in how the companies are organized, say, their centralization versus decentralization, or their differing styles of management and control. People ascribe these differences to competing values and philosophies, with one's company seen as superior and the other as backward, bureaucratic, or simply bad: "Monthly product reviews are essential in today's rapidly changing business environment; quarterly reviews are insufficient for keeping all parties informed and acting quickly when changes are required."

People begin to attack the other side and defend their own: "Quarterly reviews are just one more sign of how loosey-goosey and poorly managed their company is; we know what it takes to run an effective organization." (Of course, the other side is going through the same stage: "Monthly reviews are just one more sign of how bureaucratic and poorly managed *their* company is; we know what it takes to run an effective organization.")

Finally, people reduce the differences to competing values and philosophies. One's own company is good; theirs is backward, bureaucratic, just plain bad.

Eventually, one side "wins" as their way is adopted in the combined organization, leaving the other side feeling like losers.

Ironically, a fair amount of diversity in precombination ways of working can aid productive combination when it sparks debate and discussion of desired norms in the combined organization. When left unmanaged, however, the clash of cultures pulls sides apart rather than uniting them. Task forces (made up of employees from the partnering organizations) to study and recommend combination options—presumably to garner the best thinking from both sides—degenerate into dysfunctional groups producing decisions by default rather than by discussion. Where one side dominates the action, it forces decisions perpetuating its ways upon the other side. If more balance of power is perceived between the sides, the decision-making process is like horse trading: you can get the IT architecture, but we're going to keep our human resource policies. Either way, the low-quality results defeat the rationale for taking the time to use task forces, miss the opportunity for truly productive thinking, and leave the workforce cynical about ongoing prospects for the combined enterprise.

## The Postcombination Phase

We have received calls *eighteen months* after a combination from executives bemoaning that their best talent has bailed out, productivity has gone to hell in a handbag, and culture clash remains thick. Often this is because the executives grew impatient with planning and hurried implementation, to the extent that their two companies failed to integrate and serious declines resulted in everything from employee morale to customer satisfaction. Much can be done in this damage-control situation, but it is obviously better to preclude the need for damage control by following the successful path from the onset.

In *successful combinations,* managers and staff from both sides accept the strategic logic and understand their roles and responsibilities in making the combination work. We've worked in many companies that offered merger seminars helping to prepare managers with change management plans for implementing actions in their areas of responsibility. Obviously, many people on both sides are not involved in task forces and do not have much input into integration decisions per se. Still, we've been involved in combinations where upwards of ten thousand people were consulted by task forces and at least exposed directly to the combination process. It is important that the rest of the workforce be brought into the loop and kept informed about decisions that affect them. Moreover, distributing publications on the combination process and holding regular two-way communication sessions go a long way to ensure that a combination is managed in line with its original intent.

### Problems in the Postcombination Phase

After months of planning, the postcombination phase arrives. It requires implementing the decisions made for integrating organizations, structures, cultures, policies, practices, and people. In cases where combination planning has been more political than productive, the problems of the combination phase bleed over into the new organization. Yet even when combination planning has succeeded in identifying ways to obtain strategic synergy and in designing an organization that is more than the sum of its parts, a host of potential problems arise in the postcombination phase:

- *Renewed merger syndrome.* First, people experience a renewed surge of stress. Up to this point, many worried about their job security. Now they have to contend with new systems, coworkers, leaders, and ways of doing things. This can be an invigorating and creative period; more often than not, though, it is a confusing and chaotic time that further adds to employee stress and organizational ineffectiveness.
- *Rushed implementation.* Senior executives often hurry to get on with things and rush through implementation. Time and talent have been directed away from core business requirements during the months of combination planning, and executives grow impatient, wanting to turn their attention fully to running their business operations (or designing the next combination). Recommendations generated in task forces may identify sound approaches to extracting gains from the integrated organizations, but inattention and sloppiness in implementation regularly undercut any hope of realizing their potential.
- *Insufficient resources deployed.* Postcombination implementation problems are manifested in diverse ways. The intricacies and complexities of moving from one way of doing things to another typically are underestimated; consequently the resources

deployed for implementation—people, time, budgets—prove to be insufficient.

- *Unanticipated implementation obstacles.*  No matter how diligent the transition planning groups may have been in preparing recommendations, some pitfalls cannot be anticipated. Only when implementation begins in earnest can managers understand fully what it takes to make desired changes. A highly touted new telephone customer service center designed as part of the merger of two financial institutions debuted ominously when the higher-than-anticipated volume of calls overwhelmed the system.

- *Coordination snags.*  A whole slew of coordinative issues arise during implementation. Sometimes, coordination problems emerge within units, as with the sales staff in a high-technology alliance learning of their quotas for selling products and services but having no sales materials ready to assist them. Often, though, implementation problems occur across units. In a hospital merger, a much-publicized, state-of-the-art maternity ward sat empty for months because the legal function had not secured all the required government permits to operate the new unit.

- *Inattention to team building.*  In many cases, too, as managers and employees scurry to adopt new procedures, scant attention is given to the requirements of building postcombination teams and the desired culture. As membership or leadership changes, a team faces the dilemma of hanging on versus letting go. It takes time for new members to feel a part of the team and assume an emotional stake in its mission; they need to clearly understand what is expected of them and what they can expect of others. For teams to perform at their peak, members need to develop trust and confidence in their colleagues and superiors. But in most combinations, the requirements of team building are put off until performance problems occur. Frequently, team members reporting to a leader from the partner organization lament having to reestablish their track record. Awkwardness and insecurity prevail when a team member is not quite sure when to go to the new boss with work-related questions or when to work things out on his own. Issues of trust are exacerbated when leaders persist in handing out plum assignments to people they already know from their own organization. In some cases, disgruntled talent walks. In others, talent sticks around and subverts team performance. Eventually, the team leader reluctantly enters damage-control mode and seeks assistance in putting the fragmented team back together.

- *Culture by default, not by design.* In the postcombination phase, the cultural norms developed in the relatively unfrozen combination period are refrozen or reinforced. This usually occurs by default rather than design. Typically, leadership has done an inadequate job of articulating a desired new culture. So the norms that employees see during the combination phase—such as constricted communication—solidify into employee expectations of what life will be like in the postcombination organization. In an acquired manufacturing firm that had enjoyed excellent employee-management relations as an independent company, employees felt abandoned as their leaders concentrated on managing relations with the new owners during the combination phase. Morale plummeted, and a union drive ensued. Leadership turned their attention back to the employees and successfully fought off the unionization effort. But the battle required considerable resources, and the effort to rebuild leadership credibility, as measured in biannual employee surveys, took several years.

- *Unintended impact on employee attitudes and hence business performance.* The human side of implementation is easily overlooked. The opportunity to engage people in the change process and obtain their psychological ownership of new methods, processes, and systems gets missed as implementation occurs in a hasty, top-down, by-the-book manner. Employees—many of whom had a hand in designing the old ways—resist adopting new practices.

   It is extremely frustrating to people in the postcombination organization to sense that they now have targets, goals, and expectations upon which their job evaluations, pay increases, and promotional opportunities are based, but they do not have all the tools, information, and other resources required to perform well. Scarce time, if any, is allotted to train people in new systems or procedures, or to let them experiment with new approaches to getting work done. Compounding this concern is the desire to make a good impression on new bosses and coworkers. Although learning by trial and error is common and effective in getting people to adopt new methods, the notion of learning through mistakes troubles individuals who want to get out of the blocks quickly and make good first impressions.

• *Missed opportunities for organizational enhancement.* Even in cases where leadership does a good job of articulating the desired culture for the combined organization, its efforts frequently are undercut by reward, information, and other systems that continue to reinforce the ways of the precombination organizations. Executives at two consumer products companies coming together in a merger hoped to use the combination as an opportunity to break traditional hierarchical "silos" on both sides. Yet no systems were established to speed information across business units, whether through formal MIS systems or informal opportunities for managers to meet and share ideas and insights across groups. People regressed back to their prior behaviors rather than establish connections across business units.

## Long-Term Human Costs of Mismanaged Combinations

The impact of a poorly managed combination lingers for years. It is measured in the drain on both human resources and operational results. Executives planning a combination must consider not only the short-term consequences of a crisis-management orientation and distraction from performance but also the enduring and unintended consequences for employee attitudes and behaviors and for organizational effectiveness and performance.

### Psychological Reactions to Transition

"Survivor guilt," a well-documented reaction to (in this case) reductions in the workforce,[8] leaves employees feeling culpable for having been spared and depressed at their inability to avert future layoffs. During combinations, organizations often inadvertently hurt the most those employees they least wish to alienate: the ones who are loyal to the organization at the outset. If faithful employees feel that layoffs are unfair, their loyalty drops more sharply than that of less-committed survivors.[9] Insensitive dismissals also hurt a firm's reputation, making future recruitment of desired talent more difficult.

Two enduring symptoms of the survivor syndrome are erosion of employee confidence in their leadership and an increase in cynicism and distrust. Many employees wonder why their leaders were not proactive in minimizing employee stress or preventing culture clash in a combination. Not seeing much value derived from past combinations, employees sense that management is motivated by short-term greed rather than building long-term benefits for customers or employees.

Many employees who retain jobs breathe a momentary sigh of relief but then develop a dismal outlook as they assess the post-combination organization. Survivors feel sad about the past and anxious about the future. People miss their former mentors, coworkers, assignments, or accustomed ways of doing things. They also miss their former political connections to the powerful decision makers in their organization. And when they set their sights on the future, people become further dismayed. All signs point to fewer opportunities for advancement as a restructuring eliminates traditional career paths or a merger brings on board more competitors for fewer rungs up the corporate ladder. No one knows what becomes of the people farmed out to new alliances.

What most concerns survivors of combinations is the perceived loss of control over their working lives. No matter how well you perform on the job, your track record can be erased, or your very employment taken away, in an ensuing transition. The rapid pace of change in today's business world means that your position, pet project, or potential for advancement can be eliminated at a moment's notice, with nothing you can do to counteract it. Interviewed a year after his telecommunications company was acquired, a midlevel marketing manager articulated this control issue: "I used to think that if I did my job well, completed my projects on time and in fine manner, I would be able to control my fate. That's no longer true. This merger is bigger than I am. I've seen other managers from our side—people who clearly were good, if not excellent, performers—get the shaft. I didn't ask to be acquired, but now my track record doesn't count for anything. I'm at the mercy of some bureaucrat at headquarters. I'm no longer the master of my own fate."

## Behavioral Reactions to Transition

In a combination, one of the few areas employees feel they have control over is whether to stay or leave the company. The best and the brightest among the workforce, those with the skills and experience most in demand, are the most marketable and most likely to walk away. Recruiters swarm over companies engaged in combinations; talented employees are vulnerable to poaching competitors. Retaining key personnel and trained employees influences overall business success. Professional intellect creates most of the value in the new economy of the postindustrial information age.[10] Therefore mismanaged combinations have the potential to destroy a firm's human capital. As an experienced merger manager notes, "An organization can burn down and be rebuilt. If you run out of money, you may be able to borrow more. But, if you lose people, you're dead."[11] Loss of expertise and the departure of key role models further demotivates remaining employees.

Employees in many combining organizations see themselves working harder but not smarter. One likened his situation to that of a chicken with its head cut off, frantically moving about with no sense of direction or hope for survival. Another talked about struggling to keep her head above water; she knew what to do but was weighed down by a heavy workload and competing demands. Compounding the sheer volume of work confronting people in a combination is a lack of direction in prioritizing which tasks to tackle first. Further, risk taking plummets following a combination. Employees self-impose pressure not to make waves or take risks, just at the time when innovation and creativity can yield tremendous returns. Further cuts may be in the offing, and no one wants a blemished record when the next list of victims is drawn up. Role ambiguity also paralyzes people in combinations, as they wonder who is responsible for what and who to go to for what decisions.

According to one combination veteran, these psychological and behavioral reactions to a combination prompt many employees to "withdraw their personal and professional power from their jobs, while making it look like they're still working."[12] People's bodies show up at work, but not their hearts and souls. As executives exhort their employees to boost productivity, enhance quality, and be more globally competitive, many workers simply respond with a shrug.

## Long-Term Business Costs of Mismanaged Transitions

The unintended consequences of mismanaged combinations have been measured in financial as well as human terms. Perhaps the ultimate standard is the high rate of combinations that fail to meet their business objectives, culminating in later divestiture or write-off of an acquisition or dissolved alliance. One contributing factor is the distraction from performance that prompts a reduction in work quantity and quality. A study at Honeywell found that, on average, employees spent two hours per day obsessing on the potential impact of a combination rather than performing their work. Add this up across all employees, and it's easy to understand why combinations frequently yield such disappointing results.

Often, combining companies experience some loss in market share.[13] In manufacturing firms, customers frequently look for alternative or secondary sources of supply, just in case there is a quality problem or inventory disruption. In service organizations, as the following case shows, new prospects and even current customers often decide to avoid newly combining companies until they have stabilized:

*"Fed Up?"*

A banner headline on the front page of the business section of the *San Francisco Chronicle* cried out: "Wells' Hotline Mired by Merger." The article noted how, for the third time in six weeks, Wells Fargo Bank's telephone banking hotline all but collapsed as the company attempted to expand its system to accommodate newly acquired First Interstate Bancorp. While the Wells Fargo executive quoted in the story minimized the problem as a "growing pain," a former First Interstate customer called it "just a mess." Meanwhile, in billboard and radio ads, competitor Glendale Federal Bank asked acquired First Interstate customers if they were "fed up" and invited them to get off the Wells Fargo stagecoach and transfer their accounts.

The psychosomatic effects of living through a combination result in dramatically higher health care costs for organizations. A survey of 177 combining companies found that one-third reported an increase in workers' compensation claims over a fifteen-month period.[14] One in five companies said their workers' compensation costs increased between 50 and 100 percent. This is in spite of the fact that 37 percent of the studied companies reduced their employee head count by an average of 13 percent.

Studies document that stress-related physiological and mental health problems sustain a negative effect on the performance of substantial numbers of employees for periods ranging from six months to four years after a combination announcement.[15] The stress-related impact of a combination is little mediated by personality type, suggesting that combination stress is a universal response likely to extend through the full workforce. Moreover, the findings have been replicated even in the "friendliest" of combinations.

Mismanaged combinations mean missed opportunities to achieve the upside potential in an acquisition or alliance. A well-managed combination provides a chance to make major changes that would not be considered politically acceptable under normal business conditions. At its greatest potential, a combination is like building a whole new organization from the ground up: changing or refocusing the business mission or vision of the combined organizations, building a new culture with updated values, or rethinking and reshaping the organizational structure and design of jobs. There is no better time for a good assessment and housekeeping of procedures, systems, and work groups. Done properly, this can result in a revitalized, progressive, and more efficient organization.

## Contending with Workplace Realities

Compounding the many problems that can turn a deal sour at any of the three phases of a combination are the issues and dynamics confronted in work settings today. The vast scope of combination activity (together with the downsizings, reengineerings, and restructurings of recent years) has resulted in a set of new realities in the workplace that afflict employers and employees. These realities make the process of productive combination more difficult than ever. First, employee cynicism and distrust of leadership is at an all-time high in many work organizations. Only 20 percent of workers trust what their senior management tells them.[16] Forty-three million jobs have been erased in the United States since 1979, and nearly three-quarters of all U.S. households have had a family member, neighbor, or friend laid off. This has produced what *The New York Times* calls "the most acute job insecurity since the Depression."[17] Many people are confused and concerned that layoffs are occurring in large numbers during an economic recovery that has lasted over five years, and at companies that are doing well. This increases the difficulty of conveying to employees a rationale for why they should feel good about an impending acquisition or alliance.

Second, many employees have grown wary of so-called organizational change initiatives and of leadership's ability to produce true enhancements in their workplaces. Most efforts at large-scale change in organizations fail, produce less-than-expected results, or take much longer to implement than originally anticipated. Employees increasingly are exposed to multiple transitions: reengineering, downsizing, changes in leadership, shifts in strategy, and others—typically overlapping one another in the modern work organization. Productive combination may be seen as just another false start, fad, or "change du jour"; efforts to rally workers may get lost among all the other activities competing for air time and attention in organizations today.

A third related trend in the workplace that interferes with efforts to build value in a combination is the sense of burnout that permeates the workforce. Organizational life has an increasingly intense pace. Rampant technological change, economic development in more countries, widespread information availability, growing customer expectations, and fundamental social changes all exacerbate pressures on organizations and their employees. Employees caught up in the intensity of today's business demands liken their experience to riding in constant white water. Some turbulence can make a trip down the rapids exciting and invigorating, but constant white water overwhelms people. The announcement of an acquisition or alliance is anything but welcome to a workforce already saturated with stress and turbulence.

Finally, people see less opportunity for themselves in organizations. Downsizings and delayerings increase competition for top jobs. Most organizations have abandoned or substantially cut back management development and training programs, leaving employees to fend for themselves to obtain the skills they need for advancement. Career tracks are obscured, and employment is more transitional. The result is that the psychological work contract between employers and employees has changed. Expectations that loyalty will be rewarded with lifelong career opportunities have been replaced with the recognition that a job—and a career—can end the moment the company feels it no longer needs you. What's in it for me, people wonder, to stick around and endure the pain of transition?

## The Path Toward Productive Combination

Extraordinary demands befall executives attempting to stay on top of a combination and help people through the change. But executives are caught in a double bind: their managerial requirements are to look out for people, but their natural response is to look out for themselves.

Executives must weigh the full load of potentially harmful consequences of a mismanaged combination. *Far beyond allocating resources to transition management and away from core business, how today's combination is managed shapes the organization's operating culture, business practices, interpersonal dynamics, and employee spirit for years to come.*

In a study spanning six years, we investigated the aftermath of an acquisition of a manufacturing company by a much larger conglomerate.[18] We set out to determine the personal and situational factors that influenced people's experience of the acquisition and its implementation. We considered everything from personal demographics (age, gender, education level, tenure in the company, and so on) to such situational factors as the presence of social support in the workplace and the perceived availability of job alternatives.

The factor exerting the greatest influence was *the company's history of change management*—the extent to which employees felt they were kept informed of prior changes in the company, had a say in those changes, and understood the company's goals. Employees who held favorable views of how the company managed change in the past reacted less negatively to the acquisition. Perceptions of how the acquisition itself was managed and the extent to which employees were psychologically involved in their organization were also strongly linked to changes in employee reactions after the acquisition. The lesson here: how you manage today's combination sets the tone for how people will respond to tomorrow's.

For years now, we have been hearing that the most successful organizations are those that learn to be adaptive and successfully manage continuous change. Merger, acquisition, and alliance activity certainly brings with it powerful organizational changes, and one of the greatest challenges for today's leaders is learning how to manage the effects of these changes on people and organizational effectiveness as they work through the phases of the combination process.

This is no small matter, especially for organizations engaged in or anticipating multiple combinations. When people learn that they are being acquired or transferred to a newly formed alliance, they immediately tune into their perceptions of how the partner organization handled previous combinations. First Interstate Bank executives and employees fled like refugees rather than test their fate under the Wells Fargo regime. By contrast, Cisco Systems has been able to retain desired talent—including former CEOs—in its string of successful acquisitions because of the care it takes in each phase of the combination process.

In the following chapters, we present our approach to productive combination. We look at how to minimize the unintended impact of the many problems at each combination phase. More positively, we show how organizations, their leaders, managers, and workforces overcome these problems to create a productive combination in which the sum is greater than the parts. The next two chapters look at the precombination phase and the strategic and psychological preparation needed to ready a combination plan and the people who must bring the plan to life. This includes developing a sense of where the combination is headed, assessing potential partners in terms of organizational and cultural fit, and helping people contend with the merger syndrome. Then, we devote four chapters to the roles and responsibilities of top management, transition teams, and the overall workforce in the combination phase—identifying sources of strategic synergy, preparing integration plans, and building a desired culture. Two more chapters examine the varied requirements of the postcombination phase, including meshing organizations and practices, building positive relations within and across teams, reinforcing culture building, and helping individuals adapt to the changes surrounding them.

# Part Two

# The Precombination Phase

## Chapter Three

# Strategic and Operational Preparation

Some observers liken organizational combinations to organ transplant surgery. The latter must be well thought out and planned, and the surgical team and patient prepped, prior to the operation to allow for rapid execution and to minimize the likelihood of rejection. So too, planning and preparation are integral to success when companies join forces.

Preparation in a combination covers three areas: strategic, operational, and psychological. The strategic challenges concern key analyses that clarify and bring into focus the sources of synergy in a combination. The operational challenges involve "reality testing" potential synergies in light of the two sides' structures and cultures, and establishing the desired relationship between the two companies. The psychological challenges cover the actions required to understand the mind-sets people bring with them initially and develop over the course of a combination. This means raising people's awareness of and capacities to respond to the normal and to-be-expected stresses and strains of living through a combination.

The journey toward a successful combination begins well before dealings commence. At each step—as strategic intent and selection criteria are set; as a deal is conceived; and as potential partners are screened, assessed, and negotiated with—executives, staff specialists, and advisors need to continuously address four aspects of their potential combination:

1. *Purpose.* Define the strategic intent of the lead company or both parties, and detail the business case supporting the deal
2. *Partner.* Develop clear and cogent criteria for use in the search for a partner, assess the two companies' organizational and cul-

tural fit, and conduct due diligence in a manner that builds a deep and accurate understanding of what might be merged, aligned, or kept separate
3. *Parameters.* Establish the relationship between the parties, and delineate the desired end state of the combined organization
4. *People.* Understand and contend with the first phases of the merger syndrome and the distinct psychological patterns of perceived winners or losers in the combination

We discuss strategic and operational matters in this chapter and psychological preparation in the next. But we don't mean to imply a sequential set of analyses or actions. To the contrary, architects of successful combinations move continuously across the domains of purpose, partner, parameters, and people to deepen their awareness of who and what they are dealing with during the precombination phase and to build a workable relationship. For example, although criteria for a partner may be set early on, they have to be revisited and revised in light of new information or potential tradeoffs.

Smart managers go back to the drawing board rather than follow a preconceived plan. As an illustration, an entertainment company that wanted an alliance partner to create a worldwide distribution network instead established a series of alliances with regional partners when it could not find a satisfactory candidate.

Similarly, early expectations about how to integrate an acquisition candidate may have to be recalibrated as more is learned about the partner and its people during the courtship process. This was the case with a pharmaceutical firm that initially intended to fully integrate an acquisition but instead decided to manage several product development groups in the target company as fairly independent "skunk works." Precombination due diligence revealed that many of the key scientists involved in promising programs resisted the idea of working in what they perceived to be a large bureaucracy and were likely to defect to start-up biotech companies.

## Purpose: Putting Strategy to Work

The strategic synergies in a combination should lead to a set of decisions in the precombination phase regarding the intentions, rationale, and criteria for doing a deal. They guide eventual action for excavating sources of productive combination.

## Strategic Intent and the Business Case

Strategy setting begins with self-scrutiny of an organization's own competitive and market status, its strengths and weaknesses, along with top management's aspirations and goals. The results define a direction for increased growth, profitability, or market penetration in existing businesses, for diversification into new areas, or simply for cash investment—which may or may not involve combination activity.

In successful acquisition programs, the CEO, relevant corporate and division management, and various advisors translate these objectives into specific strategic and investment criteria. Most buying companies have standard metrics for evaluating a candidate, which include its earnings, discounted cash flow, annual return on investment, and so on. They also have objectives concerning the impact of a combination on profitability, the combined organization's earnings per share, and future funding requirements. Firms looking for joint ventures and alliances need clear boundaries regarding desired ratios of expense to return and the extent of risk and exposure that will be tolerated.

Here the typical combination and the successful combination part ways. In too many cases, financial fit receives a disproportionate amount of attention and priority in the search for a partner. In successful cases, financial criteria are respected and adhered to, but they are balanced by careful consideration of each of the synergies sought in a combination and what it will take to realize them.

> Dow's joint venture with Eli Lilly in agricultural products exemplifies the importance of this point. Dow's review of the market opportunity and industry players revealed that a DowElanco alliance could immediately open more doors and was likely to yield more future products than any of several other acquisitions being considered. It would not be as financially attractive as full ownership but would reduce risks substantially and still allow Dow to pursue other ventures to further its strategy in this marketplace.

Knowledge gained from this careful look at synergies not only sharpens the parties' assessment of their potential combination; it also enables leadership to put forward a clear and convincing rationale for the combination that goes beyond the numbers. Most combinations involve expense reduction. Executives who seek to create value have to be able to demonstrate to staff on both sides that there is more to the deal than cost cutting; this involves a crisp statement of how synergies will be realized and what it means for the people involved.

Once companies have defined their aspirations in a market or segment and then taken careful heed of customer requirements and competitive threats, the gut level consideration is "Can I do it on my own?" If the answer is that something more can be gained through a combination than through internal development or redeployment of existing assets, the path is open to a merger, acquisition, or alliance. Next comes a thorough assessment of a company's internal capabilities and delineation of what is needed from a partner. Without this mapping of desired strategic synergies, the benefits of any combination are limited and chancy.

If the true motives underlying a combination have less to do with strategy and more to do with "nonrational" forces—say, desire to run the largest company in an industry or fear of being swallowed up by competitors—then productive combination is unlikely because there are no true benefits to be reaped by joining forces. But don't think that combinations based on such motives are infrequent. A blue-ribbon panel of financial experts several years ago concluded that CEO ego was the primary force driving mergers and acquisitions in the United States.[1] More recently, a Columbia University business school study found that in essence the bigger the ego of the acquiring company's CEO the higher the premium the company is likely to pay for a target.[2]

Critical driving forces push the combination together: the need to enter new markets, or ramp up technological sophistication, or share risk in an emerging arena. Each partner analyzes and articulates its strategic intentions. These intentions, together with the sources of productive combination between the partners, form the basis for the rationale underlying the decision to combine.

### Making the Case for an Alliance

A medical laboratory services company saw opportunity in the consolidation of buyers in the $17 billion hospital and integrated delivery system (IDS) market. Given the ever-changing health care industry, the firm sought alliances with existing IDSs so that together the proactive partners could be catalysts for the changes they sought. The business case for forming alliances centered on the laboratory's need to work with IDSs and academic medical centers in order to achieve some important results:

- Capture the huge growth in the esoteric testing business

- Achieve name recognition in the marketplace

- Integrate core business and esoteric testing

- Develop a disease management strategy

- Establish a pricing position in managed care

From the IDS perspective, synergies would come from linking their systems to a common laboratory service network, ongoing cost savings, and greater revenue opportunities based on geographic breadth.

Armed with their strategy and business case, the laboratory services company's small corporate development group gained understanding and support for alliances among their own management. The opportunity to become the market leader on a national basis and, especially, to set the standard for the industry appealed to managers. With a coherent rationale explained to them, all were eager to see the alliances supported with corporate resources.

## Clear Criteria

When they have a voice in and can agree on the merits of a strategy, top executives, corporate planners, and line managers operate from a common interest and perspective. To enforce this consensus, corporate leaders assert strategic criteria and make sure the acquisition team searches for candidates that fit them.

To begin, you need to know what you are looking for in an acquisition candidate or alliance partner. Having a full and open review of these criteria allows for debate and consensus building between staff and line executives. If conflicts or confusion regarding these criteria are not aired and fully addressed up front, they will persist down the road. Second, applying these criteria religiously greatly increases the likelihood of selecting a partner that will bring true productive value to the combination rather than just making an acquisition for the sake of doing a deal. Third, understanding precisely what synergies are sought sets the stage for subsequently mining opportunities through the combination planning and implementation phases. The more unified both sides are (within and between themselves) regarding what is being sought in a combination, the more focused they can be in realizing their objectives.

Two sets of criteria help here. One is a generic set of criteria that guide a firm's overall combination program and strategy. These are characteristics of organizations that must be present in any combination partner.

*"We Do Not Go into Business . . ."*

At Emerson Electronic, three factors guide search and selection of all alliance partners:

1. We do not go into business with any company that is in a turnaround situation. If a company is in a turnaround, something is going wrong. We do not want to start an alliance by having to fix the partner's problems.

2. We do not go into business with a company that does not have good management.

3. We adhere to our core competencies. We are a manufacturing company, and we have no desire to do anything else; we simply want to do that well.[3]

The second set of criteria guide the assessment and selection of a specific partner.

*Setting the Selection Criteria*

In its effort to establish strategic alliances with other health care providers, a southern California hospital established the criteria for what it was looking for in this particular search:

- *Quality of care.* Bring a continuously improving level of quality care to the community served by the hospital.

- *Managed care market penetration.* Strengthen the bargaining position of the hospital with managed care providers. An outcome of this strength will be significantly greater market penetration by our hospital and physicians in the HMO and managed care marketplace.

- *Geographic distribution.* Enhance the geographic reach of the hospital across Los Angeles county and throughout southern California.

- *Autonomy for the hospital.* Maintain maximum autonomy for the hospital as a distinct institution. Key areas include financial integrity and control, medical staff credentialing, facility development decisions, program offerings, and budgets.

- *Partner as low-cost provider.* Promote low unit costs and a critical mass for excellence in key activities through scale. This includes administrative, financial, technical, and clinical areas of the system.

- *Vertical integration.* Promote integrated delivery of a full range of health care service offerings.

- *Prestige or image.* Associate with partners who enhance the reputation of the hospital and physicians.

- *Alignment in philosophy and goals.* Agree on the vision and mission of the hospital, philosophies of management, and the role of the community in deciding the hospital's direction.

As this list shows, selection criteria can sometimes be at odds with one another, such as finding a partner that is low-cost provider while adding prestige. So the hospital's executive team prioritized the relative importance of each criterion prior to the selection process. When it came time to evaluate choices, the team then assessed the multiple candidates and weighted the high-priority criteria accordingly.

## Partner: Search and Selection

Successful acquirers both know what they are looking for and conduct a thorough due diligence to ensure that they get what they want. Their screening of candidates covers the obvious strategic and financial criteria, but it extends to include assessments of the human and cultural elements that can undermine an otherwise sound deal. How deep is the management talent in the target? What labor relations issues lurk around the corner? How does the company go about doing its business? Is their culture a good enough fit with ours?

### Thorough Screening

The value-creating acquisition of Benham by American Century began with a screening process that integrated human and cultural issues with strategic and operational criteria. Both firms meshed along operational lines in offering only no-load mutual funds and treating small shareholders well. But as one senior executive recalled, an exchange of corporate values statements during due diligence was among the data indicating that cultural compatibility existed as well: "Their 'Guiding Principles' and our 'Statement of Beliefs' were very similar. Both companies stated 'honesty' as a fundamental belief, and in the financial services industry you don't too often see that both stated and acted out."

Similarly, architects of successful strategic alliances get an in-depth sense of what and whom they are joining forces with. They carefully evaluate a prospect's strengths and weaknesses. Alliance expert Robert Porter Lynch recommends doing a "value analysis," listing the value elements that your company can provide and the value elements you expect the other side to provide.[4] The prospective partner should be sufficiently different to make an exciting match but have enough similarity to permit a harmonious work-ing relationship. Ideally, the potential alliance partner conducts the same exercise separately, and then the parties compare notes.

In addition to an analysis of the "facts," a thorough assessment of combination candidates covers less tangible matters. First, it re-veals the motives of the sellers in an acquisition or partners in an alliance. Why does leadership of the target want to sell or join in an alliance? Are they responding to a business opportunity, or are they driven by more personal motives such as wanting to cash out their investment? Does senior leadership want to stay on board after the sale? Do you want leadership to stay? If so, will there be good chemistry between the leaders of the two sides?

Second, thorough screening gets below the top leadership and considers the mind-sets of the two management teams. How do their people feel about working with or for you? Are they looking for a savior—a company with deep pockets to fund them to glory—or are they likely to fight hard to fend off any threats to their au-tonomy after the deal closes? Does your own management team buy into this deal, or do factions exist? Where does their team stand? Are the technical and professional staff—who are outside of the inner circle but needed to make the combination work—involved in the process? Are they apt to depart after a combination is an-nounced? Even if answers to these questions are not "deal killers," they indicate what has to be done to win people over during the courtship phase.

A thorough precombination screening comes only from speak-ing directly with a good cross section of the management team from the potential partner. Automated Data Processing CEO Art Weinbach is clear on the value of face-to-face due diligence with an array of managers from potential partners: "The greater sur-prises have come to us in the people and the people relationships. We have to spend more time on the people side of the equation in the due-diligence period. That is not as simple as looking at organizational charts; it requires speaking and listening to people both for the formal business issues as well as the less formal, how-does-it-really-work issues. You learn a lot by listening."[5]

Thorough screening requires time to clarify selection criteria and to fully assess the strengths and weaknesses, as well as the motivations and mind-sets, of the potential partner. At Corning Incorporated, where 35 percent of net income is from twenty-two collaborative ventures, partner analysis begins years before formal negotiations commence. Corning managers know from their extensive background research what to expect about their prospective partner's financial condition, strategy, corporate culture, technology, and core competencies. Corning's experience is confirmed in a European study that found that the more successful and lasting organizational marriages are made between partners who have "dated" longer and know each other better.[6]

Of course, in rapidly changing industries, the notion of a multi-year lead time for assessing a combination partner may be impractical. Still, in health care, financial services, telecommunications, and other industries where extensive combination activity is expected, smart companies are at work preparing their dossiers on potential partners. They may not have the advantage of years—or even several months—of courtship, but neither are they settling for shotgun marriages.

## Diligent Due Diligence

In most combination programs, *diligence* needs to be put back into due diligence. The effectiveness of the due-diligence team hinges on the balance between what it wants to see and the rigor used in questioning what it sees. In the typical case, the financial people who dominate due-diligence teams get a sense of the partner they want and then build a case for that combination going forward. Alternatively, it is important to get people on the team who probe deeply and thoroughly enough to work backward and identify faulty assumptions and what might hinder eventual success.

Take information technology as an example. Proper due diligence ascertains, first, the extent to which the candidate's system has the capacity to meet its own current and future business needs; then it considers the compatibility between the two sides' systems both right now and following anticipated growth. If the capacity and compatibility are not present, then the cost for getting there—and the impact of that cost on the financials of the deal—need to be determined by individuals who can make a realistic (as opposed to an overly optimistic) evaluation.

Broadening the membership of the team also enhances organizational due diligence. Membership can be expanded to include both staff professionals, from such areas as human resources and information technology, and operating managers who will be working with new partners if the combination is carried out. A team of functional specialists provides a breadth of analysis that simply cannot be conducted by corporate generalists. Operations managers have a particularly important role on due-diligence teams, since they are going to have to work with the partner to make the combination a success. Middle managers can find many reasons why a deal that looks good on paper will crash upon takeoff. In addition to reviewing operational issues, they can also assess the chemistry between themselves and their counterparts. If it is not there early on, it is not likely to develop later. Differing viewpoints and preferences on how to conduct business are not in and of themselves reasons to negate a deal. But incongruent values, genuine distrust, and full-blown animosity should be noted as red flags. Of course, this assessment works both ways; partner candidates appreciate dealing face to face with executives whom they may ultimately be working with or reporting to.

Some organizations place up to twenty people on their due-diligence teams. This may be bulky up front in terms of scheduling logistics and organizing findings, but it pays off if a "showstopper" is unearthed. One organization convenes duplicate diligence teams to assess candidates and overcome the "deal fever" that frequently afflicts due diligence. Knowing that choosing a poor partner can exact a huge financial toll and be a tremendous burden on management time and energy, this company only pursues combinations that pass muster with both teams.

Due diligence is also a time to size up the breadth and depth of managerial talent in the potential partner. A study of large combinations found that 65 percent of successful acquirers reported managerial talent to be the most important instrument for creating value in a deal.[7] Smart buyers evaluate current executives but also look closely at managers within the target organization who are not yet in leadership positions.

## Cultural Due Diligence

Increasingly, executives seeking to acquire or enter into an alliance think about cultural issues during the precombination phase. There's a simple reason: if they have lived through the pain of clashing cultures in botched acquisitions or disappointing alliances, they don't want to repeat the experience as they plan future ones.

### Quantifying Cultural Due Diligence

CEO Ron Oberlander of Canadian newsprint and publication paper producer Abitibi-Price recognized that a consolidation of firms in the highly fragmented industry was inevitable. Knowing that several potential partners existed, he wanted an understanding of various cultural challenges before making a combination decision. For those firms that passed his company's strategic and financial filters, cultural fit would be used as a criterion in moving forward with a deal.

In early 1997, Oberlander and senior human resource executive Jean-Claude Casavant asked two internal organization development consultants, Michael Leckie and Pascale Carrier, to propose a methodology for assessing the cultural fit between Abitibi-Price and potential merger or acquisition candidates. They responded with a precombination cultural due-diligence process based on a Merging Cultures Evaluation Index (MCEI) that analyzes several dimensions of corporate culture. The MCEI calls for individual members of the executive teams from Abitibi-Price and potential partners to complete a questionnaire of cultural dimensions for their own firm and the other company. Individual scores are aggregated into team rankings and gaps identified, first between the two sides' self-assessments and second between both sides' self-assessments and the evaluation of them made by the other side. The summary report displays mean scores for the two companies (in Figure 3.1, circles represent one organization and squares the other) and the extent to which people within the companies agreed on the particular dimension of their culture. Executives prioritized the cultural dimensions expected to be most important to combination success and analyzed the results accordingly.

This process assumes friendly relations between the parties. In the case of a hostile or uncooperative situation, Abitibi-Price executives would couple their own assessment of the candidate with input from third parties, people like industry analysts, former executives now at other companies, or academics and reporters with knowledge of the company.

**Figure 3.1. Merging Cultures Evaluation Index (MCEI).**

| | Role/Process | | | Results |
|---|---|---|---|---|
| Role/Process Orientation versus Results Orientation | 1 | 2 | 3 | 4 5 |

| | Concentrated | | | Diffused |
|---|---|---|---|---|
| Concentrated Power versus Diffused Power | 1 | 2 | 3 | 4 5 |

| | Horizontal | | | Vertical |
|---|---|---|---|---|
| Horizontal Influence versus Vertical Influence | 1 | 2 | 3 | 4 5 |

| | Innovation | | | Traditional |
|---|---|---|---|---|
| Innovation versus Tradition | 1 | 2 | 3 | 4 5 |

| | Wide | | | Narrow |
|---|---|---|---|---|
| Wide Flow of Information versus Narrow Flow of Information | 1 | 2 | 3 | 4 5 |

| | Thinking | | | Acting |
|---|---|---|---|---|
| Problem Solving: Thinking versus Acting | 1 | 2 | 3 | 4 5 |

| | Recognition | | | Rewards |
|---|---|---|---|---|
| Rewards versus Recognition | 1 | 2 | 3 | 4 5 |

| | Consensus | Consultative | Authoritative | |
|---|---|---|---|---|
| Decision Making | 1 | 2 3 | 4 | 5 |

| | Values | Skills | Results | |
|---|---|---|---|---|
| Attributes of Valued Employees | 1 | 2 3 | 4 | 5 |

Evaluating cultural due-diligence data is not as simple as whether there's a close fit between the currently independent organizations. As depicted in Figure 3.2, a moderate degree of cultural distinctiveness is beneficial to productive combination. If it were possible to find two organizations with completely identical cultures and values guiding their behavior, the combined organization would at best be no better than the sum of the parts. Although too much distinction in underlying values and ways of approaching work is unhealthy, the best alliances and acquisitions occur when a fair amount of culture clash prompts positive debate about what is best for the postcombination organization. Ideally,

## Figure 3.2.  Cultural Differences and Combination Outcomes.

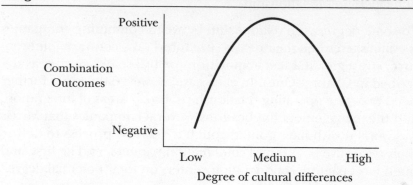

this debate includes consideration of cultural norms that may not be present in either organization separately but that may be desired for the combined organization.

## Parameters: Defining the Combination

Once companies involved in a merger, acquisition, or alliance have assessed the degree of fit between their strategies, organizations, and cultures, the central task is to integrate these dimensions into a coherent picture of the combination. This is no easy task. First, there is a tendency for buyer and seller to get mired in the details of their transaction and lose sight of the big picture. Professors David Jemison and Sim Sitkin, in their studies of the acquisition process, find that fragmentation of financial, strategic, organizational, and cultural analyses leaves the executives involved with differing—often competing—perspectives on how to put their organizations together.[8] Second, each company has its unique way of doing business; its own preferences and power structure; and a history of past decisions, forsaken options, and financial and physical investments. What appears to yield strong financial and strategic synergy between, say, two manufacturing groups may not be realizable because of incompatible structures and systems or sharp differences in cultures. In one deal we worked on, even as planners and analysts forecast savings and synergy, manufacturing managers from the two sides were engaged in "tong warfare" and lobbying their superiors to back out of the deal before it was too late.

## The Operating Relationship

To some degree, the relationship between combining companies is established when their deal is structured (as a contract, joint venture, strategic alliance, acquisition, or full-scale merger, as described in Chapter One). In each case, however, there is a further need to define operating relationships, broad areas of integration, and the management implications. Several companies that Mirvis has worked with have gone through a detailed process to define their respective powers and combination parameters. The first, and often most painful, consideration centers on their potential degree of integration (Figure 3.3).

Cross-company integration is not an all-or-nothing proposition. Options range from full consolidation to near separation of the companies, with other choices in between:

- *Separate holding company.* This is common in conglomerate mergers, where the holding company invests in an asset. It is also found in some combinations between firms in unrelated industries. As an example, this defines the link between USX and Marathon, where the lead company keeps its "hands off" the oil company's management but extracts a good deal of cash. It does not apply to most of the combinations we are discussing here.
- *Strategic control.* Here, the buyer shapes the strategy of an acquiree but exerts arm's-length control over its organization. Early on in the dealings between IBM and Lotus, there was considerable disagreement over how to position the acquiree in the parent company. Lotus CEO Jim Manzi wanted IBM to operate primarily as a "banker" for his company, whereas the parent wanted to run Lotus more or less as a subsidiary. They settled on a middle ground centered on strategic control. Interestingly, many alliances follow this pattern with the "parents."
- *Managed subsidiary.* In this traditional acquisition model, a company enters a new market or offers a new service. Ameritech's acquisition of a home-security company fits the type. The lead company foresaw a future of "smart" homes with telephones, lights, heating, appliances, and security systems interconnected via a computer. As an entrée into this market, Ameritech brought its size, market reach, and network to the

## Figure 3.3.  Degree of Integration Between Combining Companies.

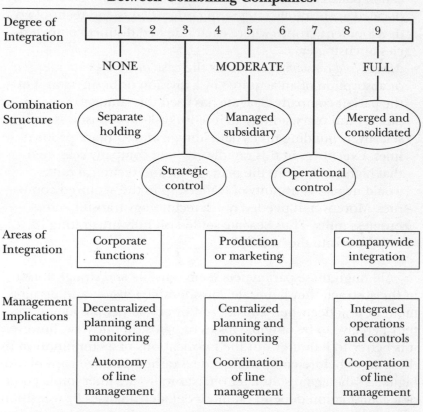

*Source:* Mirvis, P. M., and Marks, M. L. *Managing the Merger: Making It Work.* Upper Saddle River, N.J.: Prentice Hall, 1994.

deal; the acquiree had proprietary technology and product development know-how. There is no doubt that Ameritech controls strategy and budgets in this case, but local management retains its prerogatives over staffing, R&D, and operations. Many joint ventures have this flavor as well. The "parents" oversee the venture through top-down planning, monitoring, and conformance, but the general manager and staff run it as though it were their own company.

- *Operational control.* This is the desired degree of integration when two companies have overlapping capabilities; synergies depend on their combination. An illustration is the merger by composites manufacturers Hexcel and Ciba of selected fabrication plants and marketing units. Yet the combined company decided against fully integrating other plants and technology development groups where each side had distinct competencies or customers.

- *Merged and consolidated.* This is the case of a full-scale merger, or absorption of an acquiree by a division or business unit of the parent company. Seagate has used this strategy over the past several years, adding to its core disk-drive business and selectively building up its data-storage and software-product lines. Executives in this rapidly growing company reasoned that high turnover in the managerial and technical ranks would negate continuity of leadership in the acquired companies. Moreover, it needed quick technology transfer across business units. Thus Seagate settled on fully integrating its acquirees into the "family."

Although these parameters seem sensible and straightforward in the abstract, they generate considerable tension and disagreement in practice when considered by actual people facing what they perceive to be tangible losses or gains. In our view, however, it is better to hammer out the implications of a combination in these areas before completing a deal rather than see gaps or ambiguities sabotage results later on. Naturally, the finer implications of a combination depend on more detailed analyses by transition teams and negotiations between and among the executives who actually run the combined business.

## Defining the End State

In successful combinations, partners share a commonality of purpose and recognize and accept the terms of their relationship. People are then able to focus their energy on a common goal and let go of any wishful thinking that may run counter to the realities of the combination. Yet in many cases, corporate marriage contracts (like those between individuals) tend to be implicit rather than explicit, open to interpretation and misunderstanding. On the one hand, carefully defining the end state of a deal can bring the pleasantries and promises of the precombination courtship to a quick halt. On the other hand, failing to do so can lead to an even less pleasant divorce.

Although the work of achieving the desired end state involves many people, the initial step in formulating it is very much the responsibility of senior executives involved in doing the deal. *In the successful cases,* the senior executive from the buying side puts his cards on the table regarding expectations and assumptions for the combining organizations. The senior executive needs to think through and come to the precombination discussions with a clear sense of which aspects of this desired end state are open to negotiation and which are not—that is, which elements of the desired postcombination organization are in play and which are out of bounds during precombination discussions and subsequent planning.

With this in mind, executives who hope to combine their companies are well advised to consider and share their hopes, expectations, and biases for how the postcombination organization is to be structured. These intentions are largely determined by the degree of integration anticipated for the combined organization. We use a grid of different types of postcombination change (Figure 3.4) to help executives think through their options and clarify their intentions for their desired end state.

- *Preservation.* This is the case where the acquired company faces a modest degree of integration and retains its way of doing business. This end state is typically found in diversified companies that promote cultural pluralism, by which we mean an attempt to allow business units to coexist and retain their own cultures. To succeed, corporate management has to protect the boundary of the subsidiary or alliance partner, limiting intrusions by corporate staff and minimizing conformance to its rules and systems. Strategic synergies generated in a preservative combination come from the cross-pollination of people and work on joint programs.
- *Absorption.* Here the acquired company is absorbed by a parent and assimilated into its culture. Lead companies generally bring in new management in these cases and conform the target to corporate reporting relationships and regimens. Examples are acquisitions in the airline industry, such as American Airlines' absorption of Air California, Delta's of Western, and USAir's of Piedmont.
- *Reverse takeover.* This is the mirror image of the absorption combination. The acquired company dictates the terms of the

**Figure 3.4. Degree of Postcombination Change
Envisioned at Precombination Phase.**

|  | Absorption |  | Transformation |
|---|---|---|---|
| High | **Absorption**<br><br>Acquired company conforms to acquirer—Cultural assimilation |  | **Transformation**<br><br>Both companies find new ways of operating—Cultural transformation |
| Degree of Change in Acquired Company |  | **Best of Both**<br><br>Additive from both sides — Cultural integration |  |
| Low | **Preservation**<br><br>Acquired company retains its independence—Cultural autonomy |  | **Reverse Merger**<br><br>Unusual case of acquired company dictating terms—Cultural assimilation |

Low                                                                                   High

Degree of Change in Acquiring Company

*Source:* Mirvis, P. M., and Marks, M. L. *Managing the Merger: Making It Work.*
Upper Saddle River, N.J.: Prentice Hall, 1994.

combination and effects cultural change within the lead company. When this unusual type of combination occurs, it typically involves an acquired business unit or division absorbing
the operations of a parallel unit in the acquirer. For example,
Marriott acquired Saga and folded in its own contract food
services business.

• *The best of both.* This is the case of achieving synergy between
  companies through partial or full integration. Studies find
  this additive kind of combination to be more successful than
  others—and most fraught with risk.[9] It can also be the bloodi-
  est. Financial and operational synergies are achieved by consolidation; this means "crunching" functions together and
  often leads to reductions in workforce. The optimal result is
  the blending of both companies' policies and practices. The

merger of equals between Chemical Bank and Manufacturers Hanover and the combination of Canada's Molson Breweries and Australia's Carling O'Keefe are examples.

- *Transformation.* Here both companies undergo fundamental change following their combination. Synergies come not simply from reorganizing the businesses but from reinventing the company. This is the trickiest of all the combination types, requiring significant investment and inventive management. Transformation poses a sharp break from the past. Existing practices and routines must be abandoned and new ones discovered and developed. In integrating Pfizer's Animal Health Group and SmithKline Beecham's animal health products business in Europe, President Pedro Lichtinger transformed two orthodox operations into a new organization geared toward the emerging realities of the European Community. In doing so, he broke down traditional country-specific structures and cultures and forged a pan-European strategy, structure, team, and identity as the parties merged.

Frequently, the senior executive enters a combination with intentions that functions end up at various points on the grid of Figure 3.4. A company might be purchased, say, with the intention to absorb it into the lead firm's financial regimens, adopt its marketing savvy, and select the best of both sides' approaches to operations. The point is that the executive has a picture of where she wants the combination to end and makes those intentions clear to all parties. Certainly, this end state may change as the partners learn more about each other, and about opportunities and challenges that arise during the combination planning and implementation phases; but both sides enter the combination with a shared sense of the desired end state.

## Cards on the Table

Articulating the desired end state provides an early opportunity to clear the air regarding any misperceptions or fantasies about how the two sides will coexist in the combined organization. False expectations abound in combinations. Sometimes, people innocently misinterpret what they hear because the partners use language inconsistently. Other times, being in a state of psychological denial interferes with the partners' truly hearing what is being stated. Still

other times, a partner knows quite well what is being said, but pre-
sumes that its own political skills will reign and change the situation as the organizations come together.

Beyond checking misperceptions, a well-articulated desired
end state contributes to successful combination in other important
ways. First, it communicates to the workforce that their leadership
has a solid sense of where to take the combination. This drastically
differs from the "Oh no, here we go again" cynicism that accom-
panies most change efforts in organizations today. Second, it gives
people something tangible to talk about rather than turn to the
worst-case scenarios, rumors, and nay-saying that predominate in
most combinations. Third, a clear and understood desired end
state guides combination planning and implementation. Busy executives—and those who check which way the wind is blowing before committing to a course of action—do not want to spend time
on combination planning task forces studying options and making
recommendations, only to have them shot down by the senior executive because they did not fit some preconceived expectations
of what was being looked for.

A well-articulated end state has certain key components:

- *Strategic end state.* Strategy guides not only the decision to combine and the search for a partner but also the purpose of the
  combined organization itself. An alliance requires a clear,
  well-defined strategy of who's doing what and why. It needs
  meat and definition if it is to win over those who are responsible for its future success. An acquisition especially needs early
  direction and a coherent strategy because buyers often have a
  self-serving image of how to win and sellers seldom have their
  act together. Top management on both sides have to work together to reestablish the combination's raison d'être in light of
  the synergies sought and the degree of integration required.
- *Organizational end state.* Senior executives on both sides have
  assumptions regarding organizational architecture and, often,
  different preferences for the basic design of the postcombination organization. Their inclinations for the "super-structure"
  of the organization should be debated, clarified, and then
  conveyed to senior managers and participants in the transition
  planning process as soon as possible, and shortly thereafter to
  the workforce overall. Will the combined company be more
  centralized than decentralized? Will it feature a functional

organization, lines of business, or a matrix approach? The details can be worked out by transition teams as the companies combine, but the outline needs testing and clarification early on.

- *Cultural end state.* What will the cultural end state be for the combined organization? Will one side dominate? Will cultural characteristics be sought from both organizations? Will a transformation be attempted? In cases where the lead company intends to do things its way, it is better to say so from the outset than to pretend otherwise. Stating the hard truth may alienate acquired staff early on, but over the long haul some can be brought on board by selling them on the merits of this way of doing things.

## People: Managing the Dealings

Frequently, senior executives enter a combination with different ideas about the desired end state.

### Shaking Hands, Pounding Shoes

When the CEOs of two high-technology companies shook hands on what they jointly termed a merger of equals, little did they know that they held quite different interpretations of that phrase. The target company CEO assumed it meant both sides would have equal say in combination decisions. The lead company CEO, however, intended it to mean that his side would have the final say but engage their counterparts to determine how to best implement those decisions. Both CEOs prepared their teams according to their personal interpretations; ultimately they destroyed the goodwill between them.

Executive teams from the two sides showed up for their initial combination planning meeting, which was scheduled after the combination announcement but before the legal closing. As the meeting proceeded, lead company executives grew angry at the audacity of target management, who kept offering their opinions on how things should be put together. Target company representatives, in turn, became increasingly upset as their ideas were put down or ignored. The nadir came when the lead company's head of operations took off his shoe, banged it on the table, and barked, "Don't you people understand who is in control here?" Target management stormed out of the session and returned home to complain to their CEO. Upon learning of the disastrous meeting, and feeling led on by his counterpart, the target CEO convened his board and asked them to negate the deal. The target company was in a weak financial condition, however, and the board could not justify that course of action. The deal remained, but so did the bad blood between the two sides.

It may be rare for an executive to emulate Nikita Khrushchev, but it is common for partners to enter a combination with conflicting expectations. To counter this, partners in an alliance or the lead organization in an acquisition need to clarify their intentions for the combination. This means voicing both sides' assumptions and expectations about who is in charge and the desired degree of integration, as well as how they will work together in planning and building that desired organization. Conflicts arising in the precombination negotiations either have to be hashed out or taken as a sign that the partners are not ready to join forces peaceably.

Unlike a true merger of equals or an alliance, where the partners are on relatively equal footing in their precombination dealings, an acquisition often brings together parties with substantially different circumstances. One common difference is size. When the buying side is substantially larger than the seller, it naturally assumes the dominant position and expects compliance. In turn, the dynamics of the deal may color relations between the parties. A friendly courtship presents a much different context than does a hostile takeover. Finally, there is the financial health of the target to consider. In a turnaround situation, acquired management should not expect to have much say. On the contrary, they are likely to be relieved of their jobs.

Problems can be expected when precombination promises do not match postcombination realities. A buyer might talk cooperation during the negotiations but not be in a position to deliver when dismal financial returns and target management turnover dictate a more aggressive response. Thus we counsel leaders on both sides to prepare best-case and worst-case scenarios for their combination and know what each means for eventual control of the business. In one case, this advice persuaded a group vice-president to ease off on integration so long as acquired management met its numbers. In another case, it led a business head to prepare an attractive performance-related stock option package for acquired management to ensure their full commitment to the growth of the subsidiary.

Many times a lead company CEO extols the virtues of a subsidiary and says that the parent company has much to learn from its acquiree. But group management, pressed to make the deal pay for itself, and group comptrollers, eager to consolidate control, often have different ends in mind. They may use terms like "one happy family" but mean "conquest." The problem here is that target management enters the deal with a set of expectations built upon what they hear from the CEO but at odds with what group management is expected to deliver. As the high-tech merger of equals that resulted in the shoe-banging incident shows, talking merger but acting acquisition spells disaster. It is incumbent upon the CEO, then, to either tell it straight or work with his own team to clarify and enforce the desired end state.

## Showstoppers

To help counter the pressure to do a deal, especially as momentum builds toward the end of the precombination phase, it is helpful to step back and carefully and honestly assess problems confronting the impending combination. Executives typically ignore organizational issues in the precombination phase and then undermanage them during the combination period. What should executives think about at this point, beyond the basic strategic and financial fit of the parties? Marks, working with consultants David Nadler and Marilyn Showers, distilled a list of showstoppers to consider prior to final consummation of an acquisition or alliance.[10] If present, these might lead the executive to withdraw from the deal, change the valuation of the acquisition or terms of the alliance, or allocate more resources to manage the aftermath. None of these is necessarily a showstopper in and of itself; but if enough are present and they are serious enough, the combination should be reconsidered or reconceived:

- *Distrust and incompatibility between managements.* Issues of trust and compatibility that arise as a result of the precombination planning and negotiation process may signal difficulty in working together after the deal. If the chemistry among key individuals is not good as they get to know each other, it will bring down the combination. Do you trust your potential partner?
- *Difficulties in working out governance arrangements.* Problems in working out how the combined entity is to be governed and, in particular, what the roles of key individuals will be, flag

divergent or mutually exclusive approaches to governance. Can you put up with the hassles?

- *Lack of talent to manage both ongoing operations and the transition.* Not having enough managerial talent to deal with both core business tasks and the combination puts greater demands on management than there is capacity. Can significant weaknesses in the talent of the combination partner be handled?

- *Significant coordination costs required to obtain synergies.* The reality of obtaining the hypothesized combination benefits is much more costly and time consuming than initially anticipated. Time, money, technology, and other investments required to obtain synergies may distract resources from other important areas. Can you afford it?

- *Disruptions associated with the combination.* Going through the process of combination disrupts business operations and creates significant costs, problems with customers, or opportunities for competitors. Are you prepared for this?

- *Threats to customer relationships as a result of combination.* Customers may feel differently about the combined entity because of its new ownership, its size and position, or other factors that lead them to view the new organization negatively. How loyal are your customers and theirs?

- *Incompatible values and culture.* Core values and cultures that are significantly different are very difficult to combine. Are you prepared for the battles?

- *Postcombination talent drain.* Key managerial, technical, or professional talent may not want to remain because of their feelings about the new owners or partners, the nature of the new company, or real or perceived threats to their careers. Can you replace them?

- *Negative impact on the workforce and communities.* When combination gains require significant layoffs, there may be harm to the workforce and the communities in which the company operates. What is your stance?

- *Postdeal hangover.* The process of the deal has been contentious enough to create significant bad blood that will be difficult to overcome during the combination phase. Are you ready to work together? Do you really want to?

# Precombination Planning

To this point, we have addressed the precombination preparation for doing a specific deal: determining the strategic synergies and rationale, setting criteria and searching for the partner, and clarifying the intentions and desired end state for the combination. Some firms are beginning to complement this with a more generic approach to precombination planning, particularly in industries where acquisitions and alliances have become regularly occurring events. Their aim is to have their act together when a combination opportunity arises.

As these organizations survey their competitive environments and deliberate on strategic responses, they see that combinations are increasingly important for getting them where they want to go. Knowing that acquisitions and alliances are essential to meeting their strategic objectives—and in some cases are necessary for basic survival—executives proactively take the opportunity to prepare for meeting the organizational challenges in combining entities. A small but growing number of companies have either learned from their own failed combinations or taken seriously the feeble track record of other organizations and recognized the need to beef up their readiness for combining successfully.

### An Ounce of Preparation

Kaiser Permanente, the nation's largest health maintenance organization, determined through its strategic planning process that multiple acquisitions and alliances would be essential for its long-term growth and survival in the volatile health care industry. Kaiser's leadership recognized it did not have the internal competence to identify and implement combination opportunities. Advice from external consultants, coupled with the urging of an executive with considerable combination experience who had just joined Kaiser's senior team, led to forming an internal "acquisitions and alliances SWAT team." Middle-level managers from a broad array of functions and geographical units were asked to contribute their perspectives throughout the full combination process, from target selection to integration. Team members attended a two-day offsite meeting where senior executives and external experts presented the financial, legal, operational, human resource, and cultural aspects of the combination process. They received a crash course in everything from valuation to culture clash. Nearly fifty managers "graduated" into roles that complemented staff professionals and external advisors in targeting and integrating acquisition and alliance partners.

### Seeing the Forest for the Trees

At Weyerhaeuser, the forestry and paper products giant, consolidation among other industry players and the recognition that new ventures were likely to be pursued through acquisitions and alliances prompted senior executives to enhance their awareness of combination pitfalls and success factors and their readiness to manage a combination. Finance, strategy, and human resource executives joined with operations executives who had managed previous acquisitions in the company. After hearing a presentation on the organizational and psychological challenges in the combination process, executives engaged in an earnest assessment of their acquisition performance. The open discussion of what had and had not worked in previous combinations, both inside and outside the company, led to a more thorough and rigorous regard for the full set of organizational challenges in a combination.

At both Kaiser and Weyerhaeuser, organizational preparation began well in advance of any combination activity. Even when organizations have not been this foresightful, there is still time to act after the initial combination announcement. In some large acquisitions, several months can pass while legal approval is pending. Most organizations waste this time. Others use it.

### Sounding the Depths

The executive board of a prominent multinational consumer products firm wanted to prepare for an impending merger. The session began with executives sharing their current feelings about the combination:

Despite my best efforts at acting, I cannot not hide my frustration and anxiety from my people.

I've been involved in three mergers, and I saw how in each case it ruined an organization I was very proud of.

I feel like I'm under a microscope. People are searching for any kind of signal to determine whether they should stay or go. Some of my best people are saying to me, "Am I crazy for staying here and not looking for opportunities elsewhere?"

I've already lost one key person who saw the merger and figured, Why not get out now?

I'm not worried about me. I can land on my feet. But I am worried about us as a management team. All the effort we have put into building a team and organization will go by the wayside. I'm afraid for us.

The emotion-laden testimonies set the stage for a call to action among all those in the room to manage the ensuing combination in the best way possible. Specifically, the team wanted to create a model to guide acquisition implementation. After a presentation on the acquisition process, the executive team developed a template covering strategic, organizational, human, and cultural interventions for the precombination, combination, and postcombination phases. The template genuinely was regarded as a guide and not a rigid, lockstep process. The executives realized that they were just one partner in the combination and had to engage their counterparts in accepting and (most likely) revising the template. Still, the executive team ended the session with enhanced confidence that they were on their way to managing the combination in a manner that exceeded their past experiences.

Of course, the optimism and conviction generated in this session were limited to a very few senior executives. All other employees were outside the inner circle engaged in the precombination planning. As the next chapter tells, they bring strong psychological reactions that color relations within and between parties in the early going. The work of the precombination phase, then, includes understanding and dealing with the combination's psychological challenges.

## Chapter Four

# Psychological Preparation

The CEOs of two merging industrial products companies invited Marks to lunch to discuss their upcoming combination process. In their early sixties, both men planned to remain on board for a couple more years, see the integration through, and then turn over the leadership to a younger chief executive. The courtship between the two companies had been very friendly and, as part of the deal making, the two CEOs agreed on their roles in the combined operation. One would have the title of chairman and oversee the administrative, finance, and marketing functions; the other would get the CEO title and lead sales and manufacturing. After exchanging pleasantries and ordering food, one CEO asked, "I don't understand why so many of these mergers fail. We seem to be making good progress and sorting things out." Marks replied, "Of course, things look good from your vantage point. But you're the only two people in both companies who know your titles and roles! Everyone else is wondering and worrying about what might happen to them."

In this chapter, we look at the psychological challenges in joining forces. We describe the mind-sets of buyers and sellers in an acquisition and of partners in an alliance, as well as the sources of employee stress and uncertainty in a combination. We report how organizations and their people use the precombination period to prepare psychologically for the work of combining.

## Combination Mind-Sets

Combination partners typically enter a deal with distinct mind-sets. In an acquisition, the buyer and seller usually have very different psychological perspectives on the deal. Often they bring a one-up, one-down outlook into their dealings, particularly when the ac-quiree endured a downturn in business performance and is strapped for cash. The victor-versus-vanquished outlook is also found in many mergers where one of the parties is clearly seen as the lead company. In an alliance, by contrast, the roles of lead and target are not so well delineated, but psychological factors still in-fluence the relationship. Members on one side may see themselves (or be seen by the other side) as, say, more worldly, technically so-phisticated, financially strong, or savvy in the marketplace. Yet the very premise for the alliance—that the partners will gain access to or leverage each other's technology, patents, customers, or some other capability that they do not already possess—calls for a true meeting of the minds.

Psychological mind-sets certainly influence early dealings and can dominate the critical months of transition planning and imple-mentation. They often carry over into the combined organization. Awareness of these mind-sets, both one's own and the partner's, helps both sides prepare for a successful combination.

## Mind-Set of the Buyer

To the victor go the spoils. Certainly, bidding wars and hostile takeovers are exhilarating for the winners. Even in a friendly deal, there are few moments in an executive's career that equal the in-tensity and satisfaction of buying another company.

Acquiring another organization, or assuming the role of lead party in a merger or alliance, translates into a strong air of superi-ority. Company executives have just made a big deal; they are heady, confident, and very much on a roll. This attitude frequently carries over into assumptions that the buying company's business acumen—and policies, procedures, people, and systems—are su-perior to those of the purchased firm. Being the dominant party contributes to condescending attitudes about the other side: "They're still battling the problems we solved five years ago"; "Wait until we show them how to do things"; "Our systems will bring them into the modern age."

As the combination begins, the lead company is impelled to move fast and consolidate its gains. A sense of urgency prevails in the lead organization as it wants to put plans into motion fast.

There is always something uncertain about precisely what has been bought: who they are, what they do, whether they really know how to run their business. Corporate staffers pounce on the target, to get their hands on things in a hurry.

This fuels managers' momentum in the lead company, their desire to dominate the action. They have studied the situation longer and have more detailed plans and priorities. Top management may have promised to go slow and honor traditions during the precombination negotiations, but vice presidents, corporate staffers, and managers get the taste of power and have their own designs. Moreover, they are rewarded for meeting budgets and producing results, not for how fairly or smoothly they manage the combination. As a result, lead managers often unilaterally dominate the action and impose their own integration plans. Prior promises mean nothing.

## Mind-Set of the Seller

Why is being acquired so debilitating to an organization? From the start, in the case of a hostile deal or one imposed by the board, there is a sense of violation: we have interviewed executives who liken it to rape and describe their buyer as an attacker or barbarian. Even in friendly deals, acquired managers often describe themselves as being "seduced" by promises that changes will be minimal, or as being "taken advantage of" once they are forced to accommodate the new owner's demands.

A state of shock permeates a company following an acquisition announcement. Executives wander the halls after a combination is announced, unprepared to assume new duties and responsibilities. Executive recruiter John Handy found that 90 percent of nearly one thousand senior and middle executives he studied were psychologically unprepared for the changes in status and organizational structure they would encounter following their company's acquisition.[1] Seeing and sensing the anxiety in their superiors, other employees grow anxious about the combination, how it will be managed, and their personal fate in it.

One way executives cope with their shock is defensive retreat. This allows acquired executives to regroup and reformulate a "battle plan" for countering the "enemy." At one acquired manufacturing firm, this led to a strategy of noncompliance and various tactics to resist the overtures of the lead company. Even in so-called mergers of equals, perceived fears of losing status or ways of doing things lead executives to dig in and protect their turf.

Finally, acquirees often feel powerless to defend their interests or control their fate. Even when the deal is friendly or when a company is rescued from a hostile deal by a sympathetic third party, the consequences are frequently out of acquirees' control. Sellers sometimes respond with passive or aggressive hostility, or they may withdraw in defeatism.

Many managers find that Elisabeth Kübler-Ross's stages of reaction to death and loss mirror their personal reactions to being acquired.[2] Initially, there is denial and disbelief. In shock, they deny the reality and their own vulnerability; there may be underreaction ("nothing will happen") or overreaction ("everything will change"). People in the target company then experience anger. They are angry at their leadership for selling out and cashing in. Later they will be angry with the buyer. Although expressing anger allows people to vent their emotions, many become stuck at this stage and are never able to move on to accommodate the new situation, fixating instead on what is behind them.

For those who can move forward psychologically, next comes bargaining. People's natural tendency is to look out for number one. Some leave what they consider to be a sinking ship; others try to make themselves indispensable. Some cozy up to new management and pitch their importance and value to the organization, while others guard data or customer relationships as leverage for survival.

Only after time do people accept the reality of the new situation and become ready to work with counterparts in a genuine and committed way. For some, this may be a matter of weeks or months. Others take years. Some individuals never reach the stage of acceptance.

## Mind-Set of a Partner

An alliance or joint venture provides something that even the friendliest of acquisitions never can achieve: the opportunity to test the compatibility and working style of the partners. Certainly, in an acquisition the parties can—and should—get a sense of how they work together during the precombination period. Genuine distrust or bad chemistry between the parties could be a showstopper, but in practice it gets downplayed or overlooked if the lead company sees a compelling strategic reason to go forward with the deal. Furthermore, if the lead company wants to pursue the deal—and can arrange the financing and get the backing of its board—it can unilaterally go after the target. In an alliance, both sides need to agree that going forward makes sense.

Compatibility in an alliance should not be confused with duplication. The potential benefits of a combination may not be tapped unless there are some healthy differences between the two organizations that stretch either side or both to achieve something new in the marketplace.[3] Still, the two sides' precombination mindsets make a difference in eventual success. Four key elements define the right mind-set for joining forces in an alliance or venture:

1. *Trust.* Either trust is present in the relationship—such that both partners are confident the other intends to do what it says—or it must grow through honest and reliable conduct during precombination planning. Trust cannot be negotiated as a condition for a deal, nor can a lack of it be compensated through financial or legal maneuvering or an alliance design that keeps the parties at arm's length. In short, either trust your partner or walk away.

2. *Compatibility.* Partnership implies that individuals from the combining organizations have the ability to work well with one another. At a minimum, a bond needs to form between people that allows them to resolve difficult issues and conflicts. More positively, a spirit develops that propels collaboration and eagerness to work together in the enterprise.

3. *Shared purpose.* Successful alliance partners share with their counterparts a sense of purpose and an agreeable direction.[4] Both sides are open about what they want from a combination and work together to achieve it. Each side may have distinct goals and priorities, but they rely on their interdependent interests to forge achievements.

4. *Cooperative spirit.* In an alliance, the competition that pits partners against one another in segments of their market needs to be displaced by a cooperative spirit. Partners need to believe in and find win-win resolutions to issues, and see that the structure, operations, risks, and rewards in the alliance are fairly apportioned.[5] Egos are fed by team achievements as much as by personal victories.

## Psychological Preparation

An executive we worked with several years ago suggested that preparing for a combination was like "preparing to be hit by a Mack truck." Maybe so, but at least it helps to know that others have gotten up off the pavement and gone on with their lives. Psychological preparation for a combination means raising awareness of the normal and expected mind-sets of combination partners. It alerts executives on both sides to the mind-sets of the buyer and the seller, and it holds up the mind-set of partnership as the standard to achieve.

The objective of preparation cannot be to eradicate the buyer and seller mind-sets; that would be artificial and futile. Rather, psychological preparation readies people to join forces by sensitizing them to the dynamics as the combination is negotiated and a deal is made. By raising awareness of these dynamics, buyers are more likely to sense when they are lurching into a dominating mode and curb or at least temper their actions. And they are more likely to be patient with sellers who are in denial, working through their anger, or angling for an advantage for themselves. Concurrently, sellers who are aware of the stages of dealing with loss are more apt to be in control of their emotions when interacting with counterparts from the lead organization. When aware of the mind-set of the buyer, sellers are more likely to recognize what impels power plays and efforts at domination. In many combinations in which we have been involved, employees from both sides participated in sensitization seminars to foster dialogue about their respective mind-sets. At these sessions, individuals hear about combination mind-sets, express their hopes and concerns in going forward, and learn tactics for coping with their own mind-set and that of their counterparts.

Another way to raise awareness of combination mind-sets is by educating people through readings, presentations, or discussions of the human realities of a combination. Many organizations distribute books and articles describing the mind-sets of buyer and seller, sponsor workshops in which outside experts describe the dynamics of combining, and engage executives in discussing expectations or experiences in going through combinations. In organizations with experience in combinations, veterans of previous acquisitions and alliances can share their firsthand experiences with novices.

## Consciousness-Raising Workshops

A more dynamic approach to raising awareness of these mind-sets is through an experiential activity that helps people develop a true feeling of what it is like to acquire or be acquired. In the case noted in the prior chapter, where two CEOs had different views on the meaning of their "merger of equals," Marks engaged executives from both sides in a two-day meeting that combined educational with experiential activities. The following extended case study details what happened.

### Reversing—and Rehearsing—Roles

The morning of the first day began with a presentation on human, cultural, and organizational issues in combinations, including the mind-sets of buyers and sellers. Then, executives participated in a discussion that vacillated between generic issues of buying, selling, and combining companies and specific issues in their combination. After a lunch break, the two teams went to work on a business simulation. Acquired executives played the Micro Widget Company and lead company executives the Macro Widget Company. These executives, being the competitive business people they were, threw themselves into the simulation and established strategies and tactics for maximizing their returns. Just five minutes before the close of the first day's session, however, Marks announced that the Micro Widget Company intended to acquire Macro Widget (reversing the two sides' roles in the actual deal)! Nothing further was said about the details of the acquisition, though more information was promised to be forthcoming the next morning. The meeting adjourned for day one, and the participants were invited to cocktails and dinner.

Entering the lounge, one would have thought the simulation was still on. Macro Widget executives huddled in one corner, wondering aloud about their fate at the hands of their new owners and plotting ways to resist any changes in control. Micro Widget executives, at the other end of the bar, began planning how they would establish authority in their new acquisition. Both sides continued to ask questions about the deal and its purpose and expected progress, but they learned that there was no further news available.

The next morning, combination planning sessions commenced. Meeting separately, the two groups identified their negotiating teams and readied their strategies. The targeted Macro team was determined to protect its independence despite the change in ownership. The buying Micro team aimed toward consolidating operations quickly. Note that the two teams were not coached to develop these mind-sets; rather, they developed naturally based on their roles.

Then it was announced that the two sides would participate in a series of negotiating sessions alternating with time allotted for the teams to report back to their colleagues. After three rounds of negotiations, no progress had been made; target executives were obstinate in their resistance and lead executives were growing increasingly disenchanted with the lack of progress in negotiations and planning. Marks then took on the role of the lead company CEO and asked the head of the Micro Widget negotiating team why no progress had been made on integration. In a fit of frustration at the next negotiating session, he "fired" the executive who headed the Macro Widget team. At that point an end was called to the simulation and the two sides were brought together to discuss what they had experienced.

Micro Widget company executives began by asserting how uncooperative and unrealistic their acquired counterparts had been. Macro Widget company executives, in turn, complained that the buyers never intended to listen to any input from their side, were disrespectful to them and their way of doing things, and were not willing to negotiate alternative courses for approaching the combination. Both sides were asked to describe how their feelings might influence their subsequent behaviors back on the job. (Keep in mind that the Macros were the true lead company and the Micros the acquired.) Macro Widget executives acknowledged that what they saw the Micro Widget team doing in the simulation reflected their own tendencies back in the real acquisition: they were eager to move ahead with consolidation and assumed things would go their way. More than this, however, the Macros gained a deep understanding of what it is like to have one's organization suddenly taken away in a combination. They became more sympathetic and empathetic toward the plight of their real-life acquired counterparts. The Micros, for their part, came to see how easy it was to slip into the mind-set of the buyer and dominate the action. The awareness of self and others raised in the experiential activity led to the creation of formal ground rules for combination planning. The two groups then disclosed their expectations and intentions, and the full group discussed how they could move from the mind-sets of buyers and sellers to one of partnership.

Back in the real world, as the combination became legal and integration planning hit full stride no one expected a complete turnaround in people's behaviors. Yet both sides saw enough movement in their counterparts and give-and-take in their relationship to build confidence in their ability to move forward together. Lead company executives still dominated the action, but they were careful to think through how unilateral actions on their part would affect the acquired team. They became more patient, did more explaining than dictating, and looked for opportunities for true collaboration. Acquired executives grew more tolerant of the style of the lead company but were also able to call a time-out and confront their counterparts when domination seemed extreme. Although the mind-sets of the buyer and seller would never be completely eradicated, both sides recognized when these interfered with productive combination. Operating principles endorsing quick feedback to partners staved off the potentially detrimental impact of the mind-sets.

## Commitment from Top Leadership

Another way to rein in the controlling behaviors of the lead company is to have the proper outlook modeled and managed at the top. In the merger of paper producers Abitibi-Price and Stone-Consolidated, senior team executives met early in the precombination phase, well before the deal became legal. The agenda included frank discussion about the role of the combined executive group in leading the combination and the ground rules that would guide their leadership. One ground rule directed executives to reach out to the other side as they proceeded to make staffing and integration decisions. They acknowledged that only if they practiced partnership and overcame the tendency to favor people and practices familiar from their side could midlevel managers be expected to do the same.

Middle managers who must make the deal work also manifest the mind-sets of buyer and seller. Some headiness on the part of lead company managers down the line is inevitable. *It is imperative, then, that senior executives set the proper tone, articulate the principles of integration, and bring those principles to life in their own actions.* Senior executives must also be prepared to act accordingly when the principles are not followed. A top executive from the lead company in an entertainment merger recalls, "Despite all of the urgings for partnership from our CEO, a sense of 'when in doubt, go with our way' prevailed among middle-level managers from our company. It is very difficult to get people to put aside their way of doing things." In this case, senior executives from the lead company listened and responded to complaints from acquired executives and spent time coaching their own middle managers.

The optimum form of preparation for an acquiree is frank communication from the buyer that clarifies intentions and reveals common ground. Many acquirees have legitimate fears of being dominated by new owners or summarily absorbed into their business. Sometimes these fears are legitimate and need to be confirmed at the outset. But this need not necessarily escalate into continuous conflict.

*Leadership Commitment in an Acquisition*

When outlet mall developer Horizon, Inc., purchased a competitor in financial straits, its CEO was crystal clear about the need to reduce costs and consolidate construction operations. In a gesture of gentility and market savvy, he agreed to retain the services of the acquiree's CEO, insisted that he continue to work with key customers, and even let him retain the title of president for a two-year period. Nevertheless, he stated in no uncertain terms that his company's headquarters would absorb much of the staff work of the acquiree and that integration would proceed according to his firm's framework and plans.

To persuade the acquiree's management of the merits of his proposals, he and his top team spent several weeks in the acquiree's home office, prior to the close of the deal, discussing the opportunity at hand, comparing respective payrolls and operating costs, and reviewing the two sides' methods of site development and management. Through fact-based and well-reasoned arguments, he eventually brought most of acquired management over to his point of view. Furthermore, his counterpart, surprised and pleased to retain the symbols of authority, did some arm-twisting to bring the remaining doubters into the fold. Here, frankly, is a case where a bit of flattery helped smooth tensions; just as important, a mix of patience, logic, and power won the day.

*Leadership Commitment in an Alliance*

In an alliance, where lead and target roles are not so clear-cut, partners are well advised to work out matters of power and commitment prior to making a deal. A lack of mutual commitment hampered the alliance between GE Information Systems and Ameritech. GEIS, seeing real growth potential in the deal, dedicated a considerable share of its resources and senior management time to the alliance. By contrast, the opportunity at hand was far less significant to the head of the much larger commercial business in Ameritech. Persuasion and pushing could only go so far in engaging a larger "mind share" in Ameritech. Retrospectively, Ameritech management acknowledged that they had been neither strategically nor psychologically prepared for the demands that the alliance made on their time and attention. Fortunately, as the partnership's returns grew, they found the time and talent to contribute their share.

# Stress and Uncertainty

Creating value through a combination requires a lot from people, whether they be executives who have to guide a transition while still running the business; task force members who have to sort through mountains of data and make recommendations; or the overall workforce who have to maintain levels of productivity, service, and quality while fretting about what will happen to them. Ignoring or insufficiently attending to the first indications of the merger syndrome has negative, not just neutral, effects on what follows. Some of these results, such as distraction from performance, have immediate implications; others, such as declining employee morale or customer service, burden organizations over the long haul. Foremost among the costs of not addressing the early mindsets of employees is losing the rare opportunity to use their unfrozen status to begin to build a better organization.

There is a critical period in shaping employee perceptions of leadership, the combination, and the emerging organization, starting with the first contacts between partners, continuing through negotiations and the announcement of the deal, and ending with its closure. With 20–20 hindsight, most executives will tell you they underestimated the job of contending with the soft issues during this stage and should have paid more attention to employee concerns and needs. Even leaders of successful combinations who took the time to understand and address employee concerns look back in awe at the magnitude of the challenges, as one reported to us:

> Historically, people from both sides were very loyal. We assumed they would trust us, and we knew we were trustworthy. In functions where we focused our attention, we handled people very well, clarifying their roles and making them feel comfortable. In areas we did not attend too closely, we lost a lot of good talent. It only takes one or two accidents to kill the goodwill and momentum we developed in addressing human issues. We were not assertive in understanding how difficult the combination was for people throughout the organization. And once a competitor hired one or two of our people and saw how good they were, it opened a flood gate. We lost scores of good people simply because we assumed loyalty and trust would make up for not attending to them.

## What Makes a Combination So Stressful

Why are combinations so stressful for executives and employees?

- *There's more work to do and less time to do it.* The sheer amount of work involved in combining two organizations—digesting enormous amounts of information and making bet-the-company decisions—is overwhelming and absorbs senior executives' time and energy. Compounding this is the pressure they encounter to maintain day-to-day results in the face of their employees' dismay and discontent. Tension filters down through an organization during the precombination phase. Staff and lower-level managers are often called upon to assemble information, without knowing the whys and wherefores. Employees are urged to keep their noses to the grindstone and not worry about the uproar around them. Meanwhile, leadership is mostly invisible; when in sight, leaders seem harried and circumspect.

- *The future is highly uncertain.* Questions abound for which no reliable answers are given. Will the deal be consummated? How will reporting relationships be structured in the new organization? Which side's policies and procedures will be followed? Will pay and benefits be affected? Will decision-making practices change? Will expected promotions or job assignments be honored? How will redundancies in staffs and functions be resolved? Will people leave or be let go?

- *This is a time of insecurity.* The rumor mill circulates horror stories that, in an acquisition, show the buyer to be rapacious or the seller's circumstances to be dire; in an alliance, they question the integrity and intentions of the partner. People congregate around coffee machines and water fountains, in lunch rooms and watering holes, to hear the latest gossip. They obsess about how the deal is going and how the combination will affect them. Many find their self-confidence being hacked away. Managers and employees who have mastered their jobs (both formal job requirements and informal customs) now find themselves worrying about what will be asked of them. This is especially troubling for good performers, who feel they will have to prove themselves to new leaders and teammates.

- *People feel they've lost control of their situation and fate.* The ability, or at least the perception of having the ability, to exert control is a powerful coping mechanism during stressful times. When people no longer have that control, they are thrust into the panic of the merger syndrome. For some, walking away from their current job is the only way they can see to exert control. Others choose less severe, but equally maladaptive, responses and seek control through politicking or sabotaging the

process. Some become paralyzed and depressed by their perceived lack of control.

## Stress Begets More Stress

Basic research on stress highlights four factors that add to the
angst:[6]

1. *The amount of stress people experience is based upon their subjective perceptions, not on any objective reality.* The personal preoccupation and rumor-mongering associated with the merger syndrome
stem from people's assessments of their situation and personal patterns of coping with stress. Certainly, objective events factor into
subjective perceptions, but the stressfulness of a situation is in the
eye of the beholder. A senior vice president at a major financial institution, who headed up three lines of business prior to a merger
with a similar-sized firm, received the same title in a combined organization but now had responsibility for two lines of business.
Both lines literally doubled in size as a result of the combination,
so an objective observer might conclude that this fellow made out
well; yet for months all he could think about was what he lost: "Why
did they take the line of business away from me? What are they trying to tell me about my career? Doesn't the CEO trust me? I'm better than the person they gave it to."

2. *The threat of an event can be as stress-inducing as the actual event.*
Threatened loss, with all of the associated worry about oneself and
one's family, can be as debilitating as actual loss. Worrying about
not fitting in, lamenting about the loss of one's track record, or ag-
onizing over what might happen to one's career all produce stress.
At this point, it matters not what senior management intends to do
but what people fear their leaders may do.

3. *The stress of an event is determined by the amount of change it implies, not necessarily whether the changes will be good or bad.* Research
shows that marriage and births can be as stressful to people as divorce and deaths. Both disrupt the status quo, entangle family and
friends, and require that people adapt to new circumstances. Most
combinations offer a mix of good things and bad. Even the most
productive combinations require adaptation and produce stress.

4. *The effects of stress are cumulative.* That even positive changes
induce stress is important to consider because the effects of stress
are cumulative. A series of small, seemingly innocuous changes can

add up to a large and significant change in the eyes of people. A proposed change in name, location, and reporting relationships stimulates fear of wholesale change. Multiple transitions—a merger preceded by waves of downsizing and restructuring—overwhelm people's capacity to cope with stress.

## Special Challenges in the Precombination Phase

These sources of stress and uncertainty afflict everyone in a deal, to a greater or lesser extent. Some selected groups of employees, however, require careful attention.

### Retaining Desired Talent

With the announcement of an impending combination comes the risk that top technical and managerial talent will leave for what appear to be greener pastures rather than await their fate in the combined organization. Technical people are extremely marketable today and can find excellent employment opportunities. They don't have to look too hard; executive recruiters swarm over firms engaged in a combination. The bait is appealing: a well-defined job with spelled-out accountability and some added salary and perks to boot. Compare that with the uncertain prospects of staying where everything seems up for grabs, where the talk is more about what is being lost than what might be gained, and where competitive momentum seems to be slowing as people turn inward and attend to the combination rather than stay focused on external customers and competitors. Frequently, top performers in a combination figure that if they have to prove themselves to new leadership, they might as well consider opportunities on the outside.

Besides the expertise they bring to a combined organization, there are special reasons to pay attention to and court top talent. Their technical experience and insider know-how is often essential in identifying and excavating sources of synergy in a combination. This is one reason why buyers pay handsome "stay bonuses" to professionals and technicians who agree to participate on transition teams for a period of, say, up to six months. In addition, their presence symbolically reminds other employees of the excellent benefits of staying on board through the transition and perhaps into the new organization. And of course, customers appreciate dealing with proven contacts as an organization goes through a combination.

Many times, high-caliber people resist joining an alliance or joint venture. They legitimately question the value of moving from their current position—with a known boss, a relatively clear career path, and an established track record—to the less certain work environment of an alliance. Some wonder about the implications for their long-term career of moving away from corporate operations to an outlying area of the business. Here, too, a financial sweetener can be effective in the form of a performance contract or bonus package.

Some advisors suggest making retention of key executives part of the deal negotiations. This makes sense if they are needed and the financial implications can be sensibly worked out. Yet many of the employment contracts we have seen emphasize financial penalties should an executive depart before the agreed-upon time—in other words, put financial handcuffs on people. It is better, in our view, to emphasize performance bonuses and enrich the payout for their growing the business.

## Winning "Their" People Over

What is also needed to retain people is a personal bond between leadership from the lead company and desired talent from the partner. The keepers have to be identified early in the precombination phase and engaged in dialogue that evinces a high regard for their talents and shows attention to their needs. *In successful combinations,* leaders find out what motivates people from the partner organizations. What would turn them on in the new organization, and what would turn them off? What perceptions do they have about its leadership and management style? What are their worst-case fears about the combination? Their best-case hopes? What job do they personally hope for? What job will they settle for?

In this respect, retention is akin to recruiting people to be part of the combined organization. Key performers can—and should— be told that they are needed and wanted, and listened to regarding what they need and want; but no promises about role, responsibilities, or reporting relationships should be made unless there is complete certainty that they can be kept. Like all employees, top talent has to endure some uncertainty as the structure and positions are sorted out. They may press for specifics about their assignment, especially when attractive job opportunities outside the company are being dangled in front of them. Here, the ambiguity enveloping them can be turned to advantage: keepers will be part of a team of people building a new and better organization. How often in people's careers are they in a position to influence the design and start-up of a new organization (or at least to design significant improvements in an ongoing operation)? The excitement and potential of two in the bush can sometimes overcome the security of one in the hand.

While money talks, additional incentives can be used to retain key talent. One is the opportunity to participate in a successful transition. In the merger of Canadian firms Abitibi-Price and Stonc-Consolidated, many Toronto-based IT professionals indicated they would not move to the combined company's new home base in Montreal. Some had spouses with career positions in Toronto, and others knew they could find IT positions with other companies there. Still, they were desperately needed to contribute to a smooth transition.

Personal attention and a clear message of the value of staying on through the transition were effective in retaining a critical mass of IT professionals. Especially powerful was the point that participating in a successful merger would benefit people's long-term career marketability. They could distinguish themselves from other equally talented technical experts by documenting on their resumes and in job interviews that they had a hand in managing a successful combination—a competency sure to be sought by potential employers anticipating their own acquisitions and alliances.

The ability of leaders to do this kind of recruiting is largely influenced by the extent to which they have their own act together. This means having a compelling strategy thought out, knowing who will be needed to effect it, and having leaders who can rally people regarding the upside of the combination. People below the top team make note of how well prepared and together their leadership seems to be, and signals sent from the top are a barometer for what life will be like during and after the combination. Early impressions matter significantly when it comes to retaining people who have opportunities elsewhere. "We could have saved some people who left," figured one CFO of a combination; "We inadvertently sent some wrong messages, and it's difficult to change those perceptions when they are in place."

*Retention at What Price?*

In the case of Hewlett Packard's acquisition of Apollo, a key question in the precombination period was what would it take to retain Apollo's top talent. HP typically hired engineers straight out of midwestern colleges and groomed them in "the HP way." Pay rates were competitive but not outstanding and were complemented by a full battery of benefits. The problem was that the acquiree was staffed by seasoned engineers who were highly paid—some of them 20–30 percent more than their counterparts. Moreover, many had received shares of ownership in their company and expected as much, or more, from their new owners.

Early proposals to merge the two engineering groups recommended a gradual leveling of pay rates between the two sides. Top-flight engineers at the acquiree balked at pay proposals and threatened to resign en masse and seek employment at start-ups. Meanwhile, hard feelings over pay differentials began to crop up among HP's engineers. The question posed here was whether or not the buyer was willing to amend its pay policies to accommodate free-agent players and risk morale problems among its home team.

In the end, HP kept its pay policies but made special deals with selected top talent in Apollo that featured signing bonuses and attractive performance-based incentives. Interestingly, IBM made such arrangements for the "stars" at Lotus as well. This is a big issue in high-tech acquisitions, one that should be carefully considered before making a deal. It is our belief that many high-tech buyers fool themselves if they think that hardware and software engineers will settle for industry-standard pay rates when they still have hopes of making millions with another start-up venture. Yet, experience shows that at least some top talent can be retained, provided the buyer is willing to ante up.

## The Acquired CEO

Many times an acquired chief executive officer is not able to function smoothly and productively in working for a parent organization. After calling the shots from the top job (and usually having a healthy severance beckoning), most acquired CEOs choose to leave and pursue other interests. Those who remain tend to have difficulty in adapting to a new regime; reporting to someone who may be younger, less experienced, or with a lower-status title, and staying out of the way of the surviving CEO. It simply is difficult for most one-time CEOs to play second fiddle after being in the lead chair.

Nevertheless, the lead company may want the acquired CEO to remain on board for a while and assist in the dual tasks of managing the combination while running the business, or even serve in a broader capacity in the parent company, perhaps heading a business group. Naturally, this is an important part of the pre-combination discussions. If there is no meeting of the minds during the negotiations, then it's unlikely to arise later on. In the meantime, the rest of the combination stalls in a wait-and-see mode until the acquired CEO's fate is settled. In cases where the acquired chief executive remains temporarily for the transition, the title, responsibilities, and time frame for the assignment also need to be clarified up front. Any ambiguity that seeps into the combination planning period is a major distraction from the work going forward, both for the acquired CEO and for the executives and employees surrounding her.

There have been some cases in which the acquired CEO remains on board and serves productively in the combined organization. These instances have key characteristics:

- *The combining CEOs share some history and friendly relations.* In two cases of CEOs remaining but not assuming the number one position—Walter Shipley in the merger of Chemical Bank and Manufacturers Hanover and Norm Augustine in the Lockheed and Martin Marietta combination—they were good friends and had a long relationship with their new chairmen, John McGuillicuddy and Dan Telep, respectively. Trust already existed in their relationships, and the players did not require a feeling-out period to determine whether they could work well together. Moreover, after years of competing in the same industries, the surviving CEOs knew that the styles of their counterparts were substantially congruent with their own and that the transition would not cause a major disruption down the road.
- *Well-defined roles and timetables.* Neither Shipley nor Augustine sat around waiting for the calendar pages to flip until they assumed the CEO position. Because both had in place clearly defined responsibilities immediately upon the combination, there was no confusion through the ranks regarding who was really in charge. And both had agreements with their new bosses as to when the leadership baton would be handed over.

- *The acquired CEO is given a "real" job.* Nothing frustrates an acquired CEO more than being relegated to a figurehead role with no real responsibility. The ego that ran a corporation needs some sense of true importance and consequence. The job can be a temporary one, such as overseeing the transition structure determining combination plans. In fact, putting someone in charge who has the stature of the former CEO sends a message that the process matters and will be balanced.
- *The acquired CEO is supported and assisted in the transition.* Cisco Systems has been able to hold onto nine of the fourteen CEOs whose companies it has acquired. In addition to being very specific about roles and expectations following the acquisition, Cisco sends someone who was brought into the company under similar circumstances to talk to newly acquired CEOs. The contact gives the CEO a primer in the style and protocol that predominate in Cisco and also provides a sympathetic ear for the acquired CEO adapting to a new corporate order. Hearing about how another person successfully maneuvered through the transition and settled productively and positively into a larger organization is a potent influence in keeping an executive with the combination.

We often spend time meeting one-on-one with acquired chief executives. Initially, we help them think about their desire and ability to head a subsidiary. The acquired CEOs frequently come to the realization that this is not what they want to do. In such a case, we work with the lead and acquired CEOs to determine whether it is best for the individual to remain on board for a period of time or leave promptly. Often, situational factors affect the decision. If there is a paucity of management talent in the combining companies, then the acquired CEO (if willing) can help out during the transition. In the merger of two energy companies, the lead company CEO had just been elected to a one-year term as president of a national industry group and was obliged to travel extensively. The acquired CEO agreed to help lead the transition planning process, but both sides determined that this would last for no more than one year. In an acquisition of a manufacturing firm by a larger competitor, some quality problems immediately prior to the merger had key customers up in arms. The acquired CEO agreed to remain for six months, with the explicit assignment of visiting customers and acting as their liaison during the transition. All parties were comfortable with this arrangement as it kept the acquired CEO away from the action inside the company.

Even when an acquired CEO is welcome to remain and wants to stay, we find ourselves doing a lot of listening and coaching with these individuals. We hear plenty about their frustrations and anxieties concerning no longer being able to call the shots. Often, the venting helps them cope, and the guided thinking about their situation helps them get in touch with their underlying emotions. We also assist acquired CEOs in their transition, coaching them on ways to make a positive contribution without bumping into the responsibilities of others on the leadership team.

At seminars on the combination process, we are frequently asked what to do with an entrepreneurial CEO who started a business and is now acquired by a large firm. The lead organization has to think long and hard about the costs and benefits of retaining the founding CEO. As stated above, it is of foremost importance to hear the person's desires. How does he or she feel about leaving behind an organization raised from infancy? How will the acquired CEO feel in a larger and more bureaucratic operation? It's also helpful to talk with the next tiers of management in the acquired firm, to get their viewpoint. They may be lost without their leader and fear that no one will look out for them in the post-combination organization. Alternatively, they may be grateful that managers with higher professionalism are taking over and replacing the idiosyncrasies and quirks of someone whose managerial skills have kept them from succeeding. As with other aspects of the combination process, it pays to assess the specific dynamics and personalities rather than follow an unyielding rule.

## Preparing the Acquired Organization for Sale

Unless the lead company intends to make a preservative acquisition and maintain an acquired firm's autonomy, the sale of a firm implies the end of its identity. The denial, shock, and anger inherent in the mind-set of an acquiree can result in inertia that plagues the target company following a sale and for months thereafter. With senior leaders preoccupied with how they may personally be affected, and thrust into a crisis-management mode, rarely is the time between announcing the combination and its legal closing used at all creatively. Yet executives at a few companies have used the precombination period to prepare for the psychological challenges of being acquired.

### Preparing to Be Acquired

When Los Angeles-based First Interstate Bank (FIB) received an unwanted takeover bid from San Francisco-headquartered Wells Fargo Bank, target CEO William Siart identified First Bank System of Minneapolis as a potential white knight acquirer. A bidding war ensued, with employees keenly rooting for First Bank. Recollecting the ruthless manner in which Wells integrated previous acquisition target Crocker Bank, and reading business press predictions of fewer job losses in California if the midwestern bank won the contest, FIB people hinged their hopes on First Bank. "We started planning early because we knew we were in for a ride," recalled FIB's Lilian Gorman, who then headed human resources.

Investigating First Bank's culture, she concluded it would manage the combination more collaboratively than Wells Fargo; and she found a close fit in the values underlying First Bank's and First Interstate's human resource philosophies. One of those values embraced a developmental approach to organizational change. Working with her staff, Gorman designed a six-month cultural integration program to develop understanding between the potential partners, identify gaps between them, and start the work of building a shared culture. Of course, FIB was the target company and could not implement such a program on its own. Yet, from early meetings with First Bank executives and reports about the company from other sources, Gorman was confident that the program developed by her staff would at the very least have a major impact on the eventual integration process.

Gorman also knew she had to address concerns of job security among her workforce. She felt her fiduciary obligation was to deliver a high-quality workforce to the buyer, whether First Bank System or Wells Fargo. Again, she did not waste the time between announcement and legal closing. Using that time to plan distinguished her from many human resource executives who, fearing for their own security, either consciously take a wait-and-see approach or subconsciously become paralyzed by the anxiety and trepidation. Gorman and her team prepared a "human resources merger response plan" to guide the allocation of effort and resources under her control. The plan anticipated the needs of various groups of employees, including potential victims of layoffs, surviving employees, and executives with employment contracts. It spanned the dimensions of the human resource function from compensation and benefits to affirmative action (Exhibit 4.1).

### Exhibit 4.1.  First Interstate Bank Human Resources Merger Response Plan.

- Clear the decks (HR staff)
    Review projects and priorities
    Eliminate non-essentials
- Engage a merger management consultant
    Identify and review consultants
    Make selection
    Develop merger management "people principles"
- Develop employee communications strategy
    Link with employee communications
    Review alternatives and media
    Prepare master Q&As
- Implement hiring freeze
    Establish exception process
- Develop morale interventions
    Recommend appropriate interventions and activities
    Create a new performance appraisal system to reward and reinforce
        the right attitudes and behaviors in the new organization
    Implement interventions
- Develop training response
    Develop and launch appropriate training response for maintaining
        productivity during transition
    Offer special programs to support employees (stress management,
        financial management, interviewing skills)
    Order career planning tools
    Respond to training policy questions
- Develop severance policy response
    Anticipate and respond to potential policy questions
    Develop a contingency negotiation posture for employee severance,
        benefits, etc.
- Development compensation and benefit response
    Prepare responses to anticipated questions
    Research and resolve "golden parachute" questions
    Advise holders on their contracts
    Consider availability of potential retention bonus strategies in view
        of rich severance package
- Visit the issues from an affirmative action/career opportunity
  perspective
    Look at processes from an affirmative-action point of view
    Review processes from a career-development point of view

Wells Fargo eventually won the bidding war and with it the right to run the acquisition however it pleased. Gorman knew her plans would never fit with Wells's approach to human resource management and did not push hard on the buyers to consider them. Although she had prepared for a broad intervention, instead she had to settle for offering basic change management workshops. Sadly unable to forward her developmental plan, Gorman confined her efforts to getting the best possible deals and protection for the thousands of First Interstate employees who would be losing their jobs in the coming months and, to the extent possible, deliver a motivated force of survivors to Wells.

In other cases we have worked on, however, there have been better results. A professional colleague of ours, Jim Gillespie, held a "grieving meeting" with executives of an acquired company where, although he was an outside consultant, he had been very much a part of the team. Together they mourned the loss of their history and operation as a public company. In addition, they prepared a thorough and thoughtful briefing on the mores of their management philosophy and used this as a means to encourage their new owners to try out a more participatory style of management—for the combination and for the parent company! In another case, Mirvis led a three-day celebration heralding the sale of King Broadcasting, which featured sessions on the mind-set of the acquiree and concluded with a moving recitation by each employee of what he or she would be leaving behind or carrying forward into an uncertain future.

## Middle Managers' Role

Middle-level managers and supervisors play a prominent role in helping the overall workforce manage stress and uncertainty during this crucial precombination period before the sale is complete and integration gets under way. In the communications arena, organizational leaders set the tone and staff communications professionals make important contributions, but employees want to be kept informed by their immediate superiors. These are the representatives of management they see everyday, and employees know how to "read" them for the subtle signals and cues that help interpret the implications of the facts being delivered.

Unfortunately, middle managers often are caught in their middle-ness. They are bombarded with questions from their subordinates but do not have the information available to those at the top. Thus, they generally need assistance in communicating: training in effective communications methods, feedback on their styles, and content in the form of question-and-answer packets and briefings. Some managers study this material and adapt it into their own words and style; others report it to employees verbatim, while still others make copies and distribute them to their teams. Any of these methods is fine, so long as managers get the word out to their people.

A large part of middle managers' communication responsibility in the early going is to establish a climate of "When the information becomes available, you will get it." Employees learn that their immediate superiors do not have all the answers. The communications imperative for superiors is to acknowledge the issues, explain why no answer is yet available, and accept responsibility of getting back to people when one is available. Still, effective communications flow upward as well as downward. Even if managers have little information to impart to employees, they can nevertheless meet with individuals or groups to solicit their concerns. In these formal or informal listening sessions, managers and superiors are well advised to stay quiet and take notes, allowing employees to express their frustrations, concerns, and hopes. At the very least, people leave the sessions knowing that their superiors have heard their agenda and will keep their concerns in mind as the combination moves forward.

Preparing supervisors and managers for their role in helping employees cope with precombination uncertainty and insecurity includes alerting them to symptoms of the merger syndrome and other ways in which their team members may respond. Superiors who recognize subordinates' emotional pain are more likely to give them the space to work through those feelings and thereby keep such emotions from resulting in harmful effects. Team leaders who anticipate roadblocks to productivity can work with employees to assess workloads, review procedures, and prioritize competing demands. Although the pain and frustration are still there and affect individual well-being and team performance, they can be acknowledged and addressed.

Of course, midlevel managers and supervisors are more than passive agents relaying the missives of senior leaders and using the tools and tactics handed to them by human resources, corporate communications, and other staff professionals. They have to take these resources, put their own spin on them, and be proactive in helping their subordinates.

*Managing the Sales Staff*

In an international consumer products merger, rumors spread quickly following the announcement that all senior sales management positions were going
to one side. Sales managers from both partners took personal responsibility for
dealing with the fallout. In the "losing" side, middle managers spent time
with their sales staff, working with them to see the facts of the deal along with
the fears, reminding them of the many upside opportunities for sales professionals in a prominent new market leader, asking them to stay focused on
their work at hand, getting them to realize the limitations and restrictions imposed on all parties prior to legal closing, and reiterating the messages given
by their CEO regarding his commitment to a fair decision-making process
when staffing choices would be made. On the "winning" side, sales managers
corralled aggressive staff who were making disparaging remarks about their
new partners, asked them to be careful of what they said to customers, and
made it clear to them that staffing selection would be based on criteria other
than which partner a salesperson happened to come from.

## Options for Employees

The workforce benefits from many of the steps taken and actions
endorsed by their leaders, managers, and supervisors. Many employees assume that once a deal is announced, there is a plan for
integration ready to go. So employees need some education on the
basics of the combination process, matters like how deals are made
even though integration plans are far from set. This preparation
also gives employees a realistic sense of time frames, at least some
opportunity to participate in the process, and help in coping with
the uncertainty and insecurity that are inevitably experienced.

Employee communications programs during the precombination phase can go a long way in feeding people's seemingly insatiable desire for information. Valid information from formal
organizational channels offsets the rumors and worst-case scenarios
that flood the employee grapevine, but it also sends a message that
executives are alert to employees' needs.

*Communicating the Full Story*

Corporate Communications Director Susan Rogers, Manager of Employee
Communications Terry Moore, and their colleagues at Abitibi-Price executed a
comprehensive communications program during the period between the an-

nouncement of the pending merger with Stone-Consolidated and the legal closing. One component was a transition newsletter, whose premier issue included a brief history of the partner company, a profile of its CEO, and details on its manufacturing facilities and product lines. Other articles provided a straightforward acknowledgment that change was inevitable for all involved, answers to questions solicited from employees, and guidance by the company's employee assistance advisor on taking control during the merger. The newsletter also featured personal commentaries from two Abitibi employees, one who had gone through a merger previously in her career and another who reflected how he coped with an earlier transfer from Toronto to Montreal.

It is the perceived lack of control over their fate that really concerns employees in a combination. In the consumer products combination, sales staff initially felt there was little they could do to boost their likelihood of being offered a job once they heard through the grapevine that the senior sales positions were going to the other side. One of the most critical aspects of preparing people for a combination is to get them to distinguish between what they can and cannot control in their work environment, and to focus on the former. Too often, people obsess on matters over which they have no control, such as why the deal was done or what senior management is and is not doing. Concerns in these areas are valid and need to be expressed, but excessive fretting about them is unproductive and only increases anxiety and frustration.

### Reclaiming a Sense of Control

At the consumer products firms, formal team meetings provided opportunities for salespeople to vent concerns and fears. Additionally, steps were taken to get employees to examine how they could exert some control over their situation. In the "losing" sales organization, internal human resources staff meet with employees to prepare a "personal contingency plan." The plan set a course of action in the event that the person voluntarily or involuntarily separated from the organization: What people would I call? What educational courses would I take? What companies would I contact? What contacts do I know (for example, recruiters, or friends at other companies)? How can I use this as an opportunity to redo my career, change industries, or start my own business? Most people never had to use their plans, but merely thinking through and writing down ideas for self-preservation helped them focus on a domain in which they had some control. Many of the salespeople were surprised and comforted when they stopped to look at the numerous options available to them.

## Preparing to Move Forward

Strategic, operational, and psychological challenges afflict all combinations, even the friendliest and most soundly conceived. The
more that these issues can be raised and worked through during
the precombination period, the more prepared people are to take
on the challenges of the combination period and contribute to
mining the strategic synergies in a combination. Precombination
planning readies people to move forward in their personal and organizational transitions. It establishes the dynamics that endure as
the combining teams come together to manage the transition from
independent precombination entities to a unified postcombination organization.

# Part Three

# The Combination Phase

## Chapter Five

# Leading the Combination

Combination leadership is a special assignment in an executive's career, not just another managerial posting. Its success depends on how well a leader effectively works the middle ground between partners and instills excitement and commitment in staff on both sides. A Federal Trade Commission panel of merger experts concluded that a firm's combination activity is influenced more by the style and personality of its CEO than by any of the analytic models and planning protocols used by corporate staff.[1] In short, the combined company is going to be shaped as the boss wants it to be: the senior executive leading the combined organization (whose title may or may not be CEO) is the driving force.

The top leadership role is typically settled as part of the deal, with criteria depending on the type of combination.

*In an acquisition,* the parent company CEO or an executive leading a business unit assumes strategic control of the combination and the acquired business. When the acquired CEO wants to stay on and the parent company consents, he reports to the parent company's CEO or business head. But this relationship can be fraught with conflict; surveys of acquired CEOs show complaints centering on loss of decision-making autonomy and constant parent-company intrusions by the parent company bureaucracy. The upshot is that if you want the acquired CEO to run the business, he needs the freedom and running room to make it pay off.[2]

If the acquired CEO departs, the challenge is to find a viable successor within the acquired company. If not, an executive from the parent company will have to run the subsidiary. The question is, who? For seasoned executives, heading an acquiree is not necessarily a desirable career move. Several executives we have worked with have described this as being in "exile" or sent out to a corporate "outpost." In taking the job, they will not as frequently see—nor be seen by—parent company executives and staff. Younger executives, hoping to make a mark, are often eager to head a subsidiary but may not be so well received by acquired managers who are between ten and twenty years senior to them. In either case, an incoming executive is seldom as knowledgeable about the business as local management and runs the risk of being ostracized as an interloper. For these reasons, we advise buyers to scrutinize their "bench strength" prior to a deal and identify two or more candidates who might step in if subsidiary management leaves. In addition to relevant commercial and industry know-how, the candidates should have tremendous interpersonal skills (as described in Chapter Four).

*In a full-scale merger,* there's less complexity but more at stake. In some cases, a CEO near retirement sees a merger as the crowning achievement and a signal to depart. We've worked on mergers where age differences between CEOs who would stay offered each a chance to leave an imprint on integration, assume somewhat different responsibilities, and clarify the passing of leadership. In the merger of Chemical Bank and Manufacturers Hanover, for example, McGuillicuddy (from Manufacturers) assumed the chairmanship for five years and Shipley (from Chemical) operated as CEO until his counterpart's retirement. That way, both could oversee the integration of their two companies yet assume somewhat different responsibilities. In the case of Time Warner, by contrast, Steve Ross ran the show while Gerry Levin broadened his experience and consolidated his power prior to ascending to the throne upon Ross's illness and death.

*In a joint venture or alliance,* there's yet another spin on leadership selection. Coleadership requires comparison of their rank in the home company, age, and ambition (young Turk looking to make a mark; seasoned hand anticipating retirement). "First among equals" is an option, as is having a single general manager (but from which side? favoring staff and proposals from their home organization? bending over backwards to accommodate their partner at the expense of good decisions?).[3]

What is most important is that the alliance leader bring passion and dedication to building a new organization in which the sum is greater than the parts, which at the least calls for considerable time, energy, and finesse to resolve continuous conflict.

Others on the combined senior team can and should assume operational responsibility for productive integration. The top executive or business head has five central tasks during the combination phase, to which we devote the rest of this chapter:

1. *Develop a vision for the combined company.* The leader keeps people focused on what is important to the success of the combination, on what has to be accomplished to realize strategic synergies and build a truly new and better organization. As it provides direction and a desired "end state," the vision gives people in both companies a shared objective in working together.
2. *Establish integration principles and priorities.* Guidelines stipulate, say, a merger of equals, or how much autonomy a subsidiary retains, or the extent of partner integration. Leaders also articulate and model ground rules for executive behavior and for setting and following priorities.
3. *Appoint senior managers to top jobs.* Top-team appointments signal what really matters in the combination and its principles; how well individual executives work together effectively determines how fully synergies are achieved.
4. *Lead the transition organization and transition teams.* Successful CEOs use the transition period not only to plan and implement integration but as well to assess talent, guide decisions, and imprint the new corporate culture.
5. *Speak to human purpose and understanding.* Both the message (personal communications and evocative language to rally the troops) and the medium (displaying empathy and understanding of people's fear of personal costs in the combination) count.

## Vision for the Combination

A few years ago, Marks led an offsite meeting of the top seventy-five executives of a merged financial services organization where one of the primary objectives was to clarify their new vision. The morning of the first day, an article appeared on the front page of *The Wall Street Journal* dubbing vision as "overrated" as a guide to organizational behavior. It cited Chrysler CEO Robert J. Eaton as an example of a top executive who disdained the "vision thing."[4] As they filed into their meeting room, many of the managers referred to the article and suggested the session might not be a good use of their time. A closer look at Eaton's remarks, however, showed his desire for the company to "stay healthy," along with his personal ambition to be the first chairman to never have to lead a Chrysler comeback. This was the essence of Eaton's vision—not especially uplifting but nevertheless clear—and it applied to the firm and to himself. He also gave clear marching orders on how to achieve this: concentrate on managing the "nuts and bolts."

Eaton's direction and guidelines gave Chrysler managers and employees a clear sense of priorities and what he expected of people. The top executives of the financial services provider took the point and spelled out their desires for the combined corporation. Energy rose as they asked what it would take to be the "premier" company in selected markets and challenged themselves with aggressive goals of return on capital and excellence in customer service. As separate companies, each had its own human resource philosophy, one emphasizing the "carrot" to motivate employees and the other the "stick" to ensure hard work and thrift. They settled on a vision that stressed the company's commitment to offer continuous training and development to employees as well as a financial stake in the company's success. Along with this was the expectation that employees would take responsibility to improve their performance and prospects, since the combined firm could no longer guarantee them a job for life.

Such visions and operating principles are especially important in a combination. People are psychologically "needy" for direction during uncertain times and become risk-averse. Their anxiety is manifest in self-imposed pressure not to try out new ways of working—at a time when initiative and innovation are needed to make the combination succeed.

### Just Point the Way

As two HMOs merged, confusion reigned among middle managers as senior management wavered on whether to aggressively pursue membership enrollment or conservatively maintain profitability. Middle managers were left paralyzed by the lack of direction and waiting to see which way they should lead their groups. The director of operations expressed the frustration: "Does senior management want us to go out and run up the membership rolls, or are they interested in protecting margins? Either one is fine by me, but someone has got to let me know which way we are going. I don't want to build an organization that is headed one way and then get chastised because I was supposed to go the other way."

Authoritative business books such as James Collins and Jerry Porras's *Built to Last* (1994) emphasize that successful companies operate with a strong and clear sense of purpose—a guiding vision.[5] That may be motivational for the lead company in a combination, but a central task of the CEO is to communicate the implications to merged management and staff and obtain their understanding and buy-in. In alliances, careful definition of direction is important, too. The issues that tend to bedevil alliances once they are operating are conflict over scope, that is, what falls within the purview of the alliance and what does not.[6] As people feel out the merits of transferring their allegiance to the emerging organization, clear direction helps them understand and look forward to what they are getting themselves into.

## Restating the Business Case

The first step for a CEO taking charge is to reiterate the business case behind the combination. Initially fashioned to convince the two boards and Wall Street analysts of the merits of the deal, the message now is directed at selling employees on why they should invest their efforts and careers in a new organization. The best-crafted messages provide a persuasive rationale for a combination, one that goes beyond the numbers and demonstrates how synergies will result in greater competitiveness, sales growth, and more opportunities (or at least a measure of job security). Even a defensive motive in a consolidating industry can be communicated as something more than an exercise in expense reduction. In Lockheed Martin, for example, the rationale for joining forces went beyond reacting to the shrinking military budget, to proactively seizing the opportunity to capture new commercial business by building on technology and expertise honed in the defense marketplace. Ironically enough, one rationale for Boeing's purchase of McDonnell Douglas was that its commercial skills could help its partner compete with Lockheed Martin in the defense business!

### Envisioning a New Industry

John Lee, a venture capitalist and turnaround artist, assumed the reins at Hexcel in the early 1990s and took the company out of bankruptcy with new financing and disciplined financial management. As the global chemicals business underwent a shake-up, Lee made a bold move and purchased the composites business of Ciba-Geigy via a complex stock exchange and additional cash and securities. No sooner was the ink dry on this deal than Lee acquired a division of Hercules. Suddenly a company nearing collapse achieved, through two combinations, a global presence in the market of structural materials used in aerospace and other industries. On a pro forma combined basis, sales would exceed $800 million in 1995. But what was their aspiration for the years thereafter?

At a series of meetings facilitated by Mirvis, Lee and his senior executives first had to grapple with "Who are we?" According to extant organizational charts, Hexcel was a mix of strategic business units that fabricated lightweight materials used in airplane interiors, boats, and skis, plus structured honeycomb products for building, transport, and some consumer goods. The boom in aerospace, modernization of railroads, and opportunities in Asia aroused the executives in attendance as they contemplated the prospects for growth in each of their strategic business units. As these several SBUs were to some extent vertically integrated (from weaving to fabrication and creation of structures), all agreed that they would have to work cooperatively and in concert to deliver high-performance products on a global scale at a reasonable cost. The questioned remained, however, of whether or not they had a common vision and aspiration.

Through a series of highly interactive dialogues, reviewing the "theory of the case" behind their combination, sizing up the competition and market trends, and sharing their own personal visions of where each would take the company as a whole, a new idea was born. Hexcel would become the "franchise player" in the still-emerging engineered composites industry. This opened up new vistas: automobiles, the wings and engines of airplanes, and a whole swath of industrial and durable goods that were currently constructed from steel or aluminum. "My God," one SBU head concluded, "We are creating an industry!" Fired up by the prospects, Lee and his team departed on a whirlwind global tour of customers and plants to prospect market opportunities and energize staff still fretting about the future of the business. At the core of the message to customers and employees alike was the vision statement created to guide the building of the new company: "Hexcel will lead the engineered composites industry in replacing the traditional materials used in constructing the world's durable goods and infrastructure. We will enhance customer satisfaction and stakeholder value by profitably supplying market needs that have a lasting economic, social, and environmental benefit." It is far too early to tell whether or not Hexcel or any other player will create an industry to rival traditional materials. But with this vision, and aspirations of growing to $2 billion in yearly sales by the end of the century, Lee has "a gleam in his eye" and his team has lifted their sights.

## Critical Success Factors

Critical success factors (CSFs) are the key results that ground the vision in performance. They are the objectives of the combination that drive integration decisions toward creation of value. The CEO has to define and ensure that these CSFs are kept front and center in the minds of managers if the combination is to succeed. They form criteria against which combination decisions and execution are evaluated. For a merged computer-products distributor, the central CSFs included increasing market share worldwide; maintaining a low-cost, efficient operation; securing the best brands; and being the easiest distributor to do business with.

*Weaving Hexcel Together*

Hexcel's CSFs were to lower the life-cycle costs of products, build a world-class proprietary technical position, provide environmentally superior product alternatives, and structure the business to operate globally with a maximum of fiscal responsibility. To achieve these aims, the combined company had to create mechanisms to coordinate work between hitherto independent SBUs and establish a workable transfer pricing system. The work began as a series of one-offs between businesses until Lee and Jürgen Habermaier, the chief executive of the Ciba side, insisted that uniform standards be developed. In the meantime, development of the corporate organization lagged behind. Understanding that none of the parties involved had the necessary skills, CFO Stephen Forsythe took charge of the corporate organization and undertook several new hires. Soon the business heads had performance measures correlated with shareholder value and compensation tied to stock performance. In turn, Hexcel's legal department rapidly ramped up its capacity to develop contracts on five continents. In most unexpected fashion, the heads of the businesses in France and the United Kingdom began to exchange production information and communicate regularly with each other's staffs. Here is a case where critical success factors were used to inform a number of integration decisions and alter managers' accustomed behavior.

## Principles and Priorities

Combinations need principles to guide behavior and decision making, particularly in the integration phase. Consider the principles governing a merger of equals we worked on several years ago:

- *Partnership:* "Merge functions and operations; maintain distinct product lines." This no-nonsense directive established expectations that corporate functions and operating units would fully combine. At the same time, the message to technologists was that many development programs would be protected.
- *Meritocracy:* "Best person, best organization." This affirmed that the combination would be a true merger of equals. But saying it is so doesn't necessarily make it so. The CEO met individually with senior executives on both sides to reinforce his intentions. Many difficult conversations were held on the value of loyalty versus meritocracy in making executive appointments.
- *Unity:* "New company, new culture." The principle here was that the combination would involve a wholesale transformation of the two companies into one. The hope was to achieve breakthrough synergies via a new organization and culture.

As high-minded as such principles sound, they naturally engender skepticism—on both sides—and are not always honored. We've entered several combinations at the stage of damage control only to find that what was supposed to be a merger of peers was turning into plunder. A CEO who pledges equality while the situation dictates more of a three-to-one ratio between top executives from the two sides looks foolish and gains nothing from the attempt at spin. If you intend to fully absorb an acquiree, then say so from the get-go and be prepared to defend your rationale. This is how we usually advise CEOs, and most find that candor is more acceptable to acquired managers than sugar-coated messages.

## Rules of the Road

Besides these formal principles of integration, there are also rules of the road to establish as guides for everyday behavior. In an entertainment industry alliance, one of the rules was to come to meetings prepared. This directly challenged one side's culture of not taking meetings seriously. Another was to accept "roughly right" decisions. This addressed the other side's cultural norm of slowing down decision making by fine-tuning details and wordsmithing language.

In another case, as a high-technology firm acquired a slightly larger competitor, the lead CEO was very clear that the objectives of the combination included not only cost savings but also the ambition to build a customer service culture second to none in the industry. He charged task forces to bring forward recommendations to demonstrably enhance the combined company's internal and external customer service. When initial task force presentations ignored improvements in customer service, the CEO responded with an unambiguous message of his seriousness: he demoted a task force chair who had publicly decried the process. Subsequent recommendations embraced the customer service principle.

In the early days of integration, first impressions set the tone for working relationships as the combination is implemented. How well the senior executive clarifies and monitors the standards and rigor of decision making during the combination period substantially determines the quality and effectiveness of the postcombination organization. It helps when the senior executive distinguishes any "absolute" principles and ground rules—those not open to negotiation—from those that may be subject to modification as they are applied through the organization.

## The CEO's Ten Commandments

Even with well-defined principles, leading people through the maze of combination issues and decisions is a mammoth task. In briefing a CEO in the high-technology industry on what to expect from and how to lead his people in a merger, Marks and colleague Peter Lawton developed a list of "The CEO's Ten Commandments" for managing a combination (Exhibit 5.1). The commandments served two valuable functions. First, they established crisp, authoritative guidelines for behavior. Managers understood what their leader expected of them and how their conduct would be appraised. Second, the process of reviewing the commandments helped the CEO himself to clarify what was needed to make the combination a success.

## Selecting the Leadership Team

The senior leadership team (usually direct reports to the top executive, but sometimes including other senior executives) amplifies or distorts the CEO's intentions in creating a productive combination. That is, members of the top team either act in concert

## Exhibit 5.1.  The CEO's Ten Commandments of Combination Leadership.

### 1. Provide Direction

- Define your own critical success factors. What has to happen in your area if this combination is to be a success?

- Focus people on short-term objectives, deadlines, and assignments–long-term strategies come later.

- Aim high and push staff hard. People are prone to introspection during a combination—challenge them and keep them busy. Turn that anxiety and stress into productive energy.

- Make history—your organization probably never needed a figurehead as much as it does right now. This is your opportunity to become a true corporate hero, part of the folklore of the organization. Be a key role model, inspire others.

### 2. Expect Change

- Expect a drop in productivity during the combination process, and an increase in the stress level.

- Prepare staff for change—they want and expect it. They want things to get better as a result of the combination.

- Expect a certain amount of resistance to change; without it you have a lethargic, complacent organization. Manage it, tell staff why they are going through this process.

- Expect power struggles by the people underneath you in the organization. These may be significantly more intense than they have been in the past.

### 3. Be Positive

- Rise above the noise and confusion, empower yourself, be upbeat and enthusiastic.

- Develop a high tolerance for ambiguity—be flexible.

- Keep a sense of humor. Try to introduce a sense of play into the process. See the humorous side of problems as they come up.

- Keep a sense of balance. Don't let yourself get overwhelmed by combination issues.

### 4. Clarify and Manage Issues

- Separate urgent from important. Avoid being sidetracked by low priority issues–make sure the priorities are clear.

- Sort out those issues that can be dealt with right away and those that can be left for awhile—get on with issues that are of high strategic importance.

- Make sure you have a clear understanding of the problems that need to be handled—don't always believe your own press releases.

### 5. Inform Yourself

- Take time to understand the psychological change process that the staff is going through—show understanding.

## Exhibit 5.1.  The CEO's Ten Commandments
## of Combination Leadership *(continued)*.

- Ask people's opinions—find out staff names, single out individuals in public, overpraise positive behaviors.
- Keep in touch with the organization and its problems—get out with the sales force and into the operating areas.
- Invite bad news—don't shoot messengers and don't settle for people telling you what they think you want to hear.
- Learn about the culture of the other organization, its history, the way it does business—even its dress code may be different.

6. **Inform Your Staff**
- Set out to clear up the unknowns and rumors, be specific and candid.
- Give staff the good news and the bad news—don't patronize people or assume that they only want to hear the good news. Level with people.
- Be available and visible to the staff—ask questions and be prepared to discuss concerns.
- Give staff a chance to ventilate and express themselves.

7. **Get Your Staff on Board**
- Be honest. Don't make promises you cannot keep just to take the heat off in a difficult situation. Rebuild your credibility—assume that staff are looking for reasons to distrust you.
- You are a new boss—remember that your staff have to decide if they want to work for you.
- Give staff reasons to believe that the combination is being well-managed; it is their future, too.

8. **Build Your Team**
- Meet with each manager, make sure each knows their decision making authority, reporting relationships, and performance expectations.
- Build confidence in your team to restore momentum to the organization.

9. **Let the Staff Manage Their Way Through It**
- Encourage initiative and risk taking. Try to shape behavior and not judge mistakes—be a good coach, not just the boss.
- Don't try to come up with all the answers. Paint broad brush strokes with your operating principles and let staff fill in the details.
- Delegate—a lot of you will be spread too thinly, and people will get demoralized.
- Give staff time to settle in and make things work.

10. **Get On With It**
- Get on with the combination process—be action-oriented.
- Take the pain and move ahead. Your staff will thank you for it.
- Create some positive improvements and high profile successes early in the game.
- Be prepared to make the tough decisions in order to minimize political behavior.

and embrace the combination principles or they go their own way. Announcing a combined organization's senior leadership team is a milestone, often the first concrete decision made. Employees size up the caliber and characteristics of the team's members and draw conclusions about what the CEO truly values in joining forces. Soon, the grapevine fills with reports about how the members are functioning, both individually and as a team. This becomes grist for the mill for middle managers and other employees who use it to determine how they should behave.

Multiple criteria influence decisions on staffing the senior team. One set has to do with characteristics of the individual. First and foremost is the person's ability to get the job done. Also important are the style and approach the individual brings to the job and the values underlying behavior. If a CEO expects and needs a high degree of collaboration among senior team members, then individual "operators" who are otherwise able may be a bad fit for the senior team. A second set of selection criteria consider the overall makeup of the top team. A staff filled with functional superstars with mediocre interpersonal skills sends the message that doing the right thing is much more valued than doing things the right way. The pendulum can swing too far, though: a senior team made up of generalists may lack the requisite technical know-how and edge. After weighing these considerations, it is often useful to pull back and consider the chemistry between the potential members and the impression the overall profile gives to the rest of the organization.

## Appointments: Before or After the Deal?

Many advisors recommend that companies make senior management appointments part of their precombination dealings. There is much to recommend this point of view. First, it foreshortens political maneuvering by executives who might otherwise spend months currying favor or discrediting their counterparts in an effort to win top jobs. Second, it gives a target company or acquiree somewhat more leverage in securing posts for its managers. Indeed, many sellers negotiate employment contracts for their senior executives as part of the sales agreement. Finally, it can help a top team in a combination to hit the ground running and present a united front to the rest of management and the workforce.

At the same time, there are decided disadvantages to making top appointments in advance of the integration period. After doing their deal, the two partners have only "a thirty-thousand foot overview" of their combined strategy, and few close-to-the-ground analyses of how to capitalize on specific synergies. The CEO of the buying or lead company often has the barest acquaintance with senior management on the other side. The two company managements have not yet looked closely at the strengths and weaknesses of different organization structures, nor considered the right mix of leadership that is needed to make the combination work. By appointing top executives from the start, companies are betting on appointees' leadership skills in advance of making informed decisions about strategy and structure.

Is it a sensible bet? There is nothing akin to a handicapper's guide to who's in the race for top jobs—no detailed information about executives' past accomplishments nor much more than hearsay about their potential to contribute in the future. A lead company CEO knows the strengths, weaknesses, and idiosyncrasies of his players, but getting reliable data on executives from the other side is problematic. Relatively few firms undertake independent professional assessments of their executives, and even fewer document their drawbacks. To the contrary, it is commonplace for acquired firms to "blow smoke" about the skills and achievements of their senior executives and to cover up their personal or professional liabilities—particularly before a sale is completed. What should a CEO make of any dirt dug up about one or another executive? How should she react when acquired managers badmouth one of their own? Inevitably, it is hard to separate the meaning of the message from the motives of the messenger. In the end, lead company CEOs tend to go with the devil they know when making appointments early on. They then hope to fix things later, if they can.

Can their mistakes be corrected? Not easily. The long-term problem with precombination appointments is that they also preordain the combined company's organization structure and staffing profile. Naming an executive from company A to run the merged manufacturing organization and another from company B to head marketing may be defensible based on their past performance. But neither may turn out to be the best choice when a combined company concludes that it has to take its manufacturing or marketing in new directions. Additionally, early appointments tend to be duplicated down the line; that is, appointed executives are most inclined to name subordinates to next-level jobs whom they know and have worked with. As a result, to complete the example, company A dominates manufacturing posts and typically adopts its own methods and systems to run combined operations. Marketing looks and operates as it did in company B prior to the combination. Such high-level horse trading worked reasonably well in the merger of Chemical Bank and Manufacturers Hanover, where each side brought distinct strengths to the table and carried them through the combination. But when the "new" Chemical subsequently merged with Chase Manhattan, it was necessary to reshuffle the deck and reorganize businesses in light of overlapping strengths and new business opportunities. Conflicts between executives in this three-way combination slowed integration substantially and provoked infighting and second guessing over who got which jobs.

### Making Appointments As You Go

Several companies we have worked with decided to make top management appointments only after their deal was complete. In the creation of Unisys, for example, CEO W. Michael Blumenthal created an interim office of the chairman to house the very top brass of Burroughs and Sperry. He then waited several months before appointing the heads of businesses and functions. This enabled transition teams to test proposed strategies and detail the most desirous organization structures to effect them. It also gave him the chance to observe and work with Sperry executives who were otherwise unfamiliar to him and to see them in action with colleagues and subordinates. This waiting period also allowed the CEO and other senior managers to get acquainted with managers at the next several layers and better gauge their potential to contribute to the new organization.

As a result, there was a good match between strategy, structure, and the skills of appointed leaders in many parts of the combined company. In several instances, more junior-level managers who demonstrated strong analytic skills and the ability to work well with others on their transition teams secured senior management posts. At the same time, some early favorites for top posts were found wanting because of their lack of teamwork or inability to contribute winning ideas about running the combined business. Still, the process was not without its costs. Paul Stern, then president of Burroughs, chafed in the "office of" post and left the company in a huff. Others took offense that they had to compete with executives of the company that they had bought.

*Keeping Talent on Board*

Prime Computer is another example of a company that used the integration period to identify executives best suited for top jobs. In this case, Prime effected an unfriendly takeover of ComputerVision, whose executives planned to depart, handsomely compensated, en masse. CEO Joe Henson used "transition contracts" to keep several of them on hand to study in detail the future of the business and its structure and staff profile. Weeks of sobering study revealed that Prime could not effectively defend its markets from new entrants, whereas CV had myriad growth opportunities. In the end, several transitional executives from CV stayed on and gained top jobs as their combination took an entirely different turn.

*Profiling Talent Through the Ranks*

The merger of two manufacturing giants provides a good example of how to carry this kind of appointment process deep into a combined organization. Top leadership in the combined company had external consultants prepare in-depth dossiers on more than one hundred prospective senior managers. These "accomplishment profiles" documented managers' performance over the course of their careers and detailed their strengths and weaknesses. Top managers then met over several days to conduct a "player draft" to select the next layers of management. A business head would first propose a draftee but then have to defend the selection to all present, who might ask questions for information or challenge the choice. In this way, senior managers had the chance to review the full roster of the future players and carefully consider where best to place them (if at all). In cases of redundancy, a top-flight performer would be recommended for a job in another division. Without this collective selection process, the star would otherwise be outplaced or else go to work for a competitor!

## Sorting out People

Obviously, our recommendation to select executives carefully rather than quickly does not apply to every combination. In the case of a modest-size acquisition, for example, an early decision in favor of retaining local management is usually prudent. In a turnaround, however, it might be better to wait and see what you have bought. With an alliance, it helps to name a general manager and leadership team from the start because oftentimes they have to launch the venture. Finally, it is important to recognize that such appointments do not apply to everyone. In our experience, roughly one-third of top-level appointments are no-brainers. In these cases, one or another of the potential appointees simply has a better track record and superior credentials. In turn, another one-third of the time there is no decision to make. Here, an executive takes a package and exits. The challenge is to use the integration period to sort out which of the remaining one-third of senior executives in competition with one another is best suited for the job, or, more crucially, to determine when none is well suited and to look for another internal candidate or hire from the outside.

Consider how staffing plays out in this case. The CEO from the lead company in a manufacturing deal announced that he wanted to manage the event more like a merger than as an acquisition. His work in assembling a senior team was made easy by a fortuitous set of circumstances. In precombination negotiations, the heads of the two businesses agreed that the acquired CEO should not be retained in the new company; he planned on retiring and devoting his time to charitable work and his hobbies. The lead company did not have a chief operating officer. With the increased size and complexity of the combined organization, the CEO offered the job to the incumbent at the target firm. The two chief financial officers had different levels of expertise. The lead company CFO was a well-seasoned professional who was comfortable working with the external banking community. The target CFO had recently been promoted into the job. With very little finance experience, he was regarded more as a chief accounting officer. He was offered, and accepted, a position reporting to the lead company CFO. The senior vice president of manufacturing in the lead company was about to reach the firm's mandatory retirement age, opening the position for his counterpart. The senior vice presidents of sales and marketing were both excellent candidates. The CEO made a decision to separate the sales and marketing positions, creating opportunities for both of them. Likewise, the two senior human resource executives were both highly regarded. The CEO decided to retain his HR executive and offered the target company executive a temporary job as transition manager for one year. This position provided a role for the executive on the senior team and bought the CEO a year to decide what ultimately to do with the outstanding executive.

## Leading the Transition

Over the past ten years, the idea of creating a transition body to study integration options and guide the combination of businesses has emerged as a best practice. The form varies, ranging from an informal kitchen cabinet of the CEO and select senior executives to a formal coordination council of top leaders and task forces representing each function or business in combining companies. The next chapter details the creation and work of this body; here we concentrate on the role of the CEO in forming and leading it.

A first consideration is what kind of transition organization to form. In cases of full-scale mergers and alliances, it is not uncommon to have the very top management work together as an oversight group and managers from each side staff transition teams for R&D, engineering, manufacturing, marketing, sales, and each of the corporate functions. By comparison, in the case of a modest-size acquisition the transition body might consist of acquired management and select parent company leaders, with integration tasks handled by functional management.

## Leadership's Role in the Integration Program

Top leadership's role is to lead the combination through this transition body by setting guidelines, overseeing analyses and findings, and fitting recommendations into the big picture. In many acquisitions and alliances, this is the senior team that will carry on as the leadership group. For example, in the combination of Pfizer's Animal Health Group and SmithKline Beecham's worldwide animal health business, the integration team included fourteen senior executives. After the combination planning was completed, four executive vice presidents left the group when it evolved into the company's executive committee.

Call it the combination coordination counsel, steering committee, the senior team, or anything else, this group plays important oversight and coordinative roles throughout the integration program:

• It gives transition planning task forces guidance for making recommendations on the alignment of people, structure, and processes.

- It reviews and evaluates task force recommendations regarding their ability to achieve the strategy and vision of the combination.
- It identifies gaps and opportunities not covered in task force recommendations and recommends solutions.
- It coordinates all major change efforts into a fully integrated, prioritized, and understandable plan.
- It anticipates the impact of change and addresses inconsistencies between the espoused operating principles and the actual management of change.
- It defines, promotes, and supports necessary changes in individual behaviors and mind-sets to successfully realize the post-combination organization.
- It acts as individual change agents across the organization, as role models supporting change efforts and providing feedback.
- It identifies means by which the organization can measure and monitor the progress of the transition.
- If the oversight group is not the regular senior executive team, it acts as a mirror to the senior team to provide the necessary reality check on their management of change in the organization.

### Synergy Teams

Boeing's acquisition of North American Rockwell is a good illustration of the organization and pacing of transition teams. Immediately after the purchase, Phil Condit, Boeing's CEO, appointed a senior executive in the Defense and Space Group to form and lead a transition organization. He first formed a top-level steering committee composed mostly of Boeing senior executives and a few respected leaders from Rockwell. Unbalanced though it seemed to some at Rockwell, this signaled clearly that this would be an acquisition and that Boeing would be calling more of the shots.

Two sets of synergy teams were then created. The growth synergy teams were chartered "to analyze market segments, customers, and competition, and to assess future trends relating to products and programs." The major teams covered space, missile systems, military aircraft, electronics, and global developments concerning modification and privatization. Subteams were formed under several of these categories. Interestingly, these teams were cochaired by Boeing and Rockwell executives. To achieve growth, it was reasoned, the two sides would have to work together collaboratively, and cochairs were both a substantive and symbolic way of stressing the importance of mutuality.

Efficiency synergy teams addressed business development, general management, information systems, operations, engineering, and human resources, among others. Their charge was "to align organizations and leverage combined capabilities," in other words, eliminate redundancies and integrate functions. Boeing exerted more influence in the leadership of these teams. The intent was straightforward: Rockwell would conform to the Boeing organization structure and adopt Boeing systems.

As the teams conducted their analyses, Alan Mulally, from the commercial side of Boeing, was named the head of Boeing Space and Defense. Comparatively young, hard-charging, and with a track record of success, Mulally was a somewhat surprising choice to many who had expected that an existing business head in defense would be named. Apart from his credentials, he would bring a fresh eye to the space and defense business and to the integration of Rockwell. By all accounts, at a meeting in the California desert he wowed both sides with a hard-headed look at market trends and competitive dynamics and an emotional appeal to work together to improve customer knowledge and deliverables. Transition team findings and recommendations were sifted and reviewed by the four hundred or so executives from both sides in attendance. It was also announced that the former Rockwell would hereafter be folded into the buyer and be called Boeing North America.

## Speed of Integration

Senior teams consistently underestimate the time and energy required to identify, assess, and address the many decisions that arise when two complex organizations combine. More than a few CEOs have done the glamour work of negotiating a deal and thereupon handed off the dirty work of meshing structures, systems, and procedures to operations managers. *In successful combinations,* by contrast, CEOs play an active role in the integration process and keep space available on their calendars for the many public and private activities required to steward a major organizational change. "We established integration as the number one priority for the year," recalled Bill Lyons, chief operating officer in the American Century/ Benham mutual fund merger, "We made it very clear in our words and actions that this attention could be placed in no more important area."

How fast should the combination proceed? On the one hand, most involved want to move forward quickly—executives to capture synergies, managers to get refocused, and employees to get on with it or at least learn of their personal fate. Corporate staffers who prepare time projections for integration invariably overestimate the ease of combining operations and underestimate the costs and time involved. Indeed, one management consulting firm recommends to its clients that all employees be assigned new jobs or "sent home" within forty-eight hours of a combination announcement. This is nonsense. Contrast that advice with the experience of a financial services industry merger veteran: "You can come in and say, 'You stay and you go,' or you can be more careful. The careful model is much more time-intensive and stressful, but well worth the investment." Or listen to a CEO who, midway through a combination, surmised, "I've learned to not move too quickly on integration decisions, because once you alleviate one concern you create another. So, I don't rush."

The senior executive has the choice of insisting upon quick combination decisions—and living with the consequences—or of directing executives to take the time to make more careful choices. Hurried decisions that result in choosing the wrong people or systems burden the combined organization. Sound planning and decision making take time. Extracting the real synergy in a combination, that is, moving from the conceptual to the true benefits of combining complex organizations, comes only after careful examination and deliberation. Realistic timetables take into account the many tasks involved in building one organization out of two:

- Validating the "real" synergies in the combination
- Giving transition teams the time and leadership to develop combination plans
- Identifying the best talent, systems, and procedures
- Helping people work through the merger syndrome
- Designing the new organization
- Revising initial plans as new data are collected and new opportunities and challenges are identified
- Giving people and processes time to sort themselves out in the new organization
- Training people on new systems
- Learning from mistakes and disseminating that learning to all parts of the organization

Realistic timetables also consider what is going on in the part-ner organizations aside from the combination. Is a crucial new product launch or an important industry event scheduled during the integration period? Is a significant upgrade to IT or imple-mentation of a major change like a reengineering project antici-pated? If so, the time and resources allocated to these events detract from managing the combination and should be reflected in expected timing.

## Focusing and Prioritizing Executive Attention

The enormous number of decisions to be made in a combination can be overwhelming. With the many options, personalities, and issues that surface, senior executives need a way to prioritize com-bination decisions so that they, along with their management teams, can focus on the issues that matter most in eventual com-bination success. We have worked with several companies to sort the issues in terms of their value to synergies and savings versus the riskiness of integration (Figure 5.1); our counsel is to move quickly in areas that yield real synergies but are relatively easy to combine. Actions here do not require extensive analysis and debate; instead, you can put energy into developing and executing implementa-tion plans. Areas that have the potential to produce high synergies and savings but are relatively difficult to combine require careful up-front study and should be the focus of transition task forces. Areas that have relatively minor impact on synergy and savings, but

### Figure 5.1.  Prioritizing Combination Issues.

|  | Low Risk in Integration | High Risk in Integration |
|---|---|---|
| High Savings and Synergy | Do It! | Study It! |
| Low Savings and Synergy | Get Around to It! | Forget It! |

Source: Mirvis, P. M., and Marks, M. L. *Managing the Merger: Making It Work.* Upper Saddle River, N.J.: Prentice Hall, 1994.

are somewhat easy to combine, can be addressed less urgently. And areas that produce little gain in synergies or savings and are difficult to combine should be dropped from consideration; they are too fraught with conflict and there are too many other issues competing for (and more worthy of) attention.

## Senior Team Development

Formal team-building activities benefit all teams in a newly combined organization. Team development at the top, however, is critically important early on. The intent is to accelerate development of open working relationships. Depending on the circumstances surrounding the combination, different forms of team building may be useful for leadership groups. In an acquisition, for example, it can be useful to hold sessions with the acquired team first. In the case of one acquiree still in shock from its sudden purchase, Mirvis facilitated a grieving meeting with management to reflect on the glory days past and mourn their loss. Only after this meeting did acquired management feel ready to engage parent company management in a more open and forthcoming manner. In the case of a friendly merger, by contrast, Mirvis had the top team participate in an outdoor team-building session where their ascent of a wall became a continuing metaphor for helping each other surmount obstacles. Whatever type of team building is conducted, the aim is to help executives sort out roles and working relations that cause confusion and conflict in the early parts of the combination phase. The point is to proactively raise and address any issues that may inhibit team effectiveness or otherwise slow down the combination process.

Senior team development affords a variety of ancillary benefits as well. First, the senior team is often made up of high-powered individuals who rose to the top of their precombination organization based on criteria inconsistent with the desired culture of the postcombination organization. Team building provides a forum in which the senior executive can reiterate and reinforce what is expected of leadership team members. Second, team building creates a setting to review and revisit where the combination is headed. The full team discusses the senior executive's vision, adds its members' viewpoints, and modifies expectations accordingly. Third, team building conducted at the top sets a standard to be upheld through the ranks. When the senior team members feel team building is a worthwhile experience, they usually conduct similar programs with their own teams and suggest that their reports do the same.

As soon as is practical after announcement of the leadership team, a team development meeting can be held. In an alliance between an entertainment company and a telecommunications firm, Marks worked with the senior team off site for three days to achieve several objectives:

- Begin the team development process by clarifying goals, roles, processes, and leadership.
- Develop a shared perspective of the alliance rationale, expectations, and targets.
- Develop initial visions of the new organization.
- Build understanding of transition management requirements, and identify issues to address.
- Define management processes and procedures for getting started (budgets, human resources, etc.).
- Identify next steps and resources for the organization, team, and individuals.

The meeting provided a focal point for gaining clarity and consensus among top leaders regarding the direction of the alliance and for determining how the members would work together as a team. It carved out time to address immediate issues, such as financial plans and human resource policies, that were required to get the alliance ready to do business. And it created opportunities for new colleagues to get to know each other as people and have some fun together.

## Human Purpose and Understanding

In most combinations, people down the line are hungry for purpose and direction. They want to contribute to the building of something special. Getting people focused on the new organization does not happen, however, until they stop licking their wounds from the past. No amount of rallying will direct and motivate people toward the desired future if they are angry, distrustful, and cynical about past leadership actions. A dose of empathy goes a long way in helping people turn the corner from the old to the new. Acknowledging that people have been through a difficult time—and accepting personal responsibility for contributing to those difficult times—is a powerful act for the leaders of combining organizations. Such mea culpas from senior executives are rare in organizations, so they succeed at grabbing people's attention and alerting employees to the fact that this transition will be managed differently.[7]

Leaders also need to prepare people for the harsh realities of the journey ahead. Effective combination planning and implementation take more time and energy than people may want to commit, answers to questions do not come quickly enough, initial decisions are second-guessed, and uncertainty and anxiety persist. Expressing empathy for having to live through the combination period is more effective in getting people focused on the right things than a message to tough things out.

## Communicating with Staff

Naturally, CEOs and senior executives having the ability and style to talk about the combination with evocative language and high energy generate more enthusiasm among staff than those who rely on written messages or who treat communications as more or less matter of fact. Still, there has to be substance to speak to an otherwise skeptical workforce.

### Sizzle and Steak

Alan Mulally's speech to a gathering of Boeing and Rockwell executives not only generated a lot of sizzle, it also featured plenty of steak. He gave a concise account of 1996 results for the businesses, pro forma combined, and then detailed the 1997 business plan. This included both firm and stretch targets to achieve for orders and profits and must-hit cost reductions. He reviewed current customer commitments and whose responsibility it was to deliver on them, and he enumerated what synergies were expected and from whom. This detailing served two purposes. First, Mulally demonstrated his understanding of Rockwell's business and showed how the parties could achieve more by working together than on their own. Second, he grounded the vision of the combination in short-term targets and deliverables. This latter point should be stressed. Many executives we have worked with speak eloquently to their vision of the combination but do not emphasize the critical need to keep the business going during the integration period. In this case, Mulally showed everyone where the rubber meets the road.

Importantly, he also spoke to the human side of the the combination. Working with internal consultant Gary Jusela, Mulally gathered data on the hopes and fears of employees and fashioned the following guidelines for the months ahead:

- Use each other's strengths.

- Help each other.

- Share everything—no secrets.

- Include everyone—share the excitement.

- Enjoy the journey and each other.

- Operate with highest integrity.

Mulally emphasized the importance of "emotional resiliency" and the need for people to take care of themselves amid the stresses and strains of integration. As a follow-up activity, a consulting firm was commissioned to advise on wellness, lead stress-management seminars, and promote emotional resiliency among employees.

## Getting Staff to Communicate

Although messages from the top and on down through the ranks are important in setting direction and reassuring worried staff, they cannot substitute for peer-to-peer communication. In most cases, this takes place around the water cooler, in the lunchroom, or in hushed tones around desks. It tends toward supposed inside dope, rumors about who's in and who's out, which side is gaining or losing, and so forth. One study found hourly and clerical staff spending two-plus hours per day talking about such matters over the first six months following a merger. Needless to say, this is time away from day-to-day performance, and it focuses attention on the downside of the deal.

### Drafting an "Elevator Speech"

In order to cut through the rumormongering and promote constructive dialogue among frontline employees, sales personnel involved in the strategic alliance of Ameritech and GE Information Systems took care to develop their "elevator speech" about the combination: a brief synopsis that could be conveyed in the time of an elevator ride. At the end of the first joint workshop to plan integration, the sales executives and reps from each side prepared a pitch on the strategic intent of the alliance, its upside, and their own concerns. All forty or so in attendance then made videos of these speeches and critiqued them in the company of peers. This gave them practice in and feedback on relating their story of the alliance. In teams, they then highlighted hopes, fears, and unanswered questions and reviewed them with the alliance coleaders. In a fishbowl-type session, containing a spokesperson from each team and the two alliance leaders and observed by the rest of the workshop, there was an open and candid discussion of these matters. As a result, the alliance leaders got a clearer picture of what was bothering the salesforce, who in turn learned answers to questions that had not been addressed. The sales teams subsequently held sessions with their peers featuring their speech plus in-depth Q & A.

By all accounts, communications sessions are well attended and generate a surprising and welcome degree of buy-in from frontline staff on both sides. In large part, the success stems from the efforts senior leadership take to promote human purpose and understanding in building the alliance: modeling effective communication, listening to upward input, sanctioning and participating in programs to address both business and interpersonal issues, and, in general, raising and keeping in front of people the requirements for effective combination. This shows how leaders in successful combinations stay on top of their leadership responsibilities and maintain a context for productive combination as managers get to work in planning and implementing the combined operation.

## Chapter Six

# The Transition Structure

A transition structure focuses executive time and talent on how to obtain the strategic synergies of a combination. This is a temporary system that usually lasts three to six months but can extend up to a year to provide for coordination and support during implementation of change. Merely putting people into transition management positions does not by itself keep a combination on a successful course. Making one plus one equal three also requires an effective structure, able leadership, and systematic work processes to guide analyses and generate progress. This means molding individual contributors into transition teams and helping them handle the many operational and political factors that can otherwise transform good ideas into bad practice.

## Transition Structures

Transition structures vary greatly from one combination to another. The size, scope, and complexity of the combination as well as the capabilities of the people available for duty all should be considered in their ultimate design. Here are some options—not mutually exclusive—that range from simple to more complicated:

- *The hierarchy.* This is a workable option when the requirements for integration are clear and new management is in place. It is typically found in combinations where a parent company acquires an unrelated business and retains its management. Transition teams may be formed to effect changes in corporate functions and adopt parent company reporting requirements. But teams in these cases are tasked primarily with implementing requirements and are supervised by their own management and business head. The appropriate parent company leader, often the head of a business group, exercises oversight and helps run interference. In mergers of smaller companies involving modest integration, it is also possible to use the newly named heads of work units or functions to drive integration under the direction of the CEO. Of course, top-down management of the transition process also occurs when new owners take control and install their own people in senior positions. However, here the process often amounts to a full makeover of the business.

- *A coordinator or project manager.* Several companies we have worked with appointed a single project manager or coordinator to oversee integration. This can be effective in cases where operating units have to combine but there is little or no controversy over what and how to integrate and power relationships between the two sides are clear and agreeable. The general manager of a joint venture serves this same function. However, it is important that the coordinator have substantive knowledge and real power, should conflicts emerge. In the case of ComputerVision's integration with Prime Computer, for example, the coordinator was the lead company CEO's right hand and earned the title of "merger czar" based on his ability to settle differences with informed "rulings."

- *A kitchen cabinet.* Where a single coordinator cannot oversee the full range of transition activities, some companies create an informal working group to monitor integration. This typically includes key executives from both sides who advise the CEO and influence function heads in the two businesses. A variation of this has natural leaders from one or both sides in a working group set the integration agenda and mark progress. Oftentimes, this group acts as a sounding board for and resource to a combination coordinator.

- *A transition organization.* In cases where integration is deep and partners hope to extract the best of both in creating the new organization, we strongly recommend creation of a parallel organization of transition teams. Our early work in Burroughs and Sperry featured this structure, which was then an innovation in combining companies. Since then, we have worked with transition bodies in several kinds of combinations. Their scope can be daunting. For instance, shortly after the Boeing/Rockwell transition organization folded its tent, a new superstructure was needed to plan the integration of the combined company with McDonnell Douglas. A long service executive, headed for retirement, was called upon by the two company CEOs to orchestrate the work of transition teams representing the commercial side of the business (involving people from Boeing, Rockwell, and Douglas) and space and defense (Boeing and McDonnell) and align them with corporate groups. Among the challenges tackled were to prepare reams of information for regulative bodies in the U.S. and Europe, address the concerns of elected officials in sixteen states and several countries, respond to the interests of several unions, and, of course, plan for the combination of 200,000 people—all within six months.

Why are we biased in favor of a transition organization? First, and most important, it creates a forum where the two sides can study and test whether or how hoped-for synergies can be realized in practice. In most instances, the two sides have not fully engaged in the strategic preparation we outlined in Chapter Three and need to catch up and gain momentum in the combination phase. Moreover, even if they have done their homework, many of the nuances and details remain that require close attention from those who are nearest to the action. The various growth and efficiency synergy teams involving managers from Boeing and Rockwell, described in the previous chapter, serve this function. We term this the knowledge-building work of the transition organization.

Second, there is the work of relationship building. In a transition organization, several layers of management, as well as professionals and sometimes frontline personnel, get the chance to think and work with their counterparts from the other organization. Here is where differences in style and culture come to light and can be worked out through substantive effort, as opposed to, say, a seminar or show-and-tell session. Frankly, nothing shatters stereotypes or supersedes differences more effectively than sharing a common problem and needing to arrive at an agreeable solution. Furthermore, building trust is integral to developing knowledge. Until the two sides get to know and trust one another, they will not reveal the details—and particularly the weak points—of how they each do their business.

Finally, there is the work of transition management. Calling on the hierarchy to simultaneously run the business as is and plan in-depth the integration of people, processes, and cultures often means that something has to give, and that's usually the work of building something innovative and new. In turn, while appointment of a coordinator and use of a kitchen cabinet have their place, integration on a fuller scale works best when key people are dedicated to planning integration and making sure that it succeeds.

### Transition Structure at Abitibi-Consolidated

In the merger of equals between paper producers Abitibi-Price and Stone-Consolidated, senior executives from both partners recognized that their integration task was much more demanding than if one side had purchased the other outright. Precombination CEOs Ron Oberlander and Jim Doughan endorsed a temporary transition structure to ensure that executive time and talent attended to merger management responsibilities along with running the regular business. Figure 6.1 shows the transition structure.

Each component of the transition structure sported specific roles and responsibilities. CEOs Doughan and Oberlander headed a steering committee of top executives to provide oversight to the transition planning process and ensure that the critical success factors were followed in merger planning. The transition teams worked closely with the regular business executives to develop strategies, recommend the postcombination organization, and guide implementation. Transition managers from both companies, Alain Grandmont and Larry Johnson, managed day-to-day integration activities and coordinated plans and actions. As an external consultant, Marks coached the CEOs on their roles, brought an outside perspective to support the transition managers and transition teams, and was charged with facilitating the overall process.

## Transition Managers

Transition managers or coordinators assume full-time responsibility—and accountability—for making integration work. The time investment required takes one or often two executives from both sides off-line for several months (and sometimes more than a year) to micromanage analyses, planning, and implementation of the combination of two companies. If an executive team does not have the bench strength to free up key people for this assignment, it can be an early warning sign that the transition will not receive the resources necessary for success.

**Figure 6.1. Transition Structure at Abitibi-Consolidated.**

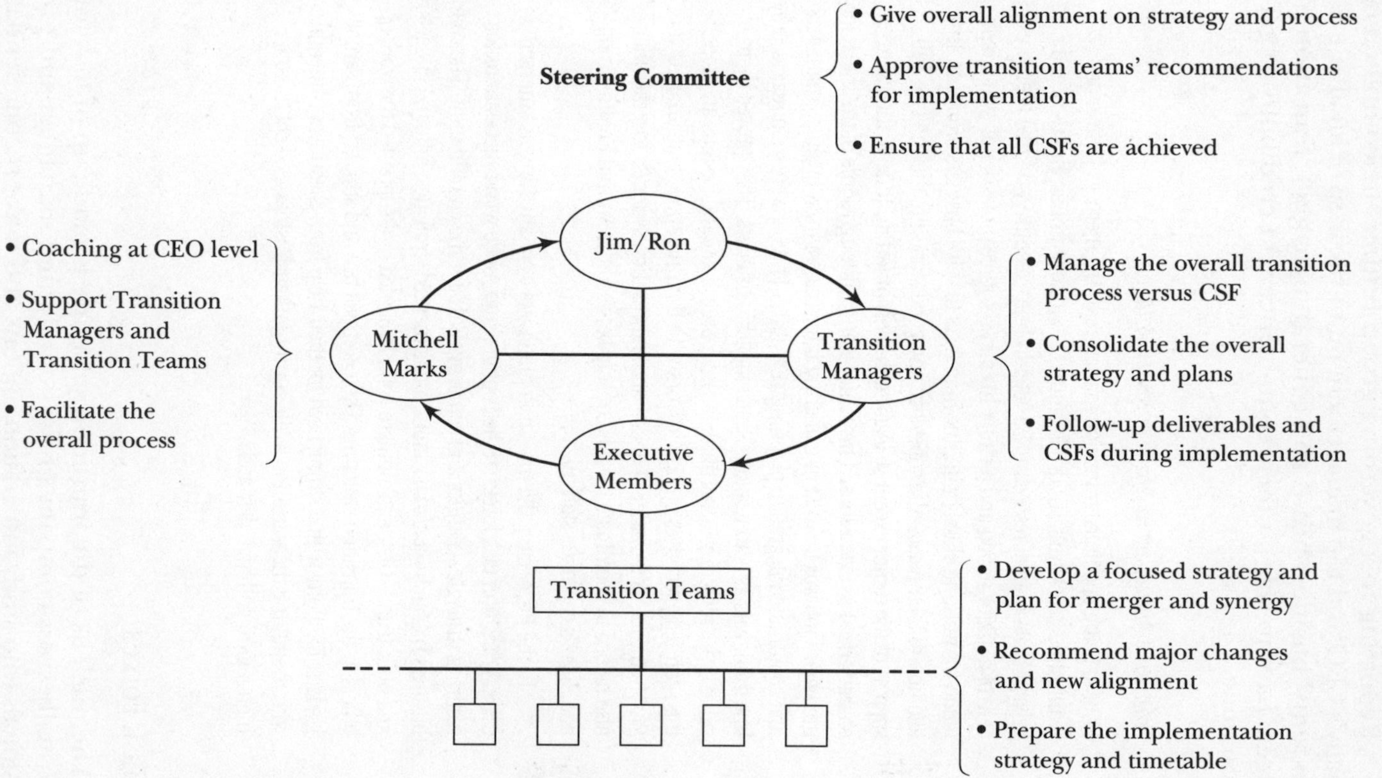

**Steering Committee**

- Give overall alignment on strategy and process
- Approve transition teams' recommendations for implementation
- Ensure that all CSFs are achieved

- Manage the overall transition process versus CSF
- Consolidate the overall strategy and plans
- Follow-up deliverables and CSFs during implementation

- Develop a focused strategy and plan for merger and synergy
- Recommend major changes and new alignment
- Prepare the implementation strategy and timetable

- Coaching at CEO level
- Support Transition Managers and Transition Teams
- Facilitate the overall process

Transition Managers

Jim/Ron

Mitchell Marks

Executive Members

Transition Teams

Reporting to a governing group (either the combined company's CEO and top management or, in the case of an alliance, the parents' business heads and general manager), transition managers have to rely on their competence and credibility to get the job done.

### Transition Managers in Pfizer Animal Health

Prior to being appointed transition managers in the merger of Pfizer and SmithKline Beecham's worldwide animal health operations, Jim Cary and Sylvia Montero were, respectively, a veteran line executive who had been president of a major region and a senior human resource professional with a reputation for working closely with line managers to solve business problems. In addition to their personal competence and good standing, they had the full support of the senior executive leading the combination. Indeed, they were characterized as extensions of his senior team. Although some of the transition manager's job was to assist in gathering information from business managers and coordinate integration planning (Exhibit 6.1), they were soon regarded by line managers as both resources and empathic listeners. They proved their value by helping executives think through organizational designs and coaching acquired executives on how to work with their new president, adapt to the Pfizer culture, and master financial and information systems. Together they also helped to coordinate the relationship between the Animal Health Group and Pfizer's corporate staff functions.

In the Pfizer case, the transition managers were anything but merger czars. Transition task forces studied options and made recommendations for securing strategic synergies and achieving CSFs for the combination. The core business hierarchy staffed positions, implemented strategies, followed budgets, and built teams. Cary and Montero complemented and supported the work of others in the transition structure. Their competence and support from senior leadership, along with a strong need for their help from executives contending with managing the transition while running their businesses, kept them in high regard and high demand.

## Task Forces

The nucleus of the transition structure is made up of task forces, usually cross-company groups of talented managers and professionals who study integration options and make recommendations

## Exhibit 6.1. Job Description for Transition Manager.

1. Support the process of consolidating the SmithKline Beecham and Pfizer Animal Health organizational structures worldwide.
   a) Support the Animal Health Group (AHG) president in selection and appointment of Management Team (MT) members.
   b) Support each MT member in design and proposal of corresponding organizational structures.
   c) Support each MT member in the selection of physical location for the new organizations around the world.
   d) Manage the proposal and approval process up the organizational ladder.

2. Coordinate with Corporate support groups in the integration of the Financial and Employee Resources systems.
   a) General ledgers
   b) Payroll
   c) Compensation systems
   d) Benefits program
   e) Information Technology systems

3. Coordinate with Corporate Finance on the acquisition financial issues. Ensure that the acquisition is non-dilutive.

4. Coordinate with Corporate support groups in determining appropriate employee relocation programs and severance programs.

5. Coordinate with the International Pharmaceuticals Group in the integration of Financial and Employee Resources systems throughout Europe, Asia, Africa/Middle East, and Latin America regions.

6. Ensure appropriate communications between AHG and Corporate groups and between AHG and other Pfizer divisions.

7. Ensure appropriate communications throughout the new AHG organization. Manage the employee communications strategy.

8. Ensure appropriate coordination and effective communications between MT members.

9. Identify and develop action plans to address cultural integration issues throughout the organization.

10. Support, coordinate, and monitor the work of external consultants in the merger integration process.

on how to design the combined organization. Typically, transition task forces address functional areas and lines of business, but sometimes they support transition management activities such as communications, training, or customer relations. Transition task forces take the raw material of vision, high-level strategy, and the hypothesized synergies identified before the deal; study the realities of the combining units and functions in light of competencies, technology, competition, and customers needs; and craft proposed actions to yield value. What these teams are called may vary (task forces, transition teams, planning committees, etc.), but what they do is universally important.

Task forces themselves are staffed by a small number of managers but can involve hundreds of employees in fact finding and analysis. In the Lotus-IBM combination, where there was substantial disparity between the two cultures and intense politicking, the combination planning process was the only forum where the two sides could have an open debate of the issues. Engagement centered around eleven functional task forces (in areas of manufacturing, marketing, sales, service, etc.) and spread to a series of initiative-based teams that resolved a number of complex organizational and product questions within the first one hundred days of the combination. The task forces and teams also defined and set priorities and monitored progress on key initiatives required to extract value from the combination.

Often there is considerable overlap between transition team members and core business managers. Especially in small and medium-size organizations, functional heads and their staff more or less constitute transition teams. In the combination of larger organizations, by contrast, only a fraction of business unit management and staff can participate on transition teams. Needless to say, matters of staffing, agenda, and team management can make or break transition teams. Even more important is the seriousness assigned to their deliberations and recommendations. Any exercise in "faux participation" (in which task forces may be convened but their work is not taken seriously) adversely affects the combination. Cynicism and distrust flourish, and subsequent efforts at participatory management are ignored. Top leadership does not have to accept task force recommendations verbatim, but it is obliged to provide feedback on why and how recommendations need to be revised. When used wisely, transition teams do not begin with a blank canvas and produce whatever inspires them. Rather, they are guided by the deal's strategy and success factors, as well as by the oversight of senior leadership.

## Benefits

Transition structures—encompassing senior leadership, coordinators, and transition teams—can yield substantial benefits beyond the immediate gains in knowledge and better relationships among upper management. For instance, in their fact finding, transition teams often involve frontline people close to the technical aspects and key business issues implicated in the combination. They also formally and informally connect with scores of other employees down the line to solicit their input and ideas and convey the progress of combination planning. This allows team members to learn much more about their partner's practices, cultures, histories, technologies, styles, and the like, all of which are needed to seriously test synergies and identify areas of fit versus misfit between the two sides.

Importantly, the transition structure can be a laboratory in which the chief executive experiments with ideas and observes the behavior of managers from the two organizations. This provides the boss with an opportunity to see how well people carry out their responsibilities, what rules they play by, how they work with others, and how they deal with stress and ambiguity. In addition to learning about managers from the other side, senior executives can also assess their own staff in a new and demanding situation. Chief executives we have worked with have used the transition structure as a testing ground to determine whom to appoint to permanent positions in the combined organization.

## Effective Transition Structures

Not all transition structures are effective. Consider this manager's experience: "The chairman brought the top ten people from both firms together and told us that we had a lot of potential if we could merge product lines and use each other's systems. He then told us that, although there would be some start-up costs, he was confident that synergies would more than outweigh these and that we shouldn't have a performance dip. The two sides were left staring at each other wondering why we were there and how we were going to make it work."[1]

Many disappointing combinations have used transition managers and task forces; just because people are assigned to manage the transition does not mean they can do so proficiently. Like the one just described, some transition teams drift aimlessly. Others succumb to politics and horse trading, making decisions based on power agendas rather than on the combination's CSFs. Sometimes, conflict erupts within teams and destroys any benefits of group decision making. In these cases, planning meetings are marked by power plays and divisiveness, not synergy seeking and the consensus required to build a new and better organization. At other times, transition teams have too little conflict and hence insufficient debate and controversy to produce productive decisions.

To identify and test sources of strategic synergy, transition teams need to conduct their work carefully and thoroughly. First, senior leadership, and then task force chairs, provides the context for transition planning. This means stating and clarifying the business case behind the combination and spelling out CSFs. It also means applying and modeling the desired operating principles.

Second, effective transition teams need to employ a credible and rigorous issue-identification and decision-making process. They collect valid data and, as dispassionately as possible, conduct an objective analysis of the data and options. There is more to this than just generic project management. Decisions have to be made with an eye not only to selecting the best from current or novel approaches but also to realistically appraising what is workable in the combined organization. In the American Century/Benham mutual fund combination, for example, the overriding rule for selecting policies and procedures from the two partners was to find "which was best for the customer." But if that option required extensive computer programming or incurred other costs or problems, then a more workable solution was sought.

Third, effective transition teams need to attend to their internal processes. Leaders and members are well advised to stay on top of the group dynamics influencing their deliberations and devote some time to group development and maintenance. Members of task forces need to maintain a sense of humor and get to know one another as people as well as professionals.

Fourth, effective transition structures also mind relations with the rest of the organization. In most instances, the transition structure is not in competition with the core business structure; on the contrary, it supports the management structure in moving from precombination to postcombination phase. Transition teams do not make high-level decisions or mandate how the firm should go about its business. Rather, transition managers facilitate the work of others, and transition task forces collect data and make recommendations. This lack of formal decision-making responsibility—coupled with respect for normal decision-making channels in the enterprise—makes the support and commitment of senior management to the transition management process essential.

## Staffing

Individuals who have most successfully filled transition roles benefit from a mix of technical expertise, managerial proficiency, and interpersonal skills. Experience helps them handle the complex workload that pulls them in many directions. They also require sensitivity to deal with the egos, anxieties, and needs of people above, below, and beside them in the organization. Beyond this, members of the transition structure should truly believe in the prospects of the combination and be genuinely excited about the opportunity at hand. *In successful combinations,* appointment as a transition manager or task force member should be regarded as an honor and a spur to career progress, not as drudgery or a sidetrack from career advancement.

Knowing the business, the competitive environment, and their functional specialty gives task force members a foundation for making a real contribution. Having strong analytical skills and the capacity to see issues from multiple perspectives helps in sorting out options. Being comfortable with exercising responsibility without complete authority helps task force members contend with the pressures that come from others outside the process. This means selecting people who are more diplomatic than political, more open-minded than narrowly focused, and more inclined to consensus than domination.

Task force members are chosen from both organizations, and from diverse functions and geographical locations. To break up traditional ways of viewing the work, put a marketing person on the operations task force and a manufacturing manager on the customer service team. Also, some fresh faces from the ranks, who have no axes to grind or people to protect, aid in generating novel approaches and fairly assessing competing options. The right mix of leaders and members results in task forces that are less likely to rely on the past practices of both partners and more likely to propose innovative courses of action. Diversity in membership allows members to reach out to a broad range of constituencies to gather data and keep people informed about combination prospects and progress.

It is just as important to consider whom *not* to give transition assignments to. Transition positions should not be staffed by second-tier managers; those seen as being farmed out or losers in the race for core business jobs will lack credibility and deflate energy toward productive combination. People with dominating personalities, poor interpersonal skills, lousy communication style, or a tendency to build personal empires at the expense of the company also do not make effective participants in the transition structure.

A task force chair stewards the group's work and exerts substantial influence on the quality and timeliness of its output. When already appointed, the leaders of businesses and functions most often serve as task force chairs or cochairs. At other times, heirs apparent serve this function. Where there is a horse race between contenders for a top job, their success as head of a task force ultimately determines whether or not they lead the combined business or function. In addition, there are instances when current management is so vested in the status quo that there is an absence of fresh thinking and give-and-take in task forces. In these cases, it can be useful to assign task force leadership to some up-and-comers and see what they have to offer. In several instances we know of, success in heading a task force resulted in a middle manager getting on the fast track to run the combined business.

## Charters

Another factor in a task force's ultimate success is the clarity of its charter and the extent to which its mission is understood and supported by both team members and those in the core business. Ineffective transition task forces trace their problems back to lack of clarity about what was expected of them. What is the group responsible for: designing a function, deciding on product lines, establishing a geographical plan of offices, recommending systems and procedures, or all the above? Where does the domain of this task force start and stop relative to other task forces and the core

business organization? Is the task force supposed to generate options, make recommendations, or make decisions? Here is the
charter developed by the service offering task force in the combination of two management consulting firms:

> The Service Offering Task Force makes recommendations to the
> Combination Steering Committee regarding the rationalization of
> practice areas in the combined organization. The Task Force will
> study and present opportunities for combining related practice
> areas from the precombination companies, recommend structures
> for the combined practice areas, propose leadership and gover-
> nance arrangements, and suggest staffing for leadership positions
> in the combined practice areas. The Task Force will also recom-
> mend any practice areas distinct to one or the other precombina-
> tion partner that should retain independent status rather than be
> rationalized with another practice area.

A transition team's charter is shaped by the desired end state
for the combination. If one company intends to absorb the other,
then the work of transition managers and task forces is to recommend how to best implement these decisions. If, alternatively, the
mandate is to select the best from both or to wholly transform operations, then fact finding and analysis is more open-ended and
the scope of task forces greatly expands. Once the regular management structure approves or revises recommendations, then the
transition manager and task forces may or may not attend to issues
of implementation. Whatever the charter of a task force is to be, it
should be discussed, clarified, and supported by all involved before moving ahead.

## Guidelines

With a clear and agreed-upon charter in hand, transition task
forces then need some guidelines to direct their work. These include a clear definition of strategy, sought-after synergies, and CSFs
as well as a no-nonsense set of combination principles issued by senior management, as outlined in the previous chapter. The vision
for the combination energizes task force members and focuses
them on what is expected from them to reach the desired end
state. Is a best-of-both combination sufficient, or should task forces
look outside existing practices and strive for breakthrough thinking? What kind of organization and culture is being sought?

Task forces also take the senior executive's principles and formulate them into their own set of rules of the road. In a high-technology alliance, one partner's culture was notorious for not taking its own past task force meetings seriously and for blatantly ignoring recommendations after they were agreed upon in meetings. Thus, in this alliance, the operations task force representing both sides established some specific ground rules:

Speak up in the room, not in the outside hallways, if you disagree with anything said.

Leave the room with consensus.

Respect task force meetings; show up on time or alert others if you will be late or absent.

Do your homework and come to meetings prepared.

Test emerging decisions with people in your work areas.

## Deliverables and Resources

Task forces also need clear deliverables and timetables. These elucidate what is expected of the task force, when, and in what format. Some CEOs only want an overview in interim reports; others demand detail. Clarity regarding the style and format of task force communications is especially important for teams led by people from the partner organization. Energy and focus that otherwise would be directed upon creating combination opportunities need not be wasted preparing overheads and scripting speeches.

Periodic reviews between the teams and top leadership aid task forces immensely. Interim reviews produce dialogue about options under investigation, clarify leadership's expectations, and inform leaders about what the task forces are learning. They circumvent the keen disappointment that develops when task forces have worked long and hard to develop a line of thinking only to have it shot down by leadership expecting—but not disclosing—that it wanted something else.

Teams require resources: staff support to assist in gathering and analyzing data, clerical support to arrange meetings and prepare documents, information technology to track and monitor work, and all sorts of logistical help to arrange travel, set schedules, etc. This sounds simple enough, but in today's era of downsized organizations, such resources may be difficult to come by, especially when the core business is vying for its share. Infrastructure has to be readied for the crunch before crises or embarrassments occur. On this point, dedicated conference rooms ensure that task forces do not have to compete with other groups for meeting space. And dedicated support staff, even temporaries hired for the purpose, ensure at the least that someone is "worrying" over all the details that would otherwise detract from team effectiveness.

## Organizing the Work

Despite their potential benefits, the sad truth is that transition task forces often produce at best mediocre recommendations, and at their worst downright antagonism among the members or between the teams and the rest of the organization. When we speak with people who have participated in or observed disappointing transition teams, they usually attribute the problems to the groups' initial launch: members embarked on their work with unclear or incongruous views on the task force's purpose, deliverables, roles and responsibilities, and operating principles. Effective transition task forces, in contrast, get kicked off in a manner that propels them forward.

Like any other start-up group, transition task forces go through stages of forming, storming, and norming before they get down to performing.[2] In the entertainment and telecommunications alliance mentioned in the previous chapter, the senior team returned from its three-day offsite meeting and sanctioned several task forces to propose ways to organize and staff functions to achieve the alliance's strategic objectives. To kick off these teams proactively and positively, Marks designed and facilitated a launch meeting for each of the task forces. Although he worked with task force leaders to craft an agenda to meet the specific needs and dynamics of each group, the meetings generally followed a two-day format.

The morning of the first day ensured that task force members received a solid foundation from which to pursue their work. This began with a review of the rationale, vision, CSFs, and operating principles of the combination and of each task force's specific charter, responsibilities, and deliverables. Each component was checked for complete understanding and support before moving to the next. The first morning also included time for the members to learn about pitfalls in group decision making and tactics for creative problem analysis, to establish their own ground rules for task force functioning, and to hear of the timetable and requested format for their work products. During the afternoon of day one and morning of day two, task forces conducted their first meetings. Then, on the afternoon of day two, task force members debriefed how the first meeting had gone and proposed any new or revised ground rules required to facilitate task force effectiveness and success. They also raised any areas of ambiguity or overlap needing coordination with other task forces.

In a concise format, this launch meeting provided opportunities for task forces to understand their responsibilities, formulate rules of the road to guide their work, experience how members deal with one another in an actual meeting, and raise issues and questions that could be brought to the combination executive committee for their immediate attention. The meeting also created opportunities for members from the partner organizations to spend time with one another and get to know each other as people. Breaks and meals were filled with informal conversations between the partners, and an evening bowling match with pizza and beer added some play time. Without some such developmental kick start like a launch meeting, task forces usually take several weeks or a few months to make this much progress.

## Knowledge Building

In cases where transition teams have to plan the full combination of companies, each side needs to teach the other how it goes about business. This can be crucial; a study by Egon Zehnder International found that the number one problem cited by 25 percent of combining organizations was a lack of understanding of their partners.[3]

Whereas the tendency to view one's own ways as superior to the other's is natural, this can be reframed so the two sides consider not only "How are we different from them?" but also "What can we learn from them?" Indeed, learning and adopting ideas from partners is part of realizing the full value of the partnership. An acquired executive in a highly successful professional-services combination credited the task force process with creating a venue in which differences could be aired: "We would not give up on our beliefs. When our buyer said something that showed they did not really understand our customer, we would fight vehemently. The lead company has to give credence and credibility to people who know the business."

To make the process work, task force members on both sides need to draw on each other's knowledge. Assessing partners' respective budgets, head counts, and operations depends on apples-to-apples comparisons. One partner may house its security and transportation office in the human resource function, while the other has them elsewhere; hence it would be unfair to compare the relative costs and staffing of the two HR groups. We used common procedures in a high-technology combination to help functional task forces compare their two sides and build the baseline knowledge required for effective combination planning:

- *Functional analysis.* A first step was to contrast the two sides' functions. Each task force identified common core functions to be analyzed and then noncore functions that would be handled separately.
- *Baselines.* Next, baseline figures of costs and head count were prepared for core areas.
- *Organization structure.* Each task force recommended an operating structure for its area of the business. They followed guidelines calling for a structure that would make things happen quickly, keep staff close to essential businesses and customers, develop broad spans of control, encourage a hands-on approach to the business, and balance supervision of staff groups against the need to service line units.
- *Staffing plan.* Lists of qualified candidates were prepared for each position below the function head, on down to first-line supervisors. This involved writing position descriptions; analyzing staffing requirements (education, previous experience, functional experience, etc.); and listing candidates along with their years of service, time in current position, precombination company affiliation, a rating of their readiness, and other pertinent information.
- *Management process and support systems.* The task force identified management policies, decision-making processes, and support systems that related directly to organization, staffing, and CSFs in the area and made recommendations for partial or complete integration.

- *Cost reductions.* Finally, each task force developed a specific cost-reduction plan. Savings came from various sources: redundant or superfluous activities; productivity improvement; make-versus-buy decisions; or choosing a more efficient way of doing things, whether based on using the best from the combining companies' existing practices or finding an altogether new way of operating.

In completing their analyses, task forces should be assisted but not overburdened with procedures. Effective transition task forces evolve and develop their own working styles. Once clarified and understood by all involved, their charter, operating principles, and deliverables are nonnegotiable. How the teams go about their work, though, is best left to the members. How often the groups meet, how the labor is divided, the agenda for specific meetings, and all the other details are up to members to determine as a group.

## Coordination

Boundaries between task forces may not be discrete; hence their work must be coordinated. The manufacturing task force cannot weigh options for how many plants will be required or affordable in the postcombination organization if it is unaware of the products task force's progress on which lines to retain or of the human resources task force's thinking on the compensation and benefits to be offered.

Various methods have been used to integrate the work of multiple transition task forces. In some cases, task force chairs can act as integrators who keep their teams abreast of the goings on of other teams. Many companies we have worked with use periodic reviews in which leaders of the transition teams come together to update one another on progress. Issues of coordination and controversy are raised and discussed by the full group after each task force presentation. Other firms rely on staff support (from people affectionately known as "runners") who move between task forces. Sitting in on one task force's meeting, they may hear an issue discussed that influences or is influenced by work being conducted by another group. Or, runners may be requested by one task force to gather information from or advocate certain viewpoints to another group. When the stakes are high, this role usually is taken by the transition manager, who has the stature and the skills to broker shared solutions across teams. In an international consumer-products merger, for example, the transition manager had to perform some shuttle diplomacy between the marketing and product task force leaders to get them to see eye-to-eye on reporting relationships between customer support staff and country managers.

Hopefully, transition teams get to the point where the leaders can talk directly to one another, without the use of third parties and in a timely manner, to compare viewpoints and determine coordinated recommendations. Often, members of one task force are invited to sit in as regular members of another. This adds to people's already crazy schedules, but over the long haul it saves a lot of grief, conflict, and reworking of recommendations.

## Transition Team Processes: Synergies Versus Politics

Besides building knowledge of what each party brings to the combination, there is also the matter of deciding how transition teams can best approach the issues. What complicates fact finding and analysis in so many cases is that the synergies sought are not well defined or can only be realized by people working together effectively. In an alliance between consulting firms, as an example, the two sides sought to pool their knowledge about information technology and change management to provide clients with a one-stop solution. This works fine in theory, but figuring out how to combine their knowledge, develop best-practice guidelines, and then prepare cross-company teams to deliver solutions to clients is where, as one consultant put it, the "rubber hit the sky." Behind each company's way of doing business are important executives and various coalitions that have lots at stake. Attempts to clarify facts and resolve differences can threaten the pecking order within companies, challenge past precedents, and put formerly friendly functions at odds or bring old enemies together, ultimately affecting who is in and out (or at least up and down) in the combined organization. There are, of course, transition teams wherein the buyer or lead investor can impose its methods and mores and run roughshod over a partner. But more often there is considerable give-and-take over both the substance of combination decisions *and* who exactly determines what results.

In order to identify different kinds of transition team agendas and processes, Mirvis and a colleague, Barbara Blumenthal, categorized them based on the partners' agreement on synergies and the stability of their relationship. A simple 2 x 2 matrix illustrates their interactive effect (Figure 6.2). To begin, the work of transition teams is greatly simplified when the partners can agree on synergies and do not have to contend with an unstable or contentious political environment. We have labeled this cell the "choir" because all concerned are figuratively ready to sing together. Next there is the case where partners cannot fully agree on synergies but have a workable relationship; this we term a "debating society" because the partners can establish ground rules for examining and deciding the issues and focus on the substance that divides them. The obverse is a "competitive sport," where the parties can agree on a game plan but cannot control who gets to play or by what rules. Finally, there is a "free-for-all," devoid of agreement on synergies and stability in the power structure.

## Lead the Choir

Some of the happy organizational marriages we have described fit this type. For instance, the merger of Chemical Bank and Manufacturers Hanover went smoothly in part because the two sides agreed on a common strategy and forestalled conflict by horse trading over who would run different parts of the combined organization. In a high-technology case, an initially contentious takeover turned collegial when the two sides agreed on what was needed

**Figure 6.2. Identifying Transition Team
Agendas and Processes.**

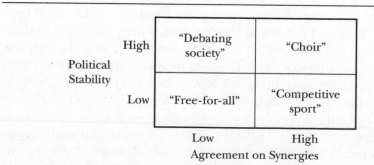

and the CEO insisted on meritocracy in decisions on organization and leadership. Here are some ideas on guiding teams in such cases:

- Establish, from the outset, any nonnegotiable strategic objectives. In the high-tech case, the CEO set out requirements to reduce costs, shed unrelated assets, and focus investments in R&D.
- Form and charge cross-company transition teams with preparing a composite picture of the marketplace and what they consider to be the ideal way to attack it. Transition teams from Chemical and Manny Hanny also prepared briefs on best practices from competitors and from companies outside their industry.
- Review team findings in open forums attended by the full cadre of senior managers. This makes the logic behind thinking visible and allows for clarifying questions and full airing of competing views.

## Conduct a Debate

When the political environment is stable, it is possible to score the merits of competing arguments about how to create value. The problems encountered by frontline staff in an alliance between French and German consulting firms was that senior management failed to establish, beyond some general bromides about collaborative synergies, what they were actually seeking in the partnership. Local managers, in turn, had no guidance on whether they were supposed to lower costs, increase revenue, or enhance the merged firm's competitive position. Furthermore, frontline consultants had no guidance on how they were supposed to work with counterparts; no mandate to build a body of knowledge from their collaborative experiences; and no one to turn to so as to resolve their conflicts over project organization, methodology, or deliverables. In this strategic and managerial vacuum, heated debate over how to meld different skills in service to a client fizzled quickly, and collaborative synergies went up in smoke.

What can partners do to foster substantive debate while getting to workable answers on the questions that matter? Besides a clearer definition of purpose and mandate to learn from one another, consider these ideas to deepen the debate:

- Select transition team cochairs who are well versed in and comfortable with the different methodologies of the two sides and not wedded to either of them. That way they can serve as informed arbiters.
- Have each side clearly present its case for how to work together. This at least forces conflicts into the open. Short-term increases in conflict might well yield longer-term benefits in improved relationships and better decisions.
- Establish selected demonstration projects where the two sides actively try to combine their skills and talents and then document the process and results. This provides a visible example of the partner's joint intent and a valuable case study for replication and improvement.

## Define the Playing Field

It is not enough for partners to agree on synergies for the game they are playing together; they also have to understand and agree to play by the rules. In the case of an acquiree purchased by a major conglomerate, local management did not appreciate that the parent company had to oversee fifty-plus unrelated subsidiaries and needed to monitor their performance in some common fashion. The acquiree's resistance to measuring performance in as much detail as was demanded raised suspicions in some circles that performance problems were being hidden and added urgency to the parent company's insistence that they conform to "standard procedures." From this experience come straightforward recommendations to guide the process of transition teams:

- *Define the rules of the game.* A buyer or lead partner will, to a greater or lesser degree, have some prerogatives that must be honored. Saying so at the outset clarifies the relative power of the partners and sets up a workable agenda.
- *Insist that people play by the rules.* When USX purchased Marathon, it was agreed that the acquiree would operate as a stand-alone business. Still, the USX chairman intervened several times when corporate staff proposed information and control requirements; in his words, he had to "call off the dogs."

- *Level the playing field.* In cases where the two sides are coequals, it is essential to set up objective criteria, to the fullest extent possible, for evaluating proposals and performance and to evaluate them fairly.

How partners study organizational options and review recommendations also invites attention. For example, one side may use transition teams to advance a divide-and-conquer strategy, the logic being it can gain more from a series of bilateral negotiations than from an overarching one. Specific functions or businesses may also gain advantage from making side deals with partner functions or by outmaneuvering them.

The obvious solution here is to place an individual or executive body in a position to police these side dealings. Another option is to bring the whole system into the room. In this way, transition team leaders and members together are exposed to the overall logic of the combination and the ways in which they contribute to or detract from it.

## Give Form to a Free-for-All

IBM's acquisition of Lotus had all the characteristics of a free-for-all. The two sides could not agree on strategy, nor was it clear that they could resolve differences amicably. After forming transition teams, the companies took innovative steps to promote dialogue and reduce mistrust. Consider some recommendations from their experiences:

- *Make analyses of the market and the logic behind the organization transparent.* In this case, the databases, analyses, and work plans of each transition team were available to other relevant parties through an electronic filing system. That way, all concerned could see and verify what was behind proposals and make any questions or challenges a part of the electronic record.
- *Prepare political maps of what is at stake for every interest in the partnership.* Recognizing that their "facts" were disputable and would not carry the day in any case, target management also devised political maps that highlighted the extent to which functions in the parent company might be affected by different strategies and identified who was open to influence.

- *Mark progress by increments.* Once the parties had access to the full range of information, options, and political ramifications on the table, they then worked a series of tactical and operational issues through to agreement. This approach enabled the two sides to work together before tackling more divisive issues.

We find that persistent and serious pressure to create value help keep political forces under control. Conflicts of interest do not vanish, but they do become manageable. At the same time, success also comes from selecting strategies that are politically feasible. This is not just a matter for top-level attention. Seemingly tactical decisions affecting businesses, functions, and employees down the line can frustrate grand strategies and produce political fallout in the ranks. However, with concerted attention to surfacing and working through their strategic disagreements, and mapping and managing the political landscape, it is possible to turn a free-for-all into a new organization and to get people with different talents and interests to sing together.

## Transition Structure Management

Once it is clear whether a team is to debate, fight, or sing together, it can reap real benefits from team building. The launch meeting is an excellent beginning, but team-building activities can be beneficial throughout the course of integration planning. Team building conducted early in a team's tenure not only identifies and addresses small issues before they mushroom into major obstacles, but it also takes a relatively well-functioning group of individuals and propels them into a highly creative, productive, and effective team.[4] This overcomes the tendency in some transition task forces to move too gingerly and waste precious time in the early weeks of the combination phase.

Both structured and unstructured team-building activities aid in developing relationships among combining managers. The launch meetings conducted in the entertainment-and-telecommunications alliance included dinners and social time to facilitate informal bonding among the task force members. In any combination, much of the work of learning about one another and each other's business gets done after hours and outside of meeting rooms. Occasional offsite meetings, recreational outings, and dinners yield important dividends, including unstructured discussions of combination issues and opportunities, and they build lasting relationships among new partners.

## Challenge Sessions

There simply is not enough time for task forces to gather and digest all the needed facts or to review and fully challenge the assumptions used in developing recommendations. Usually, once a task force centers on a course of action, commitment escalates because the costs of going back to ground zero are simply too great. To prevent escalating commitments and to reduce groupthink, it is advisable to set aside time for task forces to reevaluate previously abandoned courses of action and recalibrate the costs, risks, and benefits of the chosen courses.[5]

In addition, we also advise that there be team-on-team challenge sessions, where task forces get together to compare findings and recommendations with one another. In an alliance, teams preparing product-and-marketing plans for different industry segments presented their ideas to one another in a structured challenge session. After presenting their ideas and plans to another transition team, the presenting team would receive specific written feedback in which its proposals were ranked from 10 (complete and compelling) to 1 (dead on arrival) followed by suggestions on how to improve analyses or recommendations. Then there was a full-scale discussion of the ratings and suggestions. It is worth noting that the team providing feedback was evaluated by another transition team. This reduced the tendency to lob softballs in hopes of getting the same in return.

The transition oversight group is the final arbiter of task force recommendations. It should query task force leaders on the matter of horse trading or compromises by asking them to review their rationale for decisions and make a case for how decisions abide by the CSFs and support productive combination. It should also ask about rejected options. In some task forces, devil's advocates criticize their recommendations and speak in favor of abandoned alternatives. In one acquisition, a team undertook a role reversal wherein the buying company argued in favor of the acquired firm's methods and vice versa. This unlocked the conflict and led to a resolution of differences.

What about cases where *too little* conflict hinders a task force's work? Some task forces duck the issues and conduct their sessions like ballroom dancing, with politeness and courtesy. Here, too, top-level oversight and team building can be used to apply a healthy amount of controversy and debate to generate high-quality recommendations.

## Looking Outside of the Box

Compromises in transition planning result in compromises in combining companies. Obviously there are key strategic, financial, and operational criteria to apply when evaluating the recommendations of task forces. Our experience suggests other factors to consider in ensuring that transition teams look outside of their own situation to find best practices:

- *Reassert critical success factors.*  Senior leaders need to hold up their CSFs as criteria for evaluating the analyses of transition teams. Teams locked into we-versus-they debates need to move toward relatively more objective analyses of how well each partner's systems compare against critical success factors. A discussion of how well each system fits with the CSFs introduces the possibility that a third and novel way of doing things might be the best approach for the combined organization. And it deflects the mine-is-better-than-yours dynamic that deflates the creativity of many task forces.
- *Look at the long haul.*  Although choosing one or the other partner's systems may be appropriate for the current situation, is it suitable for the future of the combined business? This question can be a stimulus to benchmarking outside of one's industry for breakthrough ideas.
- *Bring in outsiders.*  Especially when jobs and careers are at stake, it may be necessary to bring in an outside consultant or expert who can be more objective in assessing options and evaluating recommendations.
- *Use the 80/20 rule.*  Watch out for too many supposedly new ideas. Transforming to a third way of doing things is sometimes called for, but it is always more difficult to implement than adopting current systems. If you have a solid system in

place that fits CSFs, or at least gets you 80 percent of the way there, then use it.

## Implementation

The work of transition teams does not end with developing recommendations. Many times they prepare comprehensive change management plans to complement their proposals. All too frequently, excellent work conducted by transition task forces is rejected out-of-hand by core business managers who resent being excluded from the process, are locked into their current way of doing things, or simply do not believe that anyone other than themselves could understand the true issues and opportunities and develop an optimal approach. In successful combinations, by contrast, the segue from task force planning to core business implementation better resembles a fading out and fading in of responsibilities than it does a sharp cut. Task forces need to bring core business managers into their confidence before recommendations are set in concrete, to gain the managers' input and to begin the process of transferring ownership of and support for ideas produced in the task forces.

Two sets of tasks make up implementation planning. One involves coordinating and monitoring the many changes being introduced as part of the combination. The timing and sequencing of change implementation is critically important to maintaining productivity in the switchover from the old to the new. It also has an impact on customer satisfaction and employee morale; there are few situations more deflating than the introduction of a much-heralded new system that is then bogged down by glitches and snafus. Travelers still recount the trauma of trying to board planes when the computer system shut down on "changeover" day in the 1987 acquisition of Republic Airlines by Northwest Airlines. Mindful of this sort of thing, combined companies set realistic timetables for implementing new procedures and ensure proper redundancy in systems until the changeover is complete.

The second set of tasks pertains to the human side of change. For changes recommended by transition task forces to truly engage the workforce during implementation, they should be positioned as being essential to achieving synergies and as adhering to the

combination's CSFs. When this connection is clear, recommendations have higher face validity and the path toward successful implementation is smoothed. We take up these points further in
Chapters Nine and Ten, on organization and team building.

### Midcourse Corrections

No matter how well planned change implementation might be, midcourse
corrections are commonplace in successful combinations. Take the merger of
two electronic-products distribution companies, where the CEO wanted to
build a customer service standard second to none in the industry. That critical
success factor was operationalized in task force planning as a target of next-
day delivery. In a business characterized by low margins, the CEO also set
stringent financial targets and cost-cutting goals for the combined operations.
As task forces contended with the dual requirements of enhancing service
while cutting costs, the CEO set off on a series of visits to all company locations
to communicate face-to-face to employees what would be required to achieve
the deal's strategic synergies. As part of his message, the CEO stressed that initial plans might have to be revised as the combining parties learned more
about each other and their business. He asked employees if they wanted to be
kept abreast of plans as they were being developed—with the caveat that early
announcements may be contradicted by later ones—or whether they preferred
communication only when relatively definite announcements were available.
At each location, employees clearly indicated a desire to learn as early as possible about plans in progress.

The hub of the combination planning process was the operations task
force. Its initial analyses suggested that six of the partner companies' sixteen
precombination warehouses would need to be closed in order to meet financial
targets while satisfying the criterion of next-day delivery. The senior team ap-
proved this recommendation and communicated same to the overall organization. Shortly thereafter, however, some new information surfaced that
necessitated closing three additional warehouses in order to achieve the financial goals. When leadership communicated that more warehouses needed to be
closed than originally reported, the general response among employees was
one of "Well, if this is what is required to build the best possible organization,
then this is what we have to do." Certainly there was upset among people at
the three locations newly slated for closing, but the remaining employee popu-
lation understood that the revision was the result of newly determined information and not management misdirection. They received the news with

understanding and support rather than with the cynicism and distrust that would accompany a major midcourse correction in most work organizations today.

If transition planning and implementation were simple and linear activities, then we would see many more combinations hitting their financial and strategic targets. But they are complicated and chaotic endeavors. The sheer volume of data to be collected, the large number of decisions to be made, the truly delicate process of choosing among competing systems or designing new methods, and the coordinative intricacies of addressing many simultaneous implementation issues and opportunities all contribute to the difficulty. In the meantime, management also has to build people's energy and commitment to a productive combination even as their uncertainty and fear rise.

## Chapter Seven

# Managing Uncertainty and Stress

While those involved in combination planning busy themselves with collecting data, analyzing options, and formulating recommendations, others in the organization wait to learn their fate. Even when the majority of people understand the rationale for the combination and sense that some truly productive potential can result from joining forces, they retain a constant concern for self-preservation and an equally constant craving for information about what is going on around them.

Employees experience uncertainty and insecurity in each of the phases of a combination. Initially, as a deal is rumored and then announced in the precombination phase, employees have a multitude of questions. Who are they? What are they like to work with or be a part of? Who will be in control in the new organization? What's going to happen to pay and benefits? What about that promotion or project assignment promised to me by my boss? Will I even have a job?

As teams begin to study options and make plans during the combination phase, employees wonder what is going on behind the closed doors. How are decisions being made? Who's looking out for our way of doing things? Who is my champion as staffing decisions are being made? Is the other side going to get all the good positions?

Then, with implementation in the postcombination phase, employees experience yet another wave of uncertainty and worry. What's expected of me? How do I get things done around here? Does my new boss trust me? Do I trust my new boss?

Many executives label the transition period the "twilight zone" between the old and the new: it's murky and scary to individuals who long for stability and their accustomed norms. Confusion and uncertainty reign as the organization is no longer what it was, but not yet what it intends to be.[1] People are not sure how and where they fit in, largely because the organizational structure has yet to settle into place. Control and information systems that were designed for the old regime may not be relevant to or effective in the new organization. New work teams have not yet been formed or settled into a modus operandi.

## Combination Stress Versus Commitment

Two basic tasks make up the agenda for managing employee uncertainty and insecurity in the transition. One aims to minimize the stress experienced by employees and help them cope with its effects. The second is to maximize the upside by building employee understanding of and commitment to the combination and the opportunities it offers. As Figure 7.1 shows, stress among employees rises dramatically before and during the transition and then decreases only gradually. Commitment to the new organization builds slowly. Although these patterns are inevitable, it is possible to decrease stress and increase commitment—and as a result eventually improve productivity, quality, and employee well-being—through careful management of the transition process.

**Figure 7.1. Stress and Commitment Cycles in a Combination.**

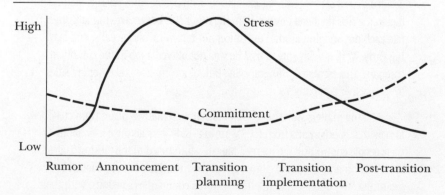

No matter how confident senior executives feel about the rationale for a combination and how much potential gain it holds for the organization and its people, employees will always experience stress and merger syndrome reactions. They are normal, natural, and to be expected in a combination. Anyone who denies susceptibility to stress and the merger syndrome is just that—in denial! The negative effects of stress and the merger syndrome cannot be eliminated. But their detrimental impact can be mollified by helping people understand and cope with their situation and supporting them in adapting to the transition.

### Managing Front-End Fears

The merger of the two international consumer products firms introduced in Chapter Four was greeted by employees, industry analysts, and the business press as a great move. Consolidation in the fragmented industry had been predicted, and observers heralded the marriage of two of the strongest players as creating the new industry leader. Share prices for both companies shot up as brokers issued buy recommendations for the stocks. Contributing to the optimism, the two highly respected CEOs both agreed to stay on, with one running manufacturing and administration and the other sales and marketing. Employee spirits rose when newspaper accounts of the deal cited the CEOs' commitment to select the best of the premerger companies and also to look for new ways of doing things in building the combined organization. As one CEO said to a major business publication, "We are not just consolidating two organizations, we are building the best organization possible to ensure our success and industry leadership for the twenty-first century."

Soon after the announcement, but before the close of the deal, rumors began to fly around both companies that the executive in charge of sales had decided to staff senior positions exclusively with people from his side. Adding fuel to the fire, the head of sales from the other side began arriving at work late each day, moping around the office, not returning phone calls, and leaving early. Word quickly spread that he was not offered a job in the combined company; this escalated into grapevine talk of a complete "takeover" of sales by the partner company.

Making matters still worse, some sales representatives heard from customers that counterparts from the "winning" side were acting cocky about their people controlling the merger. Morale plummeted in the "losing" sales organization and, eventually, throughout the firm. They felt abandoned by their CEO, who chose not to interfere with his counterpart's actions. With their own senior sales executive out of the picture, sales representatives assumed that no one would be representing them in selection decisions. When these merger syndrome symptoms were conveyed to the CEO in charge of sales, he responded, "I know it's a problem, but what can I do? I'm prevented by law from talking to their sales staff before the merger closes." (Combination partners do have to be careful about making contact with the other side during this phase. In deals involving publicly traded companies, regulations limit exchanges between the partners; in those involving privately held companies, the partners are well advised not to disclose highly sensitive competitive information until the deal closes. Still, much can be done to address employee stress and uncertainty in the front end of a combination.)

Marks began working with a team of line executives and internal human resource and communications professionals to develop a comprehensive program to minimize the unintended psychological and behavioral consequences of joining the two forces, and to maximize employee understanding of and support for the deal and the way it was being managed. Four objectives guided the program's development:

1. *Insight:* raise employees' awareness of combination-related stress and how to control it.

2. *Inspiration:* make an intellectual and emotional case for why people should let go of their accustomed ways of thinking about and doing things and accept those of the new organization.

3. *Information:* keep employees informed about the combination's purpose, promise, process, and progress.

4. *Involvement:* find ways to get people to feel more like architects of change and less like victims.

To achieve these objectives, the design team identified many leverage points that the merging senior executives could use in managing employee mind-sets. These included the executives' own actions, setting expectations for middle managers and supervisors, directing internal human resource and communications staff to develop programs, and making it clear to all employees that human responses to a combination need to be understood and addressed.

## Insight

The first step in helping people cope with combination-related stress is getting them to understand its sources and what they can do to control it. Employees engaged in a combination need to be prepared for a period of high-level activity and the pain, anxiety, and decreased productivity that lie ahead. They need to see the confusion and concerns they experience not as signs of personal weakness but as natural consequences of a deal. The emotions they feel—anger at themselves or their leaders, despair over the uncertainty of their future, and even guilt about being spared in a layoff—are legitimate reactions to the stress of a combination. Painful emotional states are more likely to become destructive (to both the individual and the organization) when they are denied or derogated as not making sense. The key is to get people to accept and control their emotional reactions to the combination, instead of letting their emotions control them.

### Road Shows and Seminars

In the consumer products firms, which were still legally separate until the combination received approval, the two CEOs took firsthand responsibility by increasing their visibility in their respective organizations. Both men scheduled "road shows" to talk with employees at each location in their firms, arranged meetings with key talent, and had informal visits with small groups of employees. In particular, the CEO from the "losing" sales side took the time to meet with his key sales staff to remind them that he knew they were talented and to let them know that they were needed to build the new organization going forward. Customers, he noted, would not tolerate the decimation of one side's sales force in the combination; nor would he. In one-on-one meetings, he acknowledged that the other CEO intended to keep his own direct reports but pointed out that no commitments had been made beyond that level. Only after the deal became legal, and sales executives from the two sides could begin communicating and exchanging information, would any additional staffing decisions be made. He pledged that a process involving managers from both parties would be used to design and staff the new sales organization, using a broad set of criteria including past performance, fit with the desired new organizational culture, and the quality of current relationships with customers.

To address concerns about his sales staff losing their champion, he vowed to personally represent them as ensuing decisions were made and to monitor the development of the sales organization. In the meantime, the CEO asked his sales staff to stay focused, to the extent they could, on their customers and the work at hand and keep contributing to company success. Note that the CEO made no promises to anyone about their job security. What he did do was acknowledge the legitimacy of their concerns, remind them that their talents were recognized and needed, alerted them to the process to be used for making decisions, and asked them to remember their short-term work responsibilities.

The CEOs also directed others to raise awareness about human reactions to a combination process. They asked their staffs to circulate articles on the merger syndrome and related literature to the workforce, as well as distribute to managers books on the human and cultural aspects of combinations. Marks was asked to design a seminar on human and organizational issues in combinations. It would provide guidelines for managing oneself and others during this stressful time and be delivered in a "separate but equal" manner, with the same format and content delivered in the two organizations.

The day-long program, on the "Challenges of Combination," combined presentations, small-group discussions, and time for individual reflection and planning (see Exhibit 7.1). The program was offered in both companies to all staff who managed people. Marks led the initial sessions with the senior teams and their direct reports. Internal resources conducted sessions with all other managers and supervisors. This cascading effort sent a message that attendance at the program was important. More important, it enabled midlevel and lower-level managers to leave the session better informed and prepared to discuss the situation with superiors who had already attended the program.

Evaluations of the seminar showed that managers received many benefits from attending the program. First, they reported a greater understanding of the potential pitfalls that bring down combinations. Second, their self-confidence was bolstered by learning that others before them had made the treacherous journey through a combination and emerged (though sometimes bruised and battered) as stronger and sturdier survivors of the corporate jungles. Third, they felt better prepared for the work-related challenges, from long hours of data gathering and task force meetings to the likelihood of less cooperation from peers or support staff obsessed with their own survival. Fourth, they appreciated the opportunity to discuss openly how managerial missteps and attendant rumors (as in the handling of senior positions in sales) were already affecting this combination. These real-life episodes brought a dose of reality to the seminar and distinguished it from a generic program on change management.

### Exhibit 7.1. Agenda for "Challenges of Combination" Seminar.

---

**Introduction**

- Welcome by CEO
- Review of seminar purpose and objectives by SVP, Human Resources

**Presentation on "Why Most Combinations Fail"**

- Small groups list "Potential Pitfalls in this Combination"
- Full group discussion of potential pitfalls

**Presentation on "The Merger Syndrome"**

- Individuals list "Ways I Can Manage Combination-Related Stress" and "How the Company Can Help People Manage Their Stress"

**Presentations on "Maintaining Productivity and Morale During a Combination" and "Managing One's Own Stress in a Combination"**

- Individuals add to and refine stress management lists
- Small groups consolidate individual lists of "Ways I Can Manage Combination-Related Stress" and "How the Company Can Help People Manage Their Stress"
- Full group discussion

**Q and A with CEO and/or other senior executives**

---

## Inspiration

In today's world of downsizing, reduced career opportunities, and a changing and less compelling psychological contract between employers and employees, inspiring people in a combination does not come easily. On an intellectual level, the CEOs in the consumer products case used their road shows and informal gatherings to present employees with a persuasive argument for why the combination made sense. They reiterated the rationale for the deal and cited its many positive reviews by the business press and investment community. People are more likely to accept the pain of a combination if they see some gain resulting from it. This vision of a new and better organization helps people divert their attention from what is being given up and toward what is being produced. It also breeds confidence (if not a sense of relief) that management has thought through where the organization is headed. And it provides a template for organizing thinking and action toward attainment of the desired end state. The workforce

needs a vision with which to align their expectations and job behaviors during a combination.

To address the healthy employee skepticism of "What's in it for
me?" the CEOs expressed the combination's potential benefits in
human as well as business terms. The strategy for the combined organization called for emphasis on growth, international business
development, and a broader product line than either precombination organization supported. This would translate into more opportunities for individuals, international assignments for those
interested in gaining global experience, and a wider array of products for salespeople to market to customers. Moreover, with its increased size and resources, the combined company could offer
career development and skills training programs not affordable in
the predecessor companies.

Inspiration has an emotional component as well as an intellectual one. Despite all of the turmoil wrought by corporate up-
heavals in recent years, our conversations with employees confirm
that people have retained the human desire to make an important
contribution in the work they do. People want to know that their
jobs make a difference and that their collective efforts result in
something special. In this case, the two CEOs made an emotional
pitch to employees framed around their own commitment to the
combination. With both men near retirement age, the combined
organization would be their legacy. They urged employees to see
the creation of a new organization as a great event in all employees' careers. "How many times in your life," asked one of the CEOs
at a visit to a manufacturing plant, "do you have the opportunity
to be in on the ground floor of the creation of a brand new company?" A value-creating combination presents leaders with the
chance to tap into and resurrect employees' aspirations to build a
new and better organization and life for themselves.

## Information

The velocity with which rumors spread through their companies
took the CEOs by surprise and prompted them to commit resources to a comprehensive communications program beginning
immediately. This distinguished them from leaders of typical combinations who nod their heads in agreement about the importance
of communications, but whose follow-on behaviors are woefully

inadequate. Managers engaged in a combination offer many excuses for not communicating to their people:

- *"There's nothing to say."* Managers are uncomfortable communicating when they themselves don't know what is in the works. They figure that employees will be skeptical if told "I don't know." In fact, especially when prepared with insight into the combination process, employees understand that integration decisions are complex and that answers to their questions may not be immediately forthcoming.
- *"I want to protect my people."* Many managers like to think that they can buffer their employees from combination-related stress; they rationalize to themselves that talk about the situation only exacerbates concerns. Rumors fill the communications void, however, and the grapevine always thrives on the downside of developments.
- *"Let the communications people do it."* Corporate communications staff can be of tremendous help, but they should not serve as the primary mouthpiece of management. Employees want to hear from and be heard by their leaders and managers, not substitutes.
- *"We've already told them that."* Employees have an insatiable thirst for information about what has happened and is happening. Regular updates, even if containing nothing new, are important reminders that management is still in touch with people's concerns.

Information contributes both substantive and symbolic value to productive combination. People want to know what is going on and why. They also, however, want the peace of mind that comes with feeling in the know. Efforts toward effective communications made by managers and staff reduce the energy expended by employees to search for answers to their questions (and, thus, their distraction from performance) and increase the accuracy of information being circulated.

Communications professional Roger D'Aprix notes varied reasons why information is so important during periods of organizational change.[2] First, effective communications create a clear and simple case for change, based on market and customer realities. The logic here is that you are asking people to accept the need to change their personal and group behavior. Most people resist that kind of change unless they recognize a strong case to embrace it.

Second, the storyline conveyed provides a context for people's work experience—a frame of reference—that allows them to put events in proper perspective. If matters are explained to them and the underlying rationale provided, employees are more likely to embrace rather than resist desired change.

A third reason why information is so important is that a comprehensive communications program has the potential to take seemingly random and even painful events and focus more on their significance than merely on the fact that they occurred. In short, it explains events rather than merely retelling them. Done right, it also depicts leadership as connected to reality. Recall the case from the previous chapter of the electronics distribution company that recanted on its initial announced plan to close six warehouses and instead decided to close nine. The front work done in setting a communications climate of full and early disclosure resulted in people's understanding and accepting the revision rather than using it as a rallying point to attack management.

Finally, effective communications show leadership actions as rational and considered. Of course, if they are neither rational nor considered, all the communications in the world are not going to change things. But if such actions are well reasoned, the resulting connections can be very reassuring and give people a sense that their leadership is on top of the game and that their own work is meaningful in getting the organization where is it headed.

### A Comprehensive Communications Program

Back at the consumer products firms, the CEOs desired to build a company where communications would be timely, open, complete, multidirectional, and checked for accuracy. Their communications program featured many such characteristics:

- *Use of multiple media.* Communication is done in writing (office memos, letters sent to employees' homes, newsletters, and question and answer packets), electronically (videos, e-mail, and telephone hotlines), and in person (large and small group presentations, one-on-one discussions, road shows).

- *Balance the upside with current realities.* Communications emphasize the positive but acknowledge problems and pain.

- *Recognize there will be more questions than answers.* Communicate what is known, and be clear about what is not known.

- *Anticipate communication breakdowns.* Recognize and speak to employee stress and "wishful hearing," both of which distort intended messages.

- *Overcommunicate.* Respond to the insatiable employee need for information, and repeat the same message through multiple channels. For example, follow paper announcements with a video.

- *Check communications.* Get feedback on clarity of understanding, and do not assume that the message received was the message sent.

- *Do it.* Recognize that effort spent up front to set the right communications tone is less costly than overcoming distrust and miscommunications down the road.

The core of the communications program was its content. In sharp contrast to the there's-nothing-to-say mentality that prevails in most combinations, top leaders in this merger found much to say. First, they reviewed the business case and strategic rationale for the combination, along with a strong argument for why maintaining the status quo was not in the best interest of either the organization or its people in an industry embarking on considerable consolidation. Second, they provided information on the partner organizations: their histories, offerings, customers, cultures, personalities, and recent accomplishments. Third, the weeks awaiting legal approval provided time to educate people on the combination process and its inherent complexities. Finally, as the senior executives prepared to combine, they decided to make use of cross-company task forces. Their intentions were announced in a memo to employees and reiterated in an article in the weekly transition newsletter that highlighted the purpose and structure of task forces as well as the criteria to be used in decision making.

Overall, the senior executives took a proactive approach to moving accurate information up and down the ranks. "We aggressively solicited the rumor mill and other communications channels," recalled one of the combining CEOs, "Human resources staff and our external consultants kept their ears to the ground and brought information quickly to the top of the organization. We found that a lot of our messages and intentions were taken out of context, so we made sure senior people went out and communicated in a timely manner before the rumor mill communicated for them." One tactic used was a toll-free telephone hotline on which employees could leave accounts of any rumors they heard. Every two weeks, a list of the "top ten rumors" was published, along with factual information addressing the content of the rumors. As the following sample rumor list shows, even when information was not yet available to respond to employee uncertainty, by raising and addressing the rumors head-on management helped the employees recognize the dubious quality of the grapevine's contents and become better "consumers" of the rumor mill.

Here are the rumors most frequently called into our toll-free telephone hotline for the past two weeks:

**Rumor:** Two hundred people are going to be laid off from headquarters.

**Fact:** Only one hundred fifty people work there.

**Rumor:** The choices we now enjoy in our employee benefit program will be eliminated once the two companies are merged.

**Fact:** No decisions regarding employee benefits have been determined. A task force will review all employee benefits and make recommendations to senior management by September 1. We will communicate any decisions to you once they are determined. In the meantime, employees from both partner organizations will continue with no changes to their current benefits packages.

## Involvement

As with other forms of organizational change, the more involved people feel in a combination, the more likely they are to understand and support its rationale, and the more they commit to successful implementation.[3] In the consumer products firms, one activity that set the pattern for fuller employee participation later on in the process was built around an early key decision regarding the location of the combined company's headquarters. More than 90 percent of all employees returned questionnaires soliciting their views on the factors that should used in selecting the site, the relative attractiveness of the business environment in the current headquarters sites, and the potentially adverse business and personal effects of locating in either city. Some also participated in focus groups to gain deeper understanding of employees' feelings and thoughts. When making the announcement of the city selected for headquarters, the CEOs cited findings from the employee research in addition to the other criteria used in making the decision.

## Managing Uncertainty During the Transition

Many of the actions initiated prior to legal closing of a deal can be extended into and through the combination phase. Senior executives still need to visit with people, acknowledge their concerns, and inspire them with a positive picture of their future organization. If anything, communications have to be increased to keep up with demand and to counter rumors, because in the combination phase there is more content and news to impart. In turn, training or sensitization seminars need to be tailored to a new phase of the combination that sometimes includes significant restructuring and layoffs, many and varied changes in policies and practices, and introduction of new leaders and a new corporate culture.

## Sensitization and Surfacing

Knowledge of the merger syndrome does not necessarily lessen stress and anxiety, but it helps people understand how they and others might be responding to the combination. Ideally, managers are given insight into the syndrome as part of their emotional preparation for a deal, and employees take part in sensitization sessions (like those conducted in the international consumer products firms) before the deal is complete. In many instances, however, the deal is done and the combination is in motion before people down the line have a chance to get together and discuss what is happening and the implications.

*Picture This*

Mirvis led a sensitization session with managers and staff at office products maker Dennison (located just outside Boston) shortly after its acquisition by its California-based competitor Avery. By this time, the combination of Avery-Dennison was signed and sealed, and Dennison employees were abuzz with rumors that their headquarters would be moved and many plants shut down. At that point, no company officer on either side had answers to their worries.

An all-staff meeting was begun with everyone in attendance asked to draw a picture of their view of the combination. Flip charts were posted around a large auditorium, and with markers in hand employees began to illustrate what was in their mind's eye: dragons breathing fire, giants clomping over villages, and diners preparing for a "feast"—with Dennison staff on the plates.

The images evoked the underlying emotion: people were fearful of being destroyed or swallowed up. Other pictures had stick figures rallying and pulling together; some even showed teams, representing the two different sides, joining forces to excite customers. These reflected the upside of the deal. The point that a picture is worth a thousand words was repeated over and over again as employees walked around the auditorium surveying visual images of their peers' hopes and fears. An intense, but often lighthearted, discussion followed involving an analysis of the themes in the pictures and their connection to the merger syndrome.

Interestingly, the CEO and head of human resources at Avery attended this session and came away better informed about their partner's mind-set and chastened over their own lack of communication to acquired employees up to that point. They reassured employees that Dennison's headquarters would remain open and become the East Coast office of the combined company. As for plant closings, nothing was promised save that business was booming and that any reductions in manufacturing staff would be based on the situation in the marketplace, rather than who bought whom. Subsequently, this picture drawing exercise was repeated in other Dennison plants and facilities and even used in workshops in Avery. Some sample drawings appear in Figure 7.2.

## Counseling and Support

Group meetings are useful forums for educating employees about merger realities and surfacing fears, but sometimes individual counseling is called for. It surely helps when employee assistance specialists are at the ready to identify people in need during a combination and provide them with advice and support. This is particularly true in cases where there are or will be evident "losers" in a combination, ranging from those with lesser responsibility to those who lose their jobs. Because there is a seeming stigma attached to seeking this help, employees often attempt to tough it out and go their own way. To counter this, EAP staff often need to work with supervisors to identify troubled staff and take care to reach out to them in ways that preserve their dignity.

It is not just everyday employees who need counseling during a combination. The aforementioned senior vice president in the financial services combination who fixated for months on the line of business he had lost benefited from counseling geared toward reality testing his perceptions of loss. In another case, a chief technology officer found herself one additional layer removed from

## Figure 7.2. Employee Drawings of
## the Impact of Their Combination.

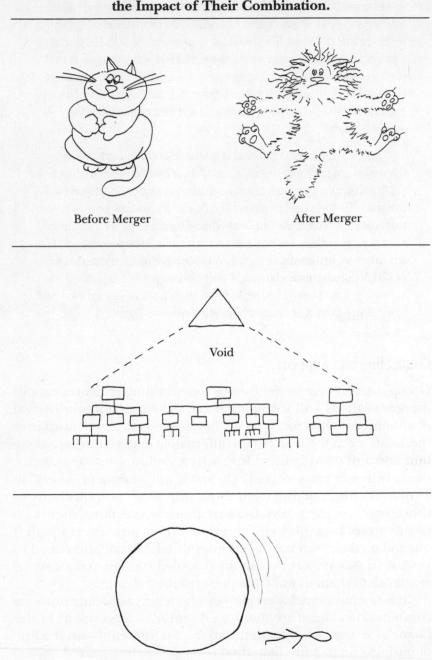

Before Merger

After Merger

Void

her mentor, the CEO, following a reorganization of top management in a merger. Furthermore, she lost some broad-based responsibility as the combined organization adopted a more decentralized approach to MIS. For several weeks, she brooded about her loss and left her own management team adrift. With appropriate counseling and a strong sense of commitment to do the right thing, she regained form and led an aggressive effort to integrate technology services and build her team. Concurrently, she also began to contact other employers, met with the CEO to discuss her needs and severance arrangements, and then, with integration complete, left to take another job.

## Walk the Talk

Inspiration bred by rallying speeches will not persevere through the combination unless leadership's actions align with the words. The operating principles for the combination and desired end state come to life through the behaviors modeled by leaders. Momentum either builds or dissipates based on what employees observe from their leadership. At the very least, consistency between words and actions subdues naysayers. Anything less promotes cynicism and distrust toward leadership and drains and diverts energy away from contributing to a productive combination.

How do executives build credibility during the transition? First, they are careful about what they say and sure about what they promise. Employees remember pledges like "We are partners in this together" and operating principles such as "equal opportunities independent of affiliation"; they weigh the words against actions (how many people from each organization are appointed to senior positions?). This is not to suggest that equality is a requirement, but if it is promised, it should be delivered. A senior executive in an alliance between two health care providers publicly praised managers from the partner as they "brought so much to the party." But he in turn ridiculed them in closed-door sessions with managers from his side. Picking up the cue, they began to disparage their counterparts. The result was an exodus of talent from the partner; first-year results were significantly below even the most conservative expectations, and the alliance itself suffered an early demise.

By contrast, combination principles, when lived up to, can be a source of confidence for people. One of the principles guiding a bank combination was to "be development-oriented." To back this up, the combined bank immediately offered new training programs in customer service and computing skills. This affirmed to employees that management was investing in them, kept many staff occupied through the planning phase of integration, and aroused their enthusiasm for working in the combined organization.

## Regular Updates

The principles and methods for effective communication hold true for all phases of the combination. In the combination phase, the purpose of the transition structure and teams, the people participating in it, the criteria they use to make recommendations, and the timetable guiding their work can all be reported. Then, as decisions are made, they can be announced through formal communications vehicles and followed up with informal in-person discussions. This one-two punch ensures that employees get a clear account of decisions and the chance to mull them over.

Employees are certain to hear the bad news through the grapevine, so it is important to promote progress made in the combination. Even small wins give a boost to people who have been cautious, or even cynical, about the combination's benefits. In a merger between two financial institutions, one based in Europe and the other in the United States, a culture clash cut deeply across national as well as corporate boundaries. Cross-border we-they feelings were pervasive, as were turf battles over who could call on new accounts. In the firm's Asia division, far from the center of conflict, representatives from the two sides joined together to call on a prominent prospect who had never done business with either side. Citing the combined resources of the two banks, the prospect became a customer. This accomplishment was widely promoted in the company newsletter and repeatedly mentioned in executive speeches. It became a symbolic point for instructing U.S. and European cross-national teams in what could be accomplished when the two sides worked together.

## Communications and Involvement down the Line

Middle-level managers and supervisors continue to relay the signals sent by senior executives as plans develop and integration begins. Their behavior either contributes to or detracts from the operating principles and success of integration. In a manufacturing combination, a general manager drew on the ideas of both sides through regular meetings and technical exchanges. He was committed to experimenting and finding best practices in building the service philosophy and systems of a combined function. Team leaders down the ranks emulated their superior's evenhanded behavior, and their newly developed suggestion system yielded five hundred recommendations for improvements in service delivery.

Many successful combinations feature creative ways to involve employees not otherwise connected to transition teams. In the combination of the American Century and Benham mutual fund groups, the executive-level task force charged with defining values for the new company commissioned focus groups to explore what employees valued about their prior companies, what they did not value, and what they felt should be carried forward in the combined organization. The task force used this employee input, along with their CEO's vision and values statements, to define a desired culture for the combined organization.

Many merging companies initially urge employees to stay away from their counterparts—no calls, no contact—and to act as though nothing is going to change. This just adds to uncertainty and creates artificial barriers between the two sides. Instead, managers and employees should reach out and build rapport. People are proud about what they bring to a combination and welcome the chance to show off their products and procedures. They are also curious about what their new partners have to offer. Two-way exchanges can take place through formal presentations, smaller show-and-tell meetings, and visits by contingents from one organization to the other. Of course, these should not be "missionary" expeditions but, instead, opportunities for all involved to show their stuff.

Throughout the transition process, people can be involved in upward communication efforts. Many organizations engage in employee "sensing" programs. Qualitative methods such as interviews and focus groups capture the detail and color of reactions to the transition process, while quantitative methods such as written surveys reach greater numbers cost-effectively. Chemical Bank surveyed a sample of employees each quarter during its combination with Manufacturers Hanover. Over the course of the integration, all employees were tapped at least once.

Furthermore, creative opportunities abound to involve employees in building the new. In one alliance we know of, employees submitted entries into a "name the new company" contest. In another case, the friendly tone of an acquisition was underscored when lead company employees brought homemade baked goods to meetings with their counterparts.

## Dealing with Redundant Staff

However much people rally to the upside of a combination, redundancy in corporate staff and capabilities in a merger or acquisition may require staff layoffs and plant closures. There are humanistic reasons for treating layoff victims fairly and compassionately, but layoff policies should be developed with an eye toward how survivors respond. As with every other management action during the combination phase, employees look for signals as to what life is going to be like in the new regime. Outplacement counseling, severance pay, extension of health insurance and other benefits, job-location assistance, and stress-management workshops are among the services that directly assist victims but also send a message to survivors that the organization cares and is ready to devote resources to soften people's landings.

Surviving employees' perceptions of the fairness of layoffs are determined by their beliefs about why the layoff occurred as well as how it was implemented.[4] They assess whether layoffs are truly necessary or are motivated by management greed or incompetence. Survivors also judge whether management could have achieved cost-savings targets through less severe methods, like attrition. The implication here is that a strong case has to be made for why a reduction in force is essential to building the desired organization.

In drawing their conclusions about what the layoff process says about their organization and its leaders, survivors consider the amount of forewarning given to victims, the frequency and content of communications about the firings, the extent to which cutbacks are shared at all levels of the organization, and, of course, how victims are treated. The criteria for the cuts are also weighed. The specific criteria tend to be less important than whether those criteria are administered accurately and consistently. If leadership says that layoffs will be determined on the basis of performance and contribution but supervisors and managers are allowed to retain their favored people, then employee despair and distrust grow as quickly as faith and trust in the new organization decline. Certainly, exceptions to any rule must be allowed, but the reasons need to be explained. Also, if merit is measured through a questionable performance-appraisal system, an otherwise well-intentioned decision may be viewed as unfair.

A particularly sticky situation is when the partner organizations' performance appraisal systems either measure different factors or are used differently. In the staffing of a health care alliance, for example, one medical center's culture called for using the performance review process as a developmental tool and emphasized areas for growth. This resulted in generally lower ratings for employees relative to counterparts from the alliance partner, where inflated performance ratings were the norm. To make apples-to-apples comparisons in people and ratings, one has to address discrepancies in performance measures and how they are used. Sometimes, it is best to abandon past metrics and engage partners in determining an appraisal system that is more attuned to the needs of the postcombination organization and less to the old ways.

Finally, successful combinations allow time for people to grieve the loss of their coworkers when layoffs are required. The mourning process is natural, and people will not be ready to move ahead to the challenges and prospects of the new organization if they have not worked through their loss. All societies have some form of mourning ceremony or ritual to help people deal with the loss of family and friends. Organizations, too, can sanction such rituals to help individual people grieve loss, let go of old attachments, and prepare themselves for new realities. Individual managers need not wait for formal company programs to help survivors mourn; listening sympathetically helps individuals work through their grief and anger over reductions in force. It also contributes to building a bond between superior and subordinate in the new organization.

## Moving On

Managing people in a combination is delicate. All actions create reactions, and even the best intentions misfire. In the combination of two brewers, for example, management attempted to appease union officials and layoff victims through generous severance payments. This prompted surviving employees to feel like they were suckers; many cried out, "Give me one of those fat severance checks, and I'll take my chances out on the street!" Creating dissatisfaction with the status quo and a sense of urgency for change are two basic principles of effective change management. Pain creates energy for change, yet pain can also create energy that is counterproductive.[5] The challenge is to develop methods of helping people cope with uncertainty, loss, and transition that catalyze action toward the desired objectives of the postcombination organization.

How does this happen? The answer lies first in careful selection, and then mainly in accountability for the desired behaviors. Once leaders make perfectly clear what they expect and need from people to make the combination work, then they seek out and appoint to positions those who can enact the desired behaviors. Compromises made in staffing always exact a toll in the combined organization. Although sorting out expectations and experimenting with new methods are part of the transition from old to new, the time for moving on arrives and individuals either have to get on board or get off the train. The senior executives we have seen leading productive combination laid out in unambiguous terms what is expected of their management team and then were willing to back up their words with actions such as demoting or even firing people who did not abide by the operating principles. They do this not impulsively but only after clearly setting out expectations, providing feedback and support for desired change, and allowing time for individuals to let go of old attachments and get on board. After a realistic assessment of the situation, however, they act decisively. It is time to move forward.

## Chapter Eight

# The Clash of Cultures

Operating in a corporate culture is a lot like breathing. You don't notice your breathing, you just do it. You may be aware of your breathing now, because we have called it to your attention. If someone were to approach you from behind, cup their hands firmly over your mouth and nostrils, threatening your ability to breathe, then you would certainly pay attention to breathing.

In typical combinations, culture building is an afterthought. Early in the process, executives downplay the importance of culture through offhand comments: "We're the same kind of people," "We're all bankers, so there is no culture clash," or "The more I look, the more I see how similar we are." With perfect hindsight, these same executives later bemoan their inattention to the differences in culture and values that set so many combinations on the wrong course. Studies conducted of combinations in a variety of countries find that senior executives rate "underestimating the importance and difficulty of combining cultures" as a major oversight in integration efforts. In Britain, for example, where acquirers on average pay a 40 percent premium over prebid stock market valuation, executives cited "culture compatibility" as being significantly more important than price paid in determining merger outcomes.[1]

## Culture in Combinations

Culture encompasses the way things get done in an organization. It can be observed in every aspect of organizational activity. Consider some examples of cultural factors in combinations:

- Do managers make quick decisions and spend time selling others on their merits, or do they take time up front to build consensus and then implement decisions relatively quickly? This is always a difference between American and Japanese companies involved in an alliance.

- Does a business have monthly or quarterly meetings? Are there formal presentations, or do managers roll up their sleeves? Is the emphasis mostly on financials or on all aspects of the operation? We observe such differences in many acquisitions where the parent looks for a full-scale presentation and focuses its comments on the numbers, while acquired management is accustomed to a real dialogue that looks at all aspects of the business.

- Does an organization typically attempt to promote people from within, or does it go outside to find the best person possible? We have observed many alliances and mergers in which one side proudly boasts how it "values its people" and the other how it "does what it takes" to build its competitiveness.

Of course, organizational members are not just influenced by their company culture overall. There are subcultures within companies that center around divisions, specialities, or occupational groups. Engineers from two combining companies, for instance, may have more in common than the engineers do with the marketers in the same company. The same may be true of blue-collar workers or women in executive ranks. In many large companies, built through combinations, there are often subcultures based on people's prior affiliations. Years ago, we were introduced to the senior executive team from the former Sperry Corporation. After meeting one particular individual, our host whispered, "He's an RCA guy." Sperry had acquired RCA's computer operations twenty-five years earlier, but in certain laboratories technicians still wore their RCA lab coats and name badges. In the executive suites, associates still labeled their coworkers by their corporate heritage.

As combinations among giants continue, executives inherit the task of breaking down disparate cultures and forging a more unified mind-set. Lockheed, as an example, encountered four distinct subcultures when it merged with Martin Marietta, which had not culturally integrated its own acquisitions of General Dynamics or GE's space business, while the latter itself had not integrated RCA's culture! Just as an organization cannot effectively run with multiple and incompatible information systems, it cannot succeed with multiple and incompatible cultures. Even GE, which retains the conglomerate form, depends on "boundarylessness" between its component parts, fosters best-practice sharing, and rotates executives across its many and varied lines of business. Looking forward, a senior vice president in a manufacturing merger of equals warned: "The worst thing that could happen as we put these companies together is to allow two separate cultures to go forward in two different directions. We have to take on the difficult work of building a shared culture now rather than allow two styles to emerge and then come back years later and wrestle with the problem."

Educators Lee Bolman and Terrence Deal call the power of a shared and cohesive culture an "invisible force" that gives a group of people its drive.[2] In particular, they note how specialized language, history, and values foster cohesion and commitment and reinforce identity. Every organization develops words, phrases, and metaphors unique to its circumstances that both reflect and shape its culture. At an industrial-products firm, for example, the language "let me tee this up with you" preceding the expression of an idea means that an immediate decision is not sought. This language lets members communicate easily with minimal misunderstanding. Additionally, in most highly successful organizations, stories keep traditions alive and provide real-life examples to guide daily behavior. An organization's history and the values that underlie its past behaviors also reinforce both current and future behaviors.

Common culture, language, and history are lost when an organization is merged or acquired. Indeed, continued reliance on that language, and reference to the glory days past, can set companies apart in a combination and emphasize differences rather than similarities in their values and experiences. This afflicted a newly formed management team following the combination of two international bank groups. A dinner, scheduled after a transition planning meeting and attended by the combined bank's North American and British executives, coincided with the retirement of a senior vice president from the lead company. After cocktails, wine with dinner, and a glass of port to accompany cigars, stories rolled out about the executive's outrageous behavior at social functions and business meetings over the years. The dinner—and in particular the story-telling—was a cherished way for people from the one side to deal with the loss of a respected and loved colleague. They roared with laughter as one hysterical tale after another was

recounted, lamented how his antics would be missed, acknowledged his many contributions to the business, and expressed genuine regret for the departure of a friend. At the same time,
attendees from the acquired side, outnumbered two to one, sat
passively and unengaged. In an impromptu debriefing a few days
later, acquired executives reported that they were somewhat put
off by what they regarded as an essentially "private" ceremony.
They acknowledged, however, that they had garnered rich insights
into the lead company's history and mores by listening to the stories and observing their counterparts' camaraderie.

## Why Company Cultures Clash

Companies have unique histories, folklore, and personalities, as
well as products, markets, and ways of running the business. Typically, people are proud of their company cultures or at a minimum
have learned how to operate effectively within them. A combination brings together companies with different cultures. What people notice first are differences between the two company cultures
and what makes their own unique. Think, for example, of travel-
ing abroad. What one notices is how a foreign land is different
from one's homeland. The same is true of a combination: people
notice how their own company is different from a partner's and
begin to pay attention to what makes their company unique.

### Stages of Culture Clash

Indeed, the culture clash in a combination begins when people
start to pay attention to their own culture. Cultural perception
then unfolds in several steps:

1. *Perceive differences.* At this first stage, people focus on differences between the two companies in terms of the style of their
   leaders, their products and reputation, the ways they make
   decisions, the kinds of people who work in the two firms, and
   so on.
2. *Magnify differences.* Next, people begin to magnify differences
   that they observe. Instead of merely different, the partner's
   ways become "very different." Distinctions become sharper and
   more polarized. This is the start of we versus they when talking
   about cultures.

3. *Stereotypes.* Then people start to typecast others in the partner company as embodiments of the other culture. Every accountant in a parent company is characterized as a "bean counter"; every engineer in an acquired software house is a "whirly-bird," and all corporate staff are "storm troopers."

4. *Put-downs.* The culture clash reaches full height as the partner company is put down as inferior. We become the superior culture and they are denigrated. The "innovators" in an acquired firm put down their parent company managers as "pants pressers" who are more concerned with neatness than running an entrepreneurial business. In turn, the "seasoned hands" at the parent company felt obliged to teach the "greenhorns" in the entrepreneurial shop a thing or two about running a "real" business.

## Cultural Winning and Losing

When individuals in a combination turn inward, they typically come to revalue key aspects of their organization and company culture. Implicit knowledge of how their company works, and how policies and systems sustain the firm, come to be explicit as employees reflect on what might be lost in a combination. Culture clash is a threat to people who see their company as a loser in a combination. They not only see differences between the two company cultures; they feel a sense of vulnerability and fear losing their culture. As in any situation in which people experience loss, they go through predictable phases, starting with disbelief and denial, then anger, and then rejection—in this case, rejection of what might otherwise be seen as valuable and worthy of emulation in another company. As described in Chapter Four, on psychological preparation, the one-down position of an acquired or merged company puts its people on the defensive. Even as individuals begin to accept the inevitability of change in their personal circumstances, however, they still reject the idea that their company and its culture will become subordinate to another firm and its ways.

The difficulty here is that in accepting another culture's way of life they run the risk of failing as individuals and as part of an enterprise. Beliefs and values embodied in a company culture are not just about how you dress, what you pay attention to, or how you make decisions, however much these may be manifest in the surface culture of a company. At a deeper level, there is an internal consistency to cultural beliefs and values that justify a way of life. People in companies that are traditionally decentralized often believe that this gives their operation its market focus, and themselves the running room, to get close to the customer and effect change "on a dime." At least these were the themes reported in a meeting with North American Rockwell managers and engineers. The themes fit together into a recipe for success in the marketplace; take any one ingredient out—or, worse, centralize operations—and the recipe is no longer reliable. Rockwell employees fretted that they would not be successful working under more centralized Boeing's tight fist. Furthermore, they feared that the combined company would move like a snail and lose out on peripheral business. The saving grace they observed was that Airbus—a group of private and state-owned European companies—was slower still and, like English cooks and French waiters, served bland food and treated customers badly.

On the other side, culture clash affects self-described winners in a combination as well. They also notice and magnify differences in company cultures and feel a strong sense of cultural superiority. After all, their side has made the buy or is on top in the alliance, or at least they have personally prevailed in a contest with counterparts from the other organization. Affiliation with the dominant side in a deal is received as vindication that one's own ways are superior to the other side's. Headiness develops and reinforces the winner's recipe for success. Hence Boeing managers, while sensitive to the merits of decentralization in theory, were nevertheless insistent that the economies of scale and scope afforded by centralization, as well as its expertise in cross-functional coordination and project management, were the keys to competitive advantage in the marketplace.

Cultural winning and losing may not be as simple as being in the lead or target organization in a combination. In one manufacturing combination, the lead company conducted a culture-mixing experiment by shifting some of its people to a plant run by the target firm. Transferred managers complained that they were the ones being taken over, as target managers dominated interactions. This supports the view of a transition manager from a high technology alliance: "When the executive teams got together we worked well together. But when you get down into the organization you start having disconnects. The executive team can change its view of the world much more quickly than the masses below. At the operating-manager level, the old culture does not die easily." Perhaps she should count her blessings that at least the top team overcame culture clash early on.

## Characteristics of Cultures

Culture is manifest on various levels. The most apparent levels concern business-related behaviors. People notice business-related differences in combinations that are a matter of policy, practice, or custom. The surface differences are easy to identify: they are evident in annual reports; in the two companies' products and services; in the design of headquarters, facilities, and plants; and of course in the demographics of the staff and their dress and appearance. More subtle cues rise as the partners come together. At the first meeting of two executive teams in a manufacturing acquisition, with the objective of educating the partners on each other's lines of business, the lead company CEO invited target executives to make the first round of presentations. Wanting to make the best possible impression, they had produced a multimedia, full-color, computer-generated presentation. Before its conclusion, the CEO whispered to his CFO, "The first thing we are going to do to these people is get them to stop wasting money on glitzy presentations." When it came time for lead company executives to present, they did so with simple black-and-white transparencies.

Structure is another area of high visibility and consequence. There was simply no fit between buyer Boeing's centralization and acquired Rockwell's decentralization. Nor could two high-technology companies merge without selecting between one side's functional organization and the other's organization by line of business. Besides structure, there are also processes and systems to consider. Mt. Sinai and Samaritan hospitals in Milwaukee had similar organization structures, but the former had a well-entrenched bureaucracy and the latter had been through waves of downsizing, leaving it lean and mean. Here's a case, one physician opined, where the "anatomy" matched but not the "physiology." Make no mistake, cultural differences matter in a strategic alliance as well. Ameritech's preference to organize teams by product line conflicted with the integrated account teams at GE Information Services. The latter approach was used in the alliance, but not without considerable debate and second-guessing.

Business relations between organizations are complicated by differences in interpersonal norms and behavior. Acquired executives in a manufacturing firm described their lead company counterparts as very crisp and decisive, particularly when requesting information or proposing postcombination changes. Yet lead executives were viewed as keeping things close to the vest when asked questions, and unable or unwilling to respond to initiatives from the acquired partner. The acquired management team spent more time in the process of decision making and would openly put everything on the table. Both sides agreed that decision making in the acquired company was as "slow as molasses," but that side's executives countered that implementation was swift because everybody would buy in.

Differences in business-related and interpersonal behaviors between the companies led to deeper inferences about the values of the two organizations. Acquired executives came to believe that their buyer was singularly profit-oriented and populated by "numbers people" who did not care about the acquired company's operations or its people orientation. In time, buying company executives referred to their acquirees as a "bunch of kooks"!

Listen to people engaged in combinations, and you'll hear that their comments span these and other realms of culture. Although themes can be differentiated, cultures are unified and internally consistent: values are evident in behaviors, and behaviors in turn give meaning to the underlying values. This implies that changes in the way things are done in an organization (behavior) can also, over time, change fundamental values and beliefs. This is what perceived losers in a culture clash resist.

## Managing Culture Change in a Combination

Despite the cacophony of a culture clash, the opportunity to proactively build a shared culture remains one of the great benefits of joining forces. We have worked with executives who used a combination to replace entrenched aspects of their precombination culture with more desirable cultural characteristics. Two large health care systems freed themselves of bureaucratic constraints and nurtured a more entrepreneurial approach to conducting business; two consumer-products firms found a comfortable medium between one side's labored decision-making style and the other's shoot-from-the-hip approach; and two aerospace companies melded one side's engineering orientation with the other's penchant for sales and marketing.

Of course, the work of building a desired culture is difficult. It requires breaking down old norms, articulating new ones, convincing people why the new way is superior to the status quo, being patient as employees experiment with bringing their on-the-job behaviors in line with espoused cultural norms, and reinforcing the new ways through rewards and recognition. All of this takes time. People who study culture change in organizations say it takes seven to ten years to break down the old and build the new culture. Our experience is that, in an acquisition or alliance, this time frame can be shortened considerably. In particular, the unfreezing associated with a combination gives executives a head start in culture change.

## Easing Culture Clash

Easing culture clash rests on acknowledging its presence, educating employees as to its dynamics, and preparing people to appreciate how initial impressions influence enduring cultural perceptions between the partners. Several companies we have advised include modules for easing culture clash between combining entities in workshops and training programs they offer to enhance employee insight into the combination process. These sessions aim at getting people to recognize differences between the companies and to expect a clash of cultures. Sensitizing people to the sources and symptoms of culture clash helps them understand that these dynamics prevail in any combination and, if left unmanaged, can create fissures. Other organizations educate employees about culture clash and prepare them for minimizing its adverse impact through newsletter articles, videos, in-person speeches, and other communication vehicles.

Companies are wise to ease culture clash early in the combination process. To guide its alliances, for example, Emerson Electronics sets up an internal management board consisting of operating executives from the partner organization and representatives from Emerson management. One member from Emerson is charged with protecting the partner from being "Emersonized" as planning ensues and integration decisions are made. Other companies take care as to whom they put in contact with the other side. Managers known to be power-imposing, dominating, and in general lacking in diplomatic skills are kept away from the combination action. Sometimes they are kept off planning groups; at other times—to ensure they have as little contact with new partners as possible—they are "shipped off to Siberia" for a temporary assignment far removed from integration activities while first impressions between the parties are forming.

## Respecting Cultures

The overriding principle for minimizing the unintended consequences of culture clash during the early phase of contacts is to respect premerger cultures. This is true even if the ultimate intention is to absorb a company and assimilate its culture. Managers who display consideration for their partner's way of doing things, rather than denigrate it, are likely to gain a reciprocal sense of respect for their own culture. In cases where one side's culture is going to dominate, respectfulness aids in helping employees see what the lead company is all about and has to offer in the way of structure, processes, and business behavior. And in cases where a new culture is being built—either through transformation or by selecting the best from both organizations—a tone of cross-cultural consideration helps employees open up to different ways of doing things rather than tightly hold on to their ways.

One simple way to show respect for the other side's culture is to ask its people how and why they do things. Most appreciate the chance to describe how they go about their work. Keep in mind that many of the people from the partner organization helped contribute to and shape its history. Their contribution needs to be honored. Nothing accomplishes this better than to inquire about individual contributions and achievements over the course of their careers. Informal and spontaneous opportunities to ask partners about their ways of doing things are both welcome and informative. An executive walking through a work area can simply stop and ask people to describe their work and what they like about their company. Naturally, tone is important here; the question should come off as an honest inquiry rather than a challenge or a bit of spying.

## Systematically Learning About Partners' Cultures

Informal questioning and respectful show-and-tells help educate partners on observable behaviors, but they cannot uncover the more deeply rooted values and basic philosophies that underlie those behaviors. To understand a culture, you need to appreciate the whys behind the whats that you observe. Many misunderstandings and communication breakdowns result from managers' lacking the means to decode, translate, and contextualize the overt messages and publicly available information about their partners. Unless key players from the combining organizations learn to read these deeper roots of the other side's culture, then mutual working relations remain under threat.

Some practices have been developed to help combining managers gain a deep understanding about each organization's culture and ways of doing business. Edgar Schein proposes an insider-outsider relationship to achieve this understanding.[3] A manager from organization A visits as an outsider to organization B to share experiences and knowledge with the insider manager. Through the interaction of A sharing her perceptions with B, who has implicit knowledge of why things are done the way they are, cultural norms and values become explicit to both. In simple terms, this intervention is based on the notion that the outsider perceives everything but understands nothing while the insider understands everything but perceives nothing.

We use a hands-on cultural-clarification activity to help teams joining forces in a merger, acquisition, or alliance learn about one another. Its objectives are, first, to raise emerging cultural perceptions and stereotypes between the partners and, second, to initiate dialogue on the desired cultural end state for the combination. The activity is built around having each partner group make three lists: (1) how we view our organization's culture, (2) how we view the other side's culture, and (3) how we think the other side views our culture. The rosters include business practices, interpersonal behaviors, and values. Importantly, participants are instructed to include characteristics that either have been experienced firsthand or heard about secondhand. The intention here is to unearth all the perceptions and stereotypes that are circulating regarding the partner.

Figure 8.1 shows a sample of the output from this activity conducted with the combining senior executives from an energy-industry alliance. The two groups had been working together for about two months, so they had plenty of time to develop initial impressions of each other. In the lists, we see how both sides tend to describe their own culture positively and be more critical of the other side's culture. For example, company A views itself as having a balanced business and technical approach but regards company B as being financially driven; the implication is that company A regards B's technological expertise as inferior to its own. Note that, in its self-description, B recognizes it puts a priority on financial performance, but nowhere does it indicate any technical inferiority. Yet executives from company B know how A feels about their technological capabilities. In fact this was a sore point for them, and it surfaced in the ensuing discussion.

Frequently, the two sides agree on their differences. In the energy alliance, company B has a behavioral norm of confronting people head-on over disagreements. They cite this in their roster (in Figure 8.1) as "push back required." Executives from A describe it as "in your face" and "decisions don't hold—need to argue and revisit." Interestingly, executives from B know this behavior irritates the "too polite" A group. In their list of how they think A views them, the company B executives unambiguously report "rude, in your face." When this cultural distinction was aired, it led to a discussion between the two groups regarding the desired norms for their combined culture. Both sides agreed that A's style was too reserved and polite; a faster-paced style of decision making and more head-on debate of the issues were required. But A's executives felt that B's style went too far in the other direction. Together, the two groups settled on a desired end state of "polite confrontation": speak up and challenge, but not rudely.

This example shows two of the values of the culture clarification process. First, it reveals for both partners the language that is used behind closed doors as one side discusses the other. What B values as "push back," A distastefully regards as "rude." Second, this activity engages the two sides in discussing which aspects of the existing cultures should be retained in the combination and which should not be carried forward. Sometimes, as in the polite versus push back example, the end result is a hybrid born from the two precombination cultures. Or the partners may agree that one side's norms are preferable. In this actual case, both sides admired B's efforts at pushing decision making down the hierarchy through empowerment and identified this as a component of the desired postcombination culture. Other times, partners agree that a characteristic shared by the two sides should not be carried forward. When this culture clarification exercise was used in a large bank merger, both sides characterized their cultures as bureaucratic, and

# Figure 8.1. How Two Companies View Each Other's Cultures.

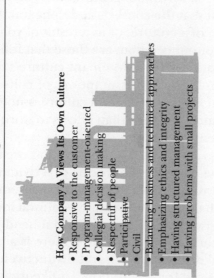

**How Company A Views Its Own Culture**
- Responsive to the customer
- Program-management-oriented
- Collegial decision making
- Respectful of people
- Participative
- Civil
- Balancing business and technical approaches
- Emphasizing ethics and integrity
- Having structured management
- Having problems with small projects

**How Company A Thinks Company B Views A's Culture**
- Bureaucratic
- Consensus decisions
- Gentleman's club vs. "hard assess"
- Arrogant
- Layers of management
- Respected competitor
- Willing to take business and technical risks
- Overfacilitized

**How Company B Views Company A's Culture**
- Bureaucratic
- Consensus management
- Too polite
- Unwilling to change
- Vertical career path
- 1950s organization
- Decisions made at the top
- Big-customer oriented
- Project-oriented
- Too serious about themselves

**How Company B Views Its Own Culture**
- Push back required
- Empowered
- Setting the bar high
- Delayered organization and small staff
- Broader career path
- Change-oriented
- Minimal oversight
- Giving priority to financial performance
- Having sense of humor
- Preferring speed and simplicity

**How Company A Views Company B's Culture**
- In your face
- Processes not documented
- Line-of-business orientation (not project orientation)
- Decisions don't hold—need to argue and revisit
- Darwinian system
- Financially driven

**How Company B Thinks Company A Views B's Culture**
- Rude, in your face
- Undisciplined
- Nontraditional energy company
- High risk takers
- Stubborn
- Technologically neophyte

neither wanted to retain so many layers of staff and decisions approvals. Perhaps as testimony to why culture change takes so long, their follow-up action step was to establish a committee on eliminating bureaucracy!

## Levels of Acculturation

Acculturation results when contact between two autonomous cultures requires change in one group or both. There are many possible levels of acculturation in an acquisition or alliance, but Mirvis and a colleague, Amy Sales, have identified what they see as the three most prominent:[4]

1. *Cultural assimilation,* where one company absorbs the other
2. *Cultural integration,* in which the partner companies blend together
3. *Cultural pluralism,* where the partners coexist

Although, theoretically, acculturation can result in a balanced merging of two group cultures, anthropological studies suggest that this balance rarely occurs.[5] Instead, one group typically dominates the other and influences the direction of cultural change much more strongly than the subordinate group does. Interestingly, anthropologists point out that the conflicts and upheaval that come from the modernization of a culture, or as a result of voluntary migrations, are far less pronounced than are those that follow forced occupations and imposition of the dominant culture's way of life. To translate this to combinations, assumptions of cultural superiority and actions toward forcing one side's culture onto the other are met by more force and resistance than efforts to work together in building a cultural end state.

Researchers Priscilla Elsass and John Veiga argue that organizational acculturation can be described in terms of a dynamic interaction between the opposing forces of cultural differentiation (the desire of groups to maintain their separate cultural identity) and organizational integration (the organizational need for cultural groups to work together).[6] In other words, there is a natural tension between groups' desires for cultural distinctiveness and organizational forces that call for integration. Unlike individuals experiencing social acculturation, organization members have the options of not acculturating, or withdrawing from the contact altogether. In short, they may choose to leave the organization if acculturation proves too stressful or disagreeable. They take with them the qualities of the partner that may have been sought in the postcombination, which is to say, the key building blocks needed for a productive combination.

## Integration and Culture

Leaders in successful combinations understand that building a new organization also means building a common culture. Beyond surfacing the issue, how should they factor it into combination decisions? A prime consideration is their desired cultural end state, a subject we covered under strategic preparation and described as an important facet of precombination planning. As the combination unfolds, of course, executives on both sides gain a better understanding of each other's culture. It is generally prudent to revisit and revise definitions of desirable levels of acculturation. For instance, the cultural assimilation that would follow from a parent company's absorbing an acquiree might not be appropriate if, say, technical talent threatens to depart or brand identity will suffer. IBM, for example, moved from expecting to assimilate Lotus to a more pluralistic stance as its networking strategy developed through conversation with its partner. Even though Lotus is not a stand-alone business, it has nevertheless retained much of its cultural distinctiveness.

Obviously a best-of-both combination looks toward cultural integration. But will the market reward it? Is it the best model for employees? In a merger between two hospitals with different religious affiliations, for instance, attempts to create distinct medical specialties in each generated resistance from both patients and staff. Furthermore, cross-hospital meetings and dialogue were met by a collective "blah" from nonmedical staff and nurses; physicians did not even bother to attend. Thus, executives focused integration on consolidating the two back offices and a variety of administrative functions such as purchasing. In essence, a holding company was created and the two hospitals retained their unique identities in the market as well as for the majority of employees.

This is not to recommend cultural pluralism or coexistence between firms. In most cases, those outcomes imply modest integration, which is unlikely to create much in the way of synergy or produce anything more than one plus one equals two. At best, cultural pluralism results in portfolio management, and at worst it breeds bad blood, as in the alliance of KLM and Northwest where both partners think they know best how to run an airline, regularly put down each other's cultures in the business press, took their differences to court, and finally agreed to disband the alliance despite tremendous profitability. When people guided by differing values or conflicting behaviors attempt to work together and must share common systems and practices, the result can only be antagonism and in-fighting. People put their energy into fighting internal battles rather than fighting off competitors.

Let's also be clear that cultural assimilation, one side absorbing the other, can contribute to a common culture and a productive combination. PacifiCare's acquisition of the FHP health maintenance organization is a prime example. The talent, technology, services, know-how, customer contacts, and the like of the assimilated organization produced strategic synergies within the cultural framework of the lead company. It was crucial in this case that both sides understood and agreed upon the desired cultural end state. Of course, agreeing does not equate to achieving!

The point here is not to favor a priori one form of acculturation over another. Rather, our counsel is that the two sides talk things through to develop an agreeable view of the desired cultural end state and then align their actions accordingly. The dialogue begins in the precombination phase, when a combined strategy is set and synergies are defined. In a merger or acquisition, the lead company needs to clarify with its partner to what degree absorbing a target versus preserving its autonomy serves those ends and creates value. That discussion sets the framework for determining whether cultural assimilation, integration, or pluralism follows. In an alliance, ideally the two parent companies' senior managements come to some shared understanding of the desired cultural end state and quickly bring into the discussions the management who will run the combined entity.

## Synergies Versus Acculturation

Although, at the broadest level, senior executives need to decide how much to integrate two firms in their combination, when it comes to putting together, say, manufacturing or marketing, the synergies therein may dictate different levels of integration. In many high-tech acquisitions, marketing and sales in a subsidiary are absorbed into the parent company, which often has more competence and better distribution channels. But the acquiree's engineering and manufacturing are given high levels of autonomy to do their own thing. In health care combinations, back-office functions may be consolidated and systems and procedures standardized, but the delivery of care is left to each of the providers. In alliances in the oil industry, in turn, refining and distribution may be consolidated yet each company's dealerships and brand are kept separate. In all of these cases, decisions about integration hinge on the business case behind the combination.

In the same way, the case needs to be made for combining cultures, function by function. It is very likely, for example, that senior executives see a need for a common and unified culture in some areas of the combination and for more pluralism in others, as in high-tech engineering, frontline health care, and gas stations. As a result, the desired cultural end state features a mix of these options. In such cases, the senior executive needs to assert up front any expectations regarding which components of the lead or parent company's culture (that is, what values or behaviors) will prevail, where the partner's cultural autonomy will be honored, where the two intend to blend cultures, and where new cultural themes need to be developed through a transformational process. This latter point needs reinforcement. One CEO we worked with declared to his counterpart, "We have a half-ass way of communicating to people, and you have a half-ass way of doing it. If we put our two ways together, we'll make a complete ass of ourselves!" The communications transition team therefore set about benchmarking leaders in this area and devised a whole new approach to employee communications in the combined company.

When it comes to building a combined culture, partners need to declare which beliefs and values are sacrosanct and which are in play for discussion and development as combination planning and implementation move forward. Furthermore, executives need not have an intricate or fully worked out cultural end state from the very beginning. Indeed, combination partners learn a lot about each other and their cultures only after they work together and the two sides get to know each other. Nor does culture change require a complete overhaul to current values and norms. In fact, successful culture change builds on the strengths of the precombination cultures. Even when one side's culture is going to predominate over the other's in the postcombination organization, the process of changing the target still requires considerable time to break down the old and introduce the new.

How do you factor in timing and the potential for a culture clash when planning integration? We worked on a study of more than one hundred banking mergers with the Management Analysis Center of Cambridge, Massachusetts, to develop a framework for this purpose (Figure 8.2).[7] The vertical axis considers the business case for how much to integrate companies function by function. The key question is, "How important is it to integrate this function for purposes of strategy, savings, or synergy?" The horizontal axis considers the cultural case for integration; its key question is, "How easy will it be to put the two function together?" This latter question considers the degree of culture clash that will erupt and attendant consequences for staff turnover, customer defections, operational hassles, and managerial headaches.

### Mapping Cultural Integration

Several options emerge from the matrix in Figure 8.2. In the case of a high-technology combination involving software and hardware component manufacturers, senior management chose to combine quickly in the areas of marketing and product development. The two sides were familiar with each other's product lines and had worked together in several large customer accounts. As for the salesforce, the case for rapid consolidation was compelling. However, the two sides had different sales approaches, and there was a considerable risk that salespeople would leave for competitors unless their needs were

### Figure 8.2. Benefits Versus Ease of Integration.

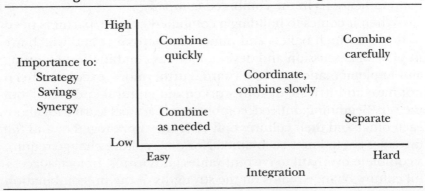

*Source:* Mirvis, P. M., and Marks, M. L. *Managing the Merger: Making It Work.* Upper Saddle River, N.J.: Prentice Hall, 1994.

addressed. Thus management went on a campaign with the combined sales-forces that involved seminars on how the product lines fit together and attractive incentives for selling package deals combining products from the two partners. In addition, there were offsite sessions held at resorts around the United States where the two salesforces could mingle and socialize, with hats, T-shirts, watches, and other corporate identity material. At these events, senior sales management did plenty of ego massaging. In a word, their aim was indeed to combine carefully.

In turn, it was decided to combine as needed several human resource programs and various policies and procedures where savings would be modest (as would the payoff). Importantly, it was decided to keep the basic research-and-development functions of the companies more or less separate. The same conclusion applied to manufacturing, where, it was reasoned, there were no short-term benefits and some risks that either side or both would miss schedules if caught up in a combination. At the same time, the company formed an internal technology council that brought together researchers and manufacturers to build camaraderie and inform strategy. This council held regular brown-bag lunches, where technicians and professionals from the two sides could mingle and compare notes. What emerged was a kind of cultural coexistence between hardware and software types under an overarching company culture of technical excellence.

Finally, it was decided to run several corporate systems—such as sales order entry, scheduling, and the like—in parallel at least through the first year of the combination. That way, sales personnel could focus on customers, and manufacturing could focus on deadlines, without the hassles and hangups entailed when integrating systems. In most instances, the lead company with its generally superior systems took over things, though in several cases new systems were developed and eased into place. The combined company today has a clear and shared culture overall, but it also has distinctive subcultures that vary by function (Figure 8.3) and, for those who still remember their days past, by precombination cultures.

## Culture Clash in International Combinations

Culture clash is exacerbated when the alliance or acquisition crosses national borders. Part of an organization's cultural heritage is linked to the history of the firm and the style of its leaders, and part is rooted in the national culture of the home country. Differences in native language, customs, business practices, and interpersonal norms all enhance the difficulty of establishing positive

**Figure 8.3. Cultural Integration Map for High-Tech Companies.**

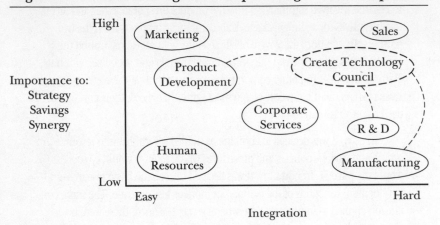

and productive working relationships. Matters of title and salutation, expectations as to dress and demeanor, and even how one shakes hands and enters a room have different meanings in different national cultures. Protocols exist, and combining managers can be put off when their customs are disregarded, inadvertently or not.

Sometimes complications arise quite innocently, as when individuals mean well but become burdened by the slowness of translating requests and documents from one language to another. Other times, difficulties stem from disrespect for the other side's norms. An alliance between U.S. and Brazilian chemical-products manufacturers set off on the wrong foot when American executives insisted their first day of meetings in Rio de Janeiro begin with a working breakfast session. This offended Brazilian counterparts who were unaccustomed and disinclined to discussing business over the morning meal.

Even when cross-border partners agree on strategic objectives during precombination negotiations, culture differences beset implementation. Differences in structuring authority can have immediate practical consequences for international acquisitions and alliances. In China, a chief engineer typically reports to the chief executive, whereas in Canada, he usually reports to the manufacturing director. A French general manager is unlikely to accept a title or position that implies anything less than the top role. Numerous other logistical and operational obstacles are soon discovered hiding behind assumed compatibility, such as different product-development standards or contrasting views of the sales process.

## Managing Culture Clash in International Combinations

Combining across national borders ratchets up the importance of understanding and respecting cultural norms and taboos. Organizations prepare managers to work more effectively in international combinations first by increasing their awareness of personal learning and communication styles and second by getting them to understand the significant aspects of their own culture, how it influences their attitudes and behaviors, and how it is perceived by others.

Cross-border culture building requires people to have the communications skills and cultural awareness to bridge differences. Some organizations only select managers with multinational experience to key positions in international alliances or to lead foreign acquisitions. Language is a fundamental consideration. Key personnel involved in international acquisitions and alliances should certainly speak the language of the country where business is to be conducted. Even if a manager can hold only a simple conversation, the other side recognizes the effort and appreciates the symbolic gesture of reaching out to their way.

Many organizations train their expatriates in the norms and business practices of other countries before sending them off to combination duty. Some go a step further and prepare people for cross-border combinations through programs that give managers insight into their own styles of sharing information, giving and receiving feedback, listening, and developing open lines of communication. These sessions also impart actions for developing a climate that recognizes differences and sees them as a positive basis for building the postcombination organization.

Although cultural boot camp helps prepare managers, front-line skirmishes inevitably occur. When they erupt into full-scale battles, the parties need to come together to mutually understand and address the underlying issues. In the acquisition of a medium-size British engineering firm by a large Swedish company, leaders invited British managers to discuss and defuse a consultant's diagnosis of cultural misunderstandings and differences.[8] At the opening of the meeting, British managers vented their feelings and frustrations with the Swedish parents—and with Swedes and Sweden in general. They identified those areas of cultural differences they found most incomprehensible in their day-to-day work and then moved on to discuss the company motto, "Be of humble spirit." For the British, "humble" was a term encoded with servility (such language confirmed their fears that they had to behave passively), whereas for the Swedish it was encoded with respect. The Swedish leadership described what they intended by the phrase, acknowledged differences in meaning from the British and Swedish perspectives, and urged their British counterparts to consider the underlying message and not the literal translation of what was meant to be a philosophy of respect and not domination. The aim of the session was to shift the British managers' perceptions of the problem and its meaning away from their ethnocentric perspective and more toward a shared perspective. Additionally, the session indicated to the British that the Swedes were sensitive to their situation and willing to work together to understand the deeper issues that were afflicting the combination.

### Culture-Building Ceremonies

A giant telecommunications merger brought together two sides with a history of bitter competition and a strong dislike for one another. Executives at the top of the combined organization forged good working relationships, but middle managers continued to hold on to their precombination attitudes and behaviors. The senior executive heading one major business unit grew increasingly pessimistic about his managers' ability and willingness to let go of the their old ways of viewing and doing things. Wanting to make a dramatic move toward building a common culture, he commissioned Marks to assist in its design and delivery.

Each of the eighty middle managers in the business unit took part in either individual or group interviews that collected their views on impediments to building a unified culture. Without much prodding, the managers offered numerous obstacles, ranging from distrust between the sides to strongly divergent precombination styles (one group viewed its counterparts as "undisciplined mavericks"; they in turn viewed the other side as "uptight clones"). At an offsite meeting, Marks reported his findings to the managers and engaged them in identifying the few critical issues that needed to be addressed for the group to move forward together. Small teams described the issues and identified actions that they and their leaders could take to minimize negative impact. A presentation on common issues and success factors in combining organizations broadened managers' awareness of actions that could be taken to build better working relationships.

The problem-identification process and presentation succeeded in raising awareness intellectually, but the managers needed to be moved at a deeper, more emotional level if they were to let go of their precombination ways. The highlight of the meeting, therefore, was a "graduation" ceremony. After the regular presentation, managers met in small groups and discussed their ideas for successful combination. They reconvened as a large group, and each was asked to write down "the three worst ways in which the merger could affect me personally." Each also received a sheet of his or her preintegration letterhead and an old business card. They were then asked to walk outside, where a wooden coffin awaited them. Off to the side, a marching band sounded a somber funeral march.

One by one, each of the eighty managers stepped up to the coffin; crumpled his or her worst-case list, letterhead, and business card; and tossed them in. As the last managers stepped back from the coffin, the group heard a low, rumbling noise. A one hundred ton paver rolled around the corner, heading straight for the group. At first the managers stood paralyzed, unsure of what was transpiring. The band broke into a rousing rendition of "On, Wisconsin," and the paver veered toward the wooden casket, flattening it and its contents. Spontaneous cheering broke out among the managers as the paver rolled back and forth over the coffin.

Abuzz with excitement, the managers went back inside. Entering the building, they received academic caps and gowns and instructions to put them on. Ushers assembled the managers into two orderly lines and marched them into an auditorium, where banners proclaiming "Congratulations, Graduates!" awaited them. Once all were seated, their senior executive welcomed them and embarked on the classic graduation speech: "The day has come for which we have all worked so hard to prepare you. It is now your turn; our destiny lies in your generation's hands." The managers sat quietly, absorbing the speech, appreciating the meaning of these words for them. Then the ushers escorted one row of graduates at a time to the stage. There, the senior executive presented each one with a diploma, a "Master's of Merger Management," and a graduation gift: one share of company stock. After they had all proceeded across the stage and back to their seats, as a group they turned the tassels on their caps from left to right, to proclamations that they had graduated into their positions as contributors in the postcombination organization.

## Protecting Core Values

When properly managed, cultural diversity benefits productive combination. If stereotyping and the tendency to put down the other side can be kept in check, clarification of differences between the partners builds insight and awareness into one's own ways of doing things as well as into those of the partner organization. Partners learn from one another and engage in constructive debate regarding which cultural characteristics best align with the combination's CSFs and best support attaining a new and better organization.

Cultural diversity, however, cannot be so extreme as to compromise the core values and philosophies that underlie either partner's culture. When the prevailing attitudes and behaviors of one partner strongly clash with the other's core values, the result is long-term conflict or organizational divorce. A key responsibility of senior executives from both sides is to define and protect the core values that support value creation in their combination. The sooner senior executive teams can understand their own values and those of their counterparts, the better able they are to assess what they have in common and what they need to espouse to make their combination work. This is why we so strongly recommend that cultural assessments be an integral part of precombination dealings and due diligence. In the typical combination, however, it is not until parties move beyond the niceties of the courting and honeymoon stages and start living and working together that they engage in deep enough interaction to promote cross-cultural understanding.

Educating people about culture clash, raising their awareness of their own and their partner's values and behaviors, and engaging them in clarifying the desired postcombination culture are among the early interventions in managing culture building. As the next chapters relate, however, individuals are likely to regress into merger syndrome reactions as combination decisions are announced and implemented. Forces holding onto the status quo strengthen. Thus, early culture-building activities must be reinforced and desired cultural behaviors and values refrozen as combined teams form, structures unfold, and new ways of doing business together commence.

# Part Four

# The Postcombination Phase

## Chapter Nine

# Building the New Organization and Culture

The postcombination phase arrives with executives in place and charged with putting their own stamp on integration plans made by transition teams. This is when the new structure fleshes out, cultural norms develop, work teams form, and individuals adapt to the many real and perceived changes enveloping them. No sharp line divides the combination and postcombination phases. Often, because of their smaller size or lesser complexity or controversy, some areas of the business are ready to integrate while others are still under review. Thus, structuring and staffing proceeds in some places well ahead of others. Similarly, even as common budgets and business plans develop, integration in such areas as information systems often lags behind.

Whenever the actual combining begins, as one manager opined, "The bullets are real." If executed badly, integration plans that are otherwise well thought out can block the realization of synergies and erode optimism about the new organization. Alternatively, effectively managed implementation can improve on integration plans and enhance the prospects of the combination. The end objective in this phase is to at least temporarily "refreeze" the work environment and enable senior leaders, managers, and workers to extract value from the combination. Of course, in today's working world of constant change, nothing is frozen for long. Perhaps it is better to say that in this phase two companies "gel" into one.

## Building the Combined Organization

By now, the senior team in the combined company is in place and takes over the duties of any coordinative body or transition management group. However, transition management responsibilities have not ended. On the contrary, the senior team's job is to manage change and address the opportunities and issues that arise in implementation.

## Top-Level Oversight

*Transition into the Postcombination Organization at Pfizer*

The Integration Team guiding the acquisition of SmithKline Beecham's animal health business into the Pfizer Animal Health Group (AHG) designed a new organization by selecting the best practices from each side and proposing some novel ways to transform the combined business. With integration plans complete and senior management appointed, the need for the team waned. AHG's president thereupon handed implementation responsibilities over to senior leaders. In looking back at their experiences, however, the newly combined management team recognized the value of focusing together on the whole of the business and operating in line with their principles and CSFs. Looking ahead, they vowed that they would as a team continue to pull in the same direction and ensure that all combining units played by the same set of rules.

With the same rigor used months earlier to develop the desired end state and guidelines for the transition, the management team defined business goals and ground rules for the new organization. The financial goals were enumerated as follows: "Become number one in every market, grow at twice the rate of the overall market, and improve profitability by at least 4 percent each year." Dubbed the "1, 2, 4 goals," these were easy to communicate and understandable to employees. They sent a message that although growth was important to the Animal Health Group, so was profitability.

The senior team also developed "guiding principles" for behavior in the combined company. Building on their transition principles, these defined how people should approach their work and how their contributions would be evaluated. Like any such pronouncements, to an outside observer the words come across as vanilla and the message sounds like motherhood and apple pie. What gave them meaning and brought them to life in this case was management's use of these principles in their ongoing review of the integration of business units:

PFIZER ANIMAL HEALTH GROUP GUIDING PRINCIPLES
- We strive to serve our customers better than any of our competitors do.

- We place the highest value on integrity.

- We manufacture products to the highest quality standards, safety, and reliability, in ways that are environmentally and socially responsible, cost-effective, and competitive.

- We value individual contributions, teamwork, and leadership ability.

- Our goal is to be the leader in those market segments in which we choose to compete.

- We are an integral part of Pfizer, Inc.

- We are recognized for the quality of our people.

- We believe that authority, responsibility, and accountability are inseparable.

- We place a high value on research.

- We are results driven.

- We value innovation and experimentation.

- We are a learning organization.

- We believe that the speed and quality of communications is a competitive advantage, and we invest in technologies and people to achieve and maintain this advantage.

There is a natural tension between individual managers who want autonomy to run their units as they see fit and the responsibility of the full team to look out for what is best for the organization overall. In the case of AHG, the top team kept its eye on the big picture to ensure that units combined synergistically and according to the guiding principles. When does top management most need to exercise such top-down oversight? It's particularly important whenever a combination seeks to blend together companies with different cultures. Take a bioengineering alliance, where the two partners came from the extremes of centralization and decentralization. In planning integration, the executives involved had staked out a middle ground, centralizing some functions and decentralizing others. Solomonic intentions aside, when implementation began all hell broke loose. Following several skirmishes between business units and staff functions, the top team went off site to address conflicts between corporate staff and lines of business. Now, with real issues and areas of identified conflict and ambiguity in front of them, the intricacies of staff-and-line working relationships could be hammered out.

Fluidity is the hallmark of successful combination management. Task force recommendations are only blueprints for integration and, as organization builders know, things change once actual construction begins. New conditions and unanticipated hindrances may require minor or even major adjustments to implementation plans. Work teams confront roadblocks and may also be dealing with a changing business environment. As the combination unfolds, senior management has the responsibility to see that new practices, policies, and procedures are in line with strategic aims and support the CSFs. The top team's job is to monitor implementation, make adjustments as needed, keep expectations clear between themselves and their managers, and promote dialogue across business units and groups. When top executives focus solely on building their own individual units, so does their middle management, and integrative synergies are lost.

### Transforming a Business Unit

Julian Gee, vice president of AHG's technical operations group prior to the SmithKline Beecham acquisition, retained that title after the combination. Technical operations saw as its mission bringing "science" to the creation, production, and sale of animal health products. Its services ranged from applied research to training nontechnical business and sales personnel. With structure and staffing set, Gee invited his top management to meet with a cross section of people from operations, marketing, central research, finance, and employee relations. He opened the meeting by presenting the model of post-combination change (see Figure 3.4). He expressed his desire to direct his organization toward the upper right-hand corner, which would amount to a transformation in the way technical operations did business. Gee's objective for the meeting was to collect ideas on how the unit should transform itself.

A breakthrough point came when each of three small discussion groups, one of people from technical operations and two of internal customers from other parts of AHG, drafted lists of desired characteristics. The technical group produced a roster composed of incremental changes in its current activities, such as running better clinical trials and speeding up regulatory approvals. The two groups of internal customers, working separately, came up with identical input (but contrary to the technical group's): get technical people much more closely involved in the business, especially in setting strategies. The message to the technical group was to step out of the laboratory and think more broadly about the business. Embracing this as the type of transformational change he was looking for, Gee used it to establish a new identity and mission for the technical group: focus on the business, not on technical perfection, irrespective of the bottom line.

Gee took advantage of AHG's "1, 2, 4" vision and guiding principles to further clarify how his group would operate in the new organization. Two months after the rollout, he convened another offsite to define what was meant by technical leadership in the animal health industry and how to achieve it by the year 2000. Again, Gee invited managers from other units in AHG. Two general themes emerged in the discussions: (1) how to achieve successful partnerships with stakeholders (both internal customers and such external groups as regulatory agencies, academia, and industry consortia) and (2) how to institutionalize AHG's thirteen guiding principles.

Through structured activities, the attendees provided rich feedback on the current behaviors of technical staff in the eyes of others at AHG. Latin American managers, for example, reported that technical staff were often dictatorial in the design of clinical trials. These field managers found that no matter what they produced, technical staff from New York headquarters invariably would redo their work. So they stopped bothering to put their best effort forward, figuring it would be changed anyway. The result was repeated paper shuffling between Latin America and New York, typically requiring four to six weeks for approval of protocols for clinical trials. After discussing the inefficiencies, Latin American managers and New York staff agreed to follow the guiding principles and embarked on a more supportive, trusting, and productive working relationship. The Latin Americans put more effort into preparing submittals and the New Yorkers backed off on making so many changes. Together the groups reduced the time required for approval from weeks to days.

## Building Cross-Functional Relations

As executives focus on building their functions and teams, fissures between interdependent units commonly develop. Indeed, responsibility for developing effective cross-unit relationships often falls through the cracks, until tension mounts or a crisis occurs. Being proactive about horizontal organization building helps keep a newly combined company aligned and averts conflicts that require considerably more effort to address later on.

### Clarifying Cross-Unit Needs

Mindful that an ounce of prevention is worth a pound of cure, Marks and consultant Marilyn Showers used an intergroup relations exercise to help AHG headquarters staff build better relations with the businesses.

One meeting brought headquarters staff directors together with executives from the field to address roadblocks to an effective working relationship. The goal was to clarify what each unit needed from the other, identify any gaps, and agree to cross-unit working arrangements. The process involved breaking the units out into separate rooms and having them respond to two generic questions: What does our group need and want from the other group? What can the other group expect from us?

The units posted their needs and expectations on flip charts and reconvened in the main meeting room. Field directors presented their cross-unit needs first. They compared their list of what field executives needed and wanted from the headquarters staff with that staff's list of "what the field executives can expect from headquarters staff." Many similarities appeared across the two lists, but some key gaps jumped out. One concerned the field directors' expectation that headquarters staff consult them early on when developing policies and establish information-reporting requirements. Staff responded that it preferred to formulate policies for the whole of the combined organization and then check them with the field. After hearing field directors give instances where consultation might have improved what in fact came across as ivory-tower policies, the headquarters staff concurred and agreed to invite representatives from each of the three regions into their planning sessions. Jointly, the two groups determined specific areas in which the field input would be of benefit, so as to not burden either side with unwarranted meetings.

After working through what was needed from headquarters staff, the focus turned to what the headquarters staff needed from the field and what field executives said could be expected from them. Again, the two groups identified and mutually addressed gaps in expectations and needs. This meeting enhanced understanding of what each group needed from the other to accomplish its objectives. It also established in the still-fledgling organization a workable process for raising and addressing issues. The cross-unit dialogue here set a new tone and demonstrated how the combination could enhance organizational effectiveness.

# Meshing Policies and Practices

Integrating systems in a large-scale combination is a complex and delicate undertaking. Thus we urge system architects and transition teams to align systems integration with long-term strategic objectives and to think through potential problems of technical glitches, operating disruptions, and a clash of cultures when choosing one side's systems over the other's.

## Integrating MIS

The chief technology officer overseeing systems integration between Chemical Bank and Manufacturers Hanover formed a joint-company transition team to develop a template for joining the two sides' information systems.

Barbara Capsalis, then CTO of the combined company, first had her team identify the myriad corporate versus line-of-business information systems and data-management practices. After several months of study, they then gave recommendations about data entry, access, and storage; the physical location of databases and facilities; various make-or-buy options; and information security. But when it came to implementing recommendations and effecting change in past practices, business heads balked and a slew of questions and conflicts confronted the new IT leadership. Who would govern the definition of databases in a more decentralized environment? Who would ensure there was compatibility between multiple systems? Current databases in the businesses focused variously on customers, transaction accounting, or traditional profit-and-loss measures. What, people asked, was corporate's need for "common" data? Would its interests prevail?

Recognizing that her function could not insist on conformity, Capsalis had the head of corporate MIS, Bruce Hasenyager, work with two consultants, Mirvis and Antonio Lucia, to develop integrative principles to guide current systems integration and future development. They interviewed the heads of each of the businesses, as well as their respective technology managers, to assess views on what sorts of principles ought to apply to systems integration and management. Needless to say, these ranged from "We need common databases and systems" to "Leave it to each business to tailor its data and systems to its own needs." It was proposed, therefore, that Capsalis form a standing committee to settle these differences and oversee implementation. This would bring together technologists and business leaders (or, to use a more generic phrase, bring the whole system into the room).

Prior to the first meeting of the council, Capsalis and Hasenyager contacted each of the proposed members to review the range of opinions and preview their suggested integrative principles. This served two purposes, educational and political. The meetings enabled the technologists to educate business heads about corporate's need for and use of a common core of bankwide data. Many were not aware of the data collected by other businesses and relished the thought of accessing it. At the same time, others were very protective of their own data and challenged corporate's position on full and open access and transparency of information. This at least identified who was for and who was against a common approach to information management.

The council met several times and through long discussion agreed on three key points:

1. We need to structure the information environment to satisfy diverse needs (top management and local, product and organization). We should define the minimum structure to provide commonality yet also provide the flexibility to add local value.

2. Information required to perform the job effectively needs to be redefined and made available with a minimum of bureaucracy.

3. We must be able to get access to relationship information from other areas.

To effect systems integration, the council devised a template for decisions, as pictured in Figure 9.1. It was agreed that information essential to top management and of strategic value would be governed by common practices instituted by the corporate IT function. In turn, information used primarily by a line of business for tactical purposes would be governed by local management. In the case of regional or globally relevant information, subcommittees of the council, composed of both corporate and appropriate business managers, would set policies. In cases of disagreement, the issues would then be brought to the council as a whole. This template was applied to twenty-plus system integration issues by the business and technology management council and used thereafter in decisions about IT architecture and data management.

## Top-Level Team Building

Statements of vision and values mean very little in a combination unless they are embodied in senior leaders' behavior; the same is

**Figure 9.1.  Chemical Bank's Information Technology (IT) Decision-Making Template.**

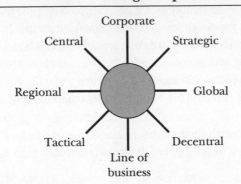

true for teamwork. As a combined business takes shape, senior executives are often confronted by confusion and conflict down the line. In response, executives issue directives or else urge that a consultant be called in to do some "team building" with middle management and supervisors. At the same time, they downplay their own lack of teamwork as a source of problems and excuse themselves from team building with such bromides as "These things take time" or "Everything will work out."

*When Bankers Bond*

The top team of Geoserve, a business unit offering back-office transaction processing and data-management services to financial institutions and businesses, faced squarely its initial everything-will-work-out attitude. Created by the merger of Chemical Bank and Manufacturers Hanover, this business unit had a mandate to grow and the resources to accomplish it. Its structural challenge was to link units organized by products or services with a market-oriented salesforce. Operating issues centered on bundling products and services, pricing, and sale through a matrix organization that featured product lines on one axis and market segments on the other. The new and unfamiliar matrix organization was identified as one obvious source of consternation down the line. Another was the growing lack of trust between sales (dominated by Chemical) and service (dominated by Manny Hanny). Behind all of this, senior sales and service executives still strongly identified with their prior companies' approaches and were unable to agree on priorities, unwilling to make decisions, and by their own admission incapable of working together.

Again, Lucia and Mirvis were asked to prepare a diagnosis of what ailed the Geoserve top team. They conducted interviews with each member and arrayed findings under the themes of goals, roles, processes, and relationships. The reasoning was straightforward: what is often characterized by people as a relationship problem has less to do with personality conflicts and more to do with conflicting work processes or roles. In turn, conflicts over processes and roles can often be traced to unclear or conflicting goals. To identify what was behind the lack of trust in this case, the consultants focused on four factors:

1. *Goals.* Although top managers in Geoserve agreed on a general strategy and business model, they had not worked out specific goals and priorities:

   "Critical success factors have not been translated into shared targets for sales and service."

   "There is no master plan for sales and service to work from."

   "What's our priority: margins or customer relationships?"

   "We need senior management commitment on products and processes."

2. *Roles.* In turn, the respective roles of senior managers were unclear and their responsibilities somewhat confused:

   "Are (sales) executives supposed to be business managers or technical experts?"

   "We present a fragmented picture to the customer. They don't know who they are dealing with and whether or not we have any authority."

   "There will always be tensions . . . but we need a long-term view of how sales and service will work together."

3. *Processes.* Disagreement over common processes exacerbated tensions between sales and service:

   "With cost data, (sales) would give away the store!"

   "(Product/Service) always asks for more and more information to make a decision."

   "There's no checks and balances."

   "We need a clearinghouse of ideas and information on competitors."

4. *Relationships.* Finally, there was bad blood between sales and service:

   "(Product/Service) doesn't trust us to tell us what's happening."

"(Sales) doesn't want to understand margins. They just want to make a sale."

"It is the 'immovable object' versus the 'irresistible force.'"

Dennis Forand, a senior vice-president in Geoserve, was neither surprised by these comments nor taken aback. He acknowledged that in creating a matrix organization, he had intermixed an organization of product chimneys with one characterized by independent sales groups. Achieving synergies meant breaking down the walls between these two sides of the matrix. Meanwhile, his own team was quarreling over matters both strategic and petty. They had not, for example, agreed on who was in charge of pricing and packaging, nor on how to communicate with each other and coordinate work. Attendance at team meetings was lax, and his direct reports were not leveling with each other.

The consultants spent two meetings reviewing the findings with the top team in Geoserve, who made little progress on the issues at hand. Forand then announced that the team needed to achieve a breakthrough or else resign itself to mediocrity. It was agreed, with some reluctance, that the group would participate in a team-building program at an offsite facility. The meeting itself featured standard teaming exercises: a check of the fit between business strategy and unit charters, articulating and prioritizing unit goals and initiatives, and then the team's rededication to its business plan. This was clarifying for all, and interactions were cordial. An analysis of the top team's roles, however, generated considerable anger and disagreement. The heat centered on who would have what authority over decisions and what they would need in the way of information and support. There was a lot of back-and-forth about the respective prerogatives of sales and service, and questions as to why so-and-so needed that information, who else would see it, and so forth. To sort through these issues, each member of the top team completed a "role contract" that addressed (1) tasks requiring partnership, (2) the person's responsibilities, and (3) the partner's responsibilities. Agreements, however, were grudging, and the team's esprit de corps faded.

To focus on interrelationships, the top team then participated in an outdoor adventure course. Through a series of initiatives, like helping one another through a rope spider web, the senior leaders practiced setting goals, assigning roles, and developing team work processes. As often happens, they improved as the day went along; people who were sometimes adversaries at work began to work together in play. The culmination of the outdoor program was a raft-building exercise where service and sales each lashed inner tubes together to form a raft, decorated it, prepared a song about Geoserve, and raced

each other across a lake. Once launched, the teams rowed feverishly and began
to bump each other's boat in an effort to win. The product/service side won the
race, but the sales side countered that its craft was the more seaworthy.
"C'mon aboard, we'll show you," one sales manager challenged. There was
scarcely a sound, and no one moved at this challenge. Then one service manager climbed on, followed by another and another. Soon the losing raft, totter-
ing under the weight, was holding both groups of managers. Together they
sang each other's songs. This event seemed to bond the senior team and rever-
berated down both sides of the matrix. With defined goals, clearer roles, and
some measure of camaraderie, the senior team went on to engage one another's subordinates and sort through many of the conflicts that slowed integration and provoked distrust.

## Culture Building

A senior vice president in an industrial-products alliance told us,
"Corporate culture is a lot like the *Queen Mary*: you don't swing it
around in five minutes. Whether our leadership likes it or not, it's
going to take a long time to implement any culture changes here."
Acculturation is a multiyear endeavor. Forces favoring the precombination ways of doing things aren't extinguished through ex-
hortations of senior management or implementation of new
policies or a new logo. Furthermore, preexisting structures, systems, and procedures often carry over into a combination, and
their retention reinforces old ways of doing things. Teams sorting
out new arrangements frequently regress to the modes of behavior prevalent in their precombination days. Individuals anxious to
prove themselves in a new situation tend to go with what they
know—which is what worked for them in the past.

### Culture Building by Design or Default?

For a corporate culture to change, change must occur at the individual level, particularly in how people interpret the environment
in which they operate.[1] To make sense of their world, people rely
on representations, or what learning theorists call mental models,
that explain the rules for getting along and getting ahead and how
things actually work.[2] These models are shortcuts that help people
select and interpret data from a universe of information that bom-
bards them. They also act as filters that cause people to reject in-

formation, interpretations, or actions that do not conform to their existing ways of looking at things or otherwise match their experiences. This is why proponents of organizational learning insist that you have to first open up mind-sets to effect individual change, and thereafter walk the talk to reinforce new knowledge and ways of doing things.

As the shock waves of the transition from old to new in a combination begin to subside, people settle into patterns of thinking and acting in their new environs. One of three scenarios prevails:

1. The combination experience does not significantly alter people's mental models, and they retain the assumptions, perceptions, and behaviors that served them in the precombination organization.
2. The combination experience alters people's mental models, and they settle into and rely upon the assumptions, perceptions, and behaviors that are reinforced *inadvertently* during the transition.
3. The combination experience alters people's mental models, and they settle into and rely upon the assumptions, perceptions, and behaviors that are reinforced *intentionally* during the transition.

There is so much real and imagined turmoil and so much at stake in a combination that people look for stability and constancy wherever they can find it. If the first scenario prevails (that is, there is no modification of people's mental models), employees hold on to accustomed ways of thinking about and doing things. Although the combination may temporarily unfreeze their mind-sets, the experience has not changed their underlying assumptions about how to operate and be effective in a new environment. There is often a certain amount of comfort in this. In one company we know of, as things settled down, employees sported badges with the moniker "I survived the merger!" In this case, unfortunately, line staff needed to effect a more substantial change but instead settled back into a comfortable routine. A wholesale reorganization nine months later forced at least two business units to "redo" their merger.

It can be argued that culture change is not always necessary in a combination, particularly when the strategy behind the deal hinges on the acquiree maintaining its independence and sense of identity. In this preservative type of acquisition, so the argument goes, the desired end state for an acquiree is to have cultural autonomy. Lotus, as an example, has retained much of its cultural distinctiveness within IBM. This has been desirable, for the sake of the marketplace and employee morale. The problem with this general scenario is that the assumptions, perceptions, and behaviors that served people well in the old days may not be appropriate in the combined organization. This is particularly true in combinations where synergies depend not on coexistence but on integrating people, structures, and cultures. As we have noted, avoiding or undermanaging culture change is especially troublesome for organizations involved in or anticipating multiple acquisitions and alliances.

The acculturation process in a full-scale combination varies in intensity between a melting pot at one extreme and a pressure cooker at the other.[3] Much depends on the degree of culture clash between combining companies and whether or not there is mutual buy-in to a desired end state. The process can be so dramatic and intense that it challenges employees' beliefs and discredits previously successful behaviors, on one or both sides of the combination. At a deep level, this may obliterate what psychologists call the cause-and-effect relationships that have guided people and replace them with new mental models. Depending on how acculturation is managed, this unlearning-relearning cycle follows one of two patterns: new perceptions and behaviors emerge by default as the result of inept or inadvertent management actions (scenario two above), or else they emerge by design as the result of proactive efforts to cast a new mold (scenario three).

### Culture by Default

A ten-year study we conducted of the white-knight acquisition of a small manufacturing company by a large conglomerate shows a case of acculturation by default.[4] The lead company's intentions were to keep the target company's top management in place. It insisted, however, that the acquiree keep far more detailed financial records and conform to its corporate reporting practices. Leaders from the acquired company lurched into crisis management as they experienced remorse at losing their independence, became overburdened by the joint responsibilities of running operations and preparing mountains of financial reports, and met among themselves to strategize how to fend off additional demands for information and conformity.

Meanwhile, parent company comptrollers and aggressive young MBAs began to question local management's resistance to preparing the complex financial analyses used by the parent to control its subsidiaries. Acquired senior management, which had maintained close informal relations with rank-and-file employees, became clannish and invisible to staff. Employees felt abandoned and out of touch with their leadership. In an attitude survey conducted a year after the combination, employees expressed how trust in management had plummeted, and employees conveyed feelings that their leaders were obsessed with the combination and not concerned about their welfare. Interviews with senior executives revealed that they were no less concerned with people but had to fight to protect them from intrusion. Yet their behavior inadvertently sent a different message to staff. One short-term implication was a union drive that, although defeated, required expending tremendous resources. The longer-term result, in this case, was "de-culturation" of the acquired company. Its prior culture was lost in the combination, but no cohesive sense of identify as part of a parent company emerged.

### Culture by Design

In sharp contrast is the case of the combination by design of two hospitals of equal size. The chief administrator, who came from one of the precombination hospitals, insisted on drawing on the best of both and used the integration period to revisit all facets of organizational effectiveness, from operating procedures to core competencies of managers. Her intentions were met with disbelief by the two management teams: those from her side assumed they would have an edge in the combined organization, while those from the other side suspected they would be at a disadvantage. Both sides were startled when she announced that every manager and supervisor would have to apply for a job in the "new" hospital and compete against one another (and perhaps outside applicants). This approach had short-term costs: a sense of abandonment by her former colleagues and some interpersonal conflict among individuals vying for jobs. But in the long run, it had the intended effect of breaking down old mind-sets and setting the stage for designing and developing a new and better organization.

## Leverage for Culture Building

If leadership has laid the foundation for culture change—by articulating a desired cultural end state, building on the strengths of current cultures, introducing new ways of doing things, and modeling desired behaviors and rewarding their adoption—then the forces for culture change have been set in motion. Now, as implementation proceeds, the requirement is to reinforce elements of the new culture. This is best achieved through using multiple leverage points.[5]

Leadership is a key leverage point. The extent to which the top executive, the senior team, and the upper management in the combined organization are aligned behind the desired end state and in sync with one another gives credibility and breathes life into messages about the new culture.

Next come the day-to-day actions of individual managers that either reinforce or conflict with the signals from above. In dealing with their direct reports, peers, and superiors, middle managers and supervisors either reinforce or weaken movement toward the desired culture through their behavior.

In turn, changes in organization can be a bane or boon to culture change. The combined company's organizational structure, business processes, measurement and appraisal systems, selection and staffing practices, and reward systems can help speed acculturation, slow it down, or run it off the tracks.

Finally, and ultimately, culture change comes about through the actions of individuals; influential people such as opinion leaders or high-profile, highly marketable individual contributors become test cases for judging whether or not a new culture takes.

### Reinforcing the Postcombination Culture

An alliance between two industrial products firms gives evidence of how multiple leverage points reinforce a desired culture. Shortly after the postcombination structure and systems were set in place, the CEO took his top team off site to discuss values that would guide behavior and goal attainment in the new organization. Before defining the agenda, however, he asked his direct reports to debate the merits of their spending time and energy—and company resources—on an ostensibly soft subject like culture. Senior team members from one side cited their prior disappointments when dealing with this subject and questioned the value of talking about culture, particularly with so many hard business issues facing them. Managers from the other side, however, recalled more favorable experiences, and after considerable back-and-forth the combined team concluded that their company could benefit from a clearer definition of the desired culture. Several potential values were nominated, discussed, and sorted into a draft statement.

The CEO next wanted to gain the buy-in of the broader management group, knowing that they had far more direct influence over large numbers of employees in the company. He convened a second offsite meeting, this time with the company's top seventy-five managers, and again tested managers' support for the concept of culture building and values clarification. In breakout groups, these managers argued the pros and cons of this work before emerging with a consensus to go forward.

Then, the seventy-five managers responded to the values proposed by the senior team. First came a test of the clarity of the draft statement of values. Returning to small groups, the managers generated questions about the meaning of some of the words and some seeming inconsistencies. When the full group reconvened, senior team members responded nondefensively about the logic of their thinking and acknowledged what now appeared to them to be contradictions. It is important to note that this was not an exercise in wordsmithing. To the contrary, managers were challenging the relative importance of values and their credibility to the workforce. Accordingly, in another round of breakout groups, managers proposed modifications to the current draft. Their input was collated overnight and used to prepare a second draft of corporate values. Early the next morning, the managers awoke to a revised draft slid under the doors of their rooms at the conference center. That day's session began with a review of this second draft.

After agreeing that this was not the time or place to quibble over semantics or to worry in too-great detail about relatively unimportant exceptions, the group developed a third draft of desired values, and a smaller number of managers were asked to make a final revision after the offsite meeting. With a rough final draft of the values statement complete, the seventy-five managers in attendance next reviewed and selected from a roster of culture-building tactics. One of the interventions selected for companywide implementation was 360 degree feedback for all managers regarding the extent to which they were living the shared values. The design called for the boss, peers, and direct reports to complete a questionnaire designed specifically to measure a focal manager's on-the-job adherence to the shared values. An outside consultant would analyze the results and feed them back, first one-on-one with the manager and then with the manager and his team. The individual feedback meeting would include a discussion of how the manager could better model the desired culture; the team meeting would attend to strengthening the desired culture in the team. Following these meetings, the manager would meet with his boss to review both personal and team action plans.

The company's human resource staff developed a questionnaire to measure the extent to which managers "walk the talk" in abiding by the shared values. For each of the twelve values, five questions were prepared. For the value "develop our people," response statements included: "The manager gives work assignments to people that stretch their current abilities," "The manager supports people's efforts to learn new skills," and "The manager gives useful feedback to people on their performance." The design called for 360 degree feedback to cascade down the company hierarchy. First up were members of the senior team. The CEO, peers on his team, and direct reports completed questionnaires for each member of the top group. After individual and team feedback meetings were conducted for the senior team, the process was replicated with their direct reports and then layer-by-layer through the organization.

This 360 degree feedback process—and the manner in which it was implemented—demonstrates the use of multiple leverage points to effect culture change. For instance, it engaged leadership at several layers in articulating the new culture and modeling new behaviors. In many work areas, the 360 degree feedback process and discussion of shared values influenced day-to-day management practice and vocabularies. Managers and subordinates would examine whether proposed decisions were consistent with their shared values before implementing them. The process involved large numbers of employees in translating high-minded values into everyday actions.

## Culture at the Working Level

One reason why it takes years and not months to change a corporate culture is that behavioral change at the top of the house cascades down to the bottom very slowly. The 360 degree feedback process described above is one way to drill-down culture change rather quickly. But effecting changes in methods of performance appraisal, promotion practices, reward systems, and the like—that is, the changes that cement new behaviors—typically covers a long time in development and implementation, and longer still to become part of the fabric of a combined company.

As important as an overall culture-building exercise can be to the success of a combination, real acculturation occurs at the working level. It is when they are on the job, in project teams or work groups, interacting with colleagues and customers, at lunch or in a car pool, and at working meetings or on a break that people are constantly making sense of their new environment and, consciously or not, deciding how to behave. Senior managers have scarcely any idea of what goes on in the workaday world of frontline staff. At most, they influence it indirectly through symbols, myriad management systems, and their own interest and example. Middle managers, especially immediate supervisors, have a far better understanding of the workings of hourly, clerical, and sales personnel and exert more influence over them. Furthermore, they have the opportunity and responsibility to fashion a working culture that, although guided by corporate values and expectations, is fitted to the needs of their operation and people.

What "levers" can managers and supervisors themselves use to build a winning work culture in a combination? Consider some examples:

- *Meetings.* In the strategic alliance between Ameritech and GEIS, alliance managers instituted fishbowl-type meetings, where a work group would review its results with managers while being observed by other work groups. The intent was to build collective intelligence about products and customers and foster norms of open dialogue and team-on-team coaching.

- *Settings.* In the combination of two high-technology companies, private offices were eliminated in regional facilities. Now salespeople work in an open space adjacent to work spaces filled by service personnel and technical support. Interactions between sales representatives have increased, as has their contact with other members of their newly formed "customer team."

- *Interactions.* In a high-technology acquisition, technologists from the acquired side were invited to join brown-bag seminars in the lead company on developments in the industry featuring well-known academics and respected innovators. After a short time, engineers from the acquired side were invited to present their work; later they hosted meetings, on a rotating basis, on their home turf.

- *Work processes.* Nothing affects culture change more at the operating level than introducing a new way of working together.

The merger of widely dispersed information technologists from Chemical Bank and Manufacturers Hanover took an upward turn when all were interconnected via Lotus Notes. Technologists from all over the globe could use this database to develop, after a fashion, a common (virtual) culture. Interestingly, the same thing is happening in parts of IBM, with the massive introduction of Notes technology from its acquiree. IBMers used to come to meetings with armloads of overheads. Now they conduct many more virtual meetings or merely plug in their personal computers when making "face time" presentations.

## Culture Training

A few companies are using advanced training tactics to accelerate the process of acculturation at the working level. These programs give frontline employees the opportunity to think through and practice behaviors consistent with the desired postcombination culture. A financial services alliance was formed with much fanfare around the company's "shared values." To underscore their commitment to these values, senior leadership charged its training professionals to develop a program to reinforce the emerging culture. One course, "Living the Shared Values," gave employees a chance to discuss and role-play the espoused values of the alliance. In the workshop, employees heard from a member of the senior team about why these particular values were chosen. To model the value of open communications, the executive described the debate and controversy that consumed the senior team as they wrestled with options.

Then, in experiential exercises, employees participated in simulated business situations. They were assigned a business circumstance and asked to act out how to handle it in line with a particular shared value. This brought the values to life, raised awareness of the intentions underlying the words, offered opportunities to practice new behaviors, and provided individuals with feedback on the degree to which they understood what was expected of them in the new organization.

As implementation proceeds, postcombination organization-building and culture-building activities contribute to realizing synergies and to setting in place the desired organization. People experience this reality in various ways, and, as the next chapter tells, it influences the important work of building teams out of individual contributors.

## Chapter Ten

# Building Postcombination Teams

After months of waiting for something to happen, hearing rumors about what might be changing, hoping for the best and fearing the worst, employees now have to get down to work and make the combination's potential come to life. They do this within the context of their work teams, which are in turn formed within the framework of the overall organization and its culture. Efforts to build combined teams are also influenced by the psychological readiness of individual members. Some may be prepared to move forward to the challenges and opportunities ahead. Others are holding onto baggage from their precombination company or from their experience of the combination to date. And some are simply bewildered about what is happening and what they are supposed to do.

## Managing Mind-Sets

For new or reappointed team leaders, the upside of a combination includes the opportunity to build a new team from scratch or, alternatively, revamp and revitalize an incumbent team. Similar to the CEO's opportunity in leading the combination, the team leader can clarify a desired end state, focus people on CSFs, and engage them in formulating operating principles that serve as rules of the road for the emerging team.

A mind-set of partnering is characterized by trust, commonality of purpose, and cooperative spirit. It goes a long way in building a team wherein goals are shared rather than disparate, enemies are located outside the organization rather than within, and issues are addressed openly and fairly rather than pushed under the rug or handled politically behind closed doors. It's obviously easier to build a team of this caliber in a combination if a team leader's own boss models similar action. Even if a superior doesn't do so, however, the opportunity remains for a team leader to exert some control and build a high-performing work group.

As the organization moves into the postcombination phase, individual employees are confronted with a multitude of changes in structure, systems, procedures, expectations, relations, and so on. This is a confusing time for many people, wrought with uncertainty and stress, especially when they have not been directly involved in decisions about their new organization. As in the other phases, lower-level employees have less control over their situation in the postcombination period than do their superiors. Yet they do have some control, and probably much more than they imagine. To help its employees, an apparel company prepared and distributed to employees a memo titled "How to Manage Change Without It Managing You." Informally referred to as an "employee survival guide," the document offered specific ways in which employees could better understand and positively influence their situation:

- *Understand what you can and cannot control.* Spend your energy on doing the former well, and do not waste it on trying to do the latter.
- *Learn about what is going on around you.* Stop and think before you act, rather than do things in an uneducated or hasty manner. Talk with people, ask questions, get information and, in general, conduct a "diagnosis" of the situation in which you find yourself.
- *Learn about what is going on inside you.* Stop and listen to your own self. What emotions are you feeling? What are you afraid of and what excites you? Determine whether you are in control of your emotions or they are in control of you.
- *Change your definition of success.* The good old days are gone, and so are some rungs from the corporate ladder. Still, you can thrive—not just survive—in the new organization. Perhaps receiving a new job assignment or being invited to participate on a special task force is today's recognition of a job well done.
- *Take personal responsibility for your situation.* The company can't plan everything for you—your career track, your training, your retirement. You have a greater-than-ever responsibility for managing your employment and career. Make your interests,

needs, and abilities known to your supervisor. Volunteer for special assignments or task forces.

- *Do the right things.* You are either contributing to or detracting from the company we are attempting to build. Align your priorities with those of the company. Reengineer your job so that what you do makes a positive contribution, eliminates waste, and is consistent with the objectives of your team, the mission of your department, and the vision of our company.

- *Let go of fear.* If you are good, your company needs and wants you. If it doesn't, someone else does.

- *Be tolerant of those around you.* This is an intense time for all of us. There is no master plan and no one has all the answers—not the company, and certainly not your boss. And just when things seem to be going in one direction, they may shift to another. This may be an important and beneficial midcourse correction, given the uncertainty and competitiveness of our industry.

- *Be tolerant of yourself.* You don't have all the answers, either. You may need to learn some new ways of doing things, along with new ways of seeing and thinking about things. Trial-and-error is a powerful way to learn, but sometimes a painful way to learn. Embrace the learning opportunity inherent in all mistakes; but don't continue to make the same mistakes over and over again.

- *Tell it like it is.* Contribute to building the best possible new organization and to a culture in which openness and honesty prevail. Speak up, point out problems, and suggest improvements. You can be direct without being nasty.

- *Anticipate the next transition.* Sooner or later, we are all going to go through another major transition. That's just how the game is played these days. Don't be like an ostrich with its head in the sand, or like a chicken running around aimlessly with its head cut off. Use your head to keep abreast of events in our company, our industry, and in the overall economy.

- *Have some fun.* Times are tough, but life is short. Being here at the creation of our new company is a special event for all of us. Make every day important and productive. Enjoy what you do and have fun doing it.

- *Take care of yourself.* Of course there will be disappointments and difficult times as we move forward together. Look out for yourself. Eat well, exercise, and talk things out with a friend, family member, or coworker. Go out dancing and let it all hang out. Or, lose yourself in a great movie or novel. Then, come back tomorrow and we'll try it again, together.

## The Psychology of Adaptation

All change, even change for the better, involves some experience of loss. In a combination that succeeds at implementing truly new and better ways of doing things, people have to give up familiar ways of working. Remember the truism that people have to let go of the old before they accept the new. Senior executives, those with the most at stake in a combination, often have the most intense reactions to the transition. Significantly, however, their adaptation to change is accelerated by the high degree of control they enjoy relative to others in the organization. As the primary designers of change, they participate in combination planning and decision-making activities; they understand why change is needed and where it is headed. All other members of the organization have less influence and a lot more uncertainty.

As Figure 10.1 shows, those at high levels begin to adapt to organizational changes well before employees at other levels. Thus, by the time executives at the top have accepted and dealt with their own feelings of loss, insecurity, and threat and are looking to the challenges ahead, people lower down may at best be in the midst of their adaptation process. In large organizations, changes may not ripple down to the lowest levels for quite a while; by then, senior executives have put their personal pain behind them and as a result appear unsympathetic to others' needs to work through the process. Either because they are impatient to move on or because they have repressed the pain of their own transition, senior executives often overlook and undermanage the human realities of the combination process.

Forces for and against desired change compete with one another throughout the combination process, with the balance constantly shifting. As time moves forward in a well-managed combination, the forces for change tend to dominate and provide the necessary impetus for letting go of the old and adapting to the new. Yet, as decisions are announced and implementation begins in earnest, a wave of resistance often swells up as people regress psychologically and behaviorally. Many employees we have inter-

## Figure 10.1. Adaptation to Transition by Hierarchical Level.

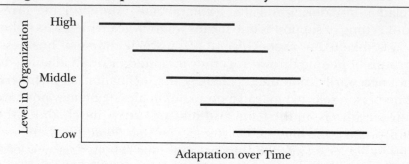

Source: Marks, M. L. *From Turmoil to Triumph: New Life After Mergers, Acquisitions, and Downsizings.* San Francisco: New Lexington Press, 1994.

viewed and surveyed report that they fall back into the merger syndrome. They become increasingly anxious, turn inward, keep score, and sometimes lash out. All the stress building up impairs their perceptions of what is going on around them and makes it hard for them to hear important and uplifting communications. This frustrates and often angers executives who are farther along in their adaptation. Expecting to lead motivated troops to charge up the hill and capture the prize awaiting them, they instead encounter a mass of doubt and confusion. Advice from an employee survival guide, however sound, only goes so far. Managers have to reenlist the troops and motivate them to action.

## Building Postcombination Teams

The work team is a focal point for realizing synergies in a combination. Even though success elsewhere in a company influences employees' sentiments about the combination, evidence from their own work teams matters most. People see their coworkers either embracing new work methods or resisting them. In addition, well-functioning work teams help individuals adapt to change. Work teams provide social support by reducing the level of stress experienced by their members and by buffering them from the physical and psychological consequences.[1] A work team with a high level of social support is not as susceptible to increased interpersonal conflicts and drags on performance that otherwise wrack work relationships during and after a combination. Moreover, the giving and getting of support is one means whereby team members bond.

Unlike teams that evolve in the normal course of business, groups of people thrown together in a merger or an alliance do not necessarily know the capabilities and inclinations of members. The person selected to lead a postcombination team may not have chosen who is on the team and may not know much about the individual contributors. Conversely, not all team members may have self-selected into the team or know much about their new leader. Thus, effective postcombination teams are built one person at a time.

The mandate for team leaders is to step back, understand mind-sets, and assess the prevailing dynamics that influence performance. Four general requirements guide effective team leaders: (1) understand the emotional states of individual contributors in the postcombination phase, (2) anticipate sources of tension in building postcombination teams, (3) mold a group of individuals into a team, and (4) develop the team proactively.

## Understanding Postcombination Mind-Sets

In forming postcombination teams, leaders face employees with very different attitudes (Exhibit 10.1). Some team members willingly let go of old attachments, adapt to new realities, and are ready to get on with the work at hand. Others want more support and more reasons to be part of the new team. Still others feel shut out and resist efforts to move forward.

Employees who get the job they wanted or expected in the combined company are usually ready to enlist in the new team. With worries about their personal fate substantially behind them, they are charged up by the challenges and opportunities of adding real value. For example, in their alliance with an established computer manufacturer, employees from a firm with a strong product-development pipeline but inefficient manufacturing and limited distribution were excited by the potential of joining forces with a company possessing these competencies. Such employees are often the mainstay of a new team; their positive attitudes can be infectious. An overly gung ho outlook, however, can alienate less-spirited employees who need more time to adapt.

### Exhibit 10.1.  Recognizing People's Mind-Sets
### in the Postcombination Phase.

**THE READY**

| | |
|---|---|
| Their situation: | Have been promoted or retained the job they want |
| | See greater opportunity to produce and advance |
| What to hope for: | Energy and excitement; charged up |
| What to watch for: | Overly aggressive; acting superior |

**THE WANTING**

| | |
|---|---|
| Their situation: | Did not receive the job they wanted or were demoted |
| | Miss former mentors, projects, and status |
| What to hope for: | Working through loss; adjusting to new realities |
| What to watch for: | Depression; anger and vindictiveness |

**THE WRUNG OUT**

| | |
|---|---|
| Their situation: | Have the same job, but things have changed |
| | More distant from leadership |
| | More competition for advancement |
| | Feel jerked around by the process |
| What to hope for: | Working through frustration; regaining footing |
| What to watch for: | Demotivation; lack of direction and purpose |

*Source:* Mirvis, P. M., and Marks, M. L. *Managing the Merger: Making It Work.*
Upper Saddle River, N.J.: Prentice Hall, 1994.

Other team members are found wanting. Perhaps they didn't get their desired job title or responsibilities, or they've been separated from their mentors or friends, or their budgets or projects have been slashed. These employees remain preoccupied with their lower-than-expected status and wonder if it is a harbinger of a dead-end career. Plainly, they need more time to sort things out.

Finally, there are employees who simply feel wrung out by the combination process. Contrary to their worst fears and best hopes, they pretty much retain the same or similar jobs and responsibilities in the combined organization. Still, they are listless and weary from the ordeal they have survived. These people often hold onto the glass-half-empty perspective, locking in on cues that the situation around them has changed for the worse. They may complain that the combined organization adds layers between them and the highest levels of management. Those previously housed close to the action at headquarters fret when they find themselves farther removed from the center of power in a new alliance start-up or in an acquired subsidiary. Upwardly mobile employees bemoan the increased competition for advancement in the combined organization.

For those charged with leading a new team, understanding a person's current emotional state is more difficult than it seems. Team members who are not close to their new boss may put on a poker face and hide their true feelings. Some simply cannot verbalize their reasons for persistent discontent. Others play up to the boss and hide their incompetence in a veil of enthusiasm and self-serving flattery. Part of the leader's responsibility in forming a new team is to ascertain the mind-set of individual members, reenlist them, and help them rededicate themselves to their jobs. Straightforward one-on-one talks between leader and team member can uncover hidden emotional states. With hard-to-read employees, involving a human resources professional, trained counselor, or even a trusted peer can open up discussion with a superior.

## Sources of Tension in Building New Teams

Team building in a combination is complicated when there are changes in leadership and membership of a team. Any one of the following factors enhances the likelihood of tension in newly formed teams:

- *A new boss.* The appointment of a new boss creates tension as subordinates naturally jockey for influence and visibility. Conflict is especially likely if a subordinate was expecting to have the new boss's job, if former peers are placed in a superior-subordinate relationship, or if the new boss comes from one partner to take over a team from the other.
- *New peers.* When combinations mix people from the partner companies, they naturally divide into coalitions and exchange confidences with former peers. This can continue the we-they feelings and force managers to take sides in resolving conflicts.

- *New methods.* Members of acquired teams not only have to adapt to job-related changes, they also have to learn the politics and protocol of operating with a new parent company. Similarly, members of teams in alliances and transformational mergers are confronted with new systems, duties, and expectations. Predictably, there is a tendency to go with what (and who) you know. This means that people may have trouble gaining access to the informal social and communication networks of the new organization and are likely to encounter untold problems in simply getting the job done through normal channels.
- *New relationships.* Diversity can enhance team creativity and performance, but it takes time to turn what initially is likely to be a source of conflict into an enhancement. The feel and flow of relatively homogeneous work teams is disrupted by people from different organizations, cultures, or countries. This raises tension levels, especially when the differences interfere with work quality or quantity.

## Molding Individuals into a Team

Three common factors frame the team leader's tasks in making individuals into team members:[2]

1. *Psychological enlistment.* People need to feel a part of the team and have an emotional stake in their team's mission.
2. *Role development.* People need to clearly understand what is expected of them and what they can expect of others.
3. *Trust and confidence.* People need to develop trust and confidence in their colleagues and superiors.

Although these needs are part of any employment situation, they become especially prominent in the context of postcombination mind-sets and dynamics (Exhibit 10.2).

### Psychological Enlistment: Forming the Team

Before signing up psychologically, employees who are reporting to new bosses, working with new peers, or contending with new procedures go through some self-examination. They ask themselves, "Do I really want to be part of this team?" Several factors influence

## Exhibit 10.2. Stages in Building a New Team.

| STAGES: | I<br>SIGNING UP | II<br>SORTING OUT | III<br>SETTLING DOWN |
|---|---|---|---|
| **Leader's Role** | | | |
| | Form the team | Establish norms | Motivate performance |
| | Set expectations | Set ground rules | Set objectives |
| **Member's Issues** | | | |
| | Inclusion— am I a member of this team or not? | Control— who is in charge? | Openness— are we achieving? |
| **Sources of Resistance** | | | |
| | Unclear sense of purpose, mission, role | Holding onto old allegiances; moves to gain advantage | Holding onto ways of doing business |
| | People on trial | Internal conflict | Clash of cultures |
| | Personal distress | Gamesmanship | Foot dragging |
| **How to Counter Resistance** | | | |
| | Rally people | Negotiate roles/ responsibilities | Performance management |
| | Personalize the sign-up | Develop role agreements | Incentives to perform |
| | Massage egos | Clarify reporting relationships | Model desired behaviors |
| | Lay it on the line | Establish ground rules | Team building |

their decision. First is their drive toward achievement: employees want to know the team's purpose and how it contributes to the overall organizational scheme. Second are facets of power motivation: employees want to know if they have to prove themselves, wonder if they'll thrive under current leadership, and question if they have any voice in matters that affect them. Finally there are needs for affiliation: they want to know if their teammates do their fair share, and if people work together well.

Obviously, enlisting employees is aided by affirmative signals that needs for achievement, power, and affiliation are being met.

Still, many people may exhibit passive or active aggression as the untoward effects of transition linger, alienating them from their new boss and peers. Leaders can take steps to lessen these sources of resistance to psychological enlistment in a team:

- *Re-recruit employees.* Team leaders who want to enlist their members can take a lesson from college recruiters courting top athletes: give people a reason for wanting to be on this team. Recruiting begins by thoughtfully assessing people's goals and aspirations, carefully considering what might moti- vate them or turn them off, and then formally signing them up. Reminding people that their importance and value to the team are recognized addresses their need for inclusion and any insecurity they may have regarding their perceived merit. Of course, in the case of highly marketable talent, it may be necessary to follow the dictum of professional recruiters and "show them the money."
- *Massage egos.* Many employees need extra reassurance of their worth, especially when they have not gained what they hoped for in the postcombination organization or when they sense they are being tested at a point in their career where their accomplishments and capabilities should be recognized. The team leader can do some stroking and ego massaging, create opportunities for some quick wins and small successes, and acknowledge their achievement. It helps also to acknowledge people's past contributions.
- *Lay it on the line.* Over time, individuals and teams have to get on with the work at hand. Employees who continue to mope around the office, bad-mouth the combination, or perform below expected levels may need a message from the boss to shape up or ship out.

### Role Development: Team Organization

After team members are in place, team leaders and members often test one another in another way: struggling to determine relative degrees of control. Group dynamics experts refer to this as the "storming" phase of group development. Leaders help their teams weather this storm by clarifying people's roles and setting ground rules. It is here that the group's modus operandi and pecking order are established and recognized.

Some predictable sources of resistance interfere with team leaders' efforts to manage these dynamics. First, managers taking over well-established groups often find people still holding on to their old allegiances and ways of doing things. Second, internal conflict can undermine team development. Some employees brownnose the boss and backstab their peers in an effort to gain power. Others gain command of their peers and orchestrate a revolt against the new boss (a classic dynamic as small groups develop). The storming phase can put team leaders in a no-win situation. If they assert their authority preemptively, conflict goes underground. But if they let conflict get out of control, the bad feelings developed may not be assuaged by later intervention.

At stake in these situations is the extent to which the team leader is able to develop esprit de corps rather than mindless obedience:

- *Negotiate roles.* Positions and players may be set, but postcombination job duties and responsibilities require clarification. In role negotiation, a technique developed by consultant Roger Harrison, a team leader and subordinates discuss expectations of roles, identify areas of conflict or ambiguity, and engage in the give-and-take of negotiating a realistic role definition acceptable to both parties.[3]
- *Establish reporting relationships.* Employees regularly complain about ambiguous reporting relationships in a combination. To counter this, team leaders should bring organizational charts to life and delineate who reports to whom and with what authority and responsibilities. This may seem foreign to organizations accustomed to fluid structures and hesitant to put on paper the extant chain of command. It is useful, however, to overstructure in the early stages of team building, when areas of responsibility are contested.
- *Set group ground rules.* Finally, there is a need to establish both formal procedures (regarding budgetary authority, communication formats, and so on), as well as informal norms (dress, timeliness, protocol, and so forth) in a team. Employees are more apt to understand and accept ground rules that are congruent with and support the desired cultural end state for the organization than ones that send a contradictory message. The legitimacy of team ground rules also grows when employ-

ees have just witnessed a combination phase in which operating principles guided and enhanced the work of planning teams.

### Trust and Confidence: Getting down to Work

Teams make their fullest contribution to the combined organization when members have trust and confidence in each other. Until now, team members have had to make individual accommodations to change; now the group must accommodate as a whole. In a chicken-and-egg predicament, team members depend on trust and confidence to operate in a fully productive mode, yet they require some evidence of productivity and reciprocity from teammates before extending that trust and confidence.

A number of factors prevent this from developing in a combined team. First, the team may need lead time to sort out new methods and procedures and a grace period to learn how to work with new systems. Second, performance expectations may differ among members of a combined team. Consider the case of a manager who insisted that his people arrive at work early and stay late. When his team was combined with another that had a more laid-back style, trouble ensued. By all accounts, the easygoing group was every bit as successful as its hard-driving counterpart. But when the hard-driving manager secured the top post, he forced his ways onto the new subordinates, who thereupon left in droves. This speaks to a third problem in achieving high performance: how to handle diversity. Naturally it is difficult to reconcile differences among team members who are used to certain ways of doing things. Can a team accommodate members who like to plan out their work in detail as well as those who take a more spontaneous approach? How about team members who yell and swear at meetings versus those who are accustomed to sober discussion and mannerly disagreement?

Organizations and even units within them have different philosophies and approaches to dealing with diversity. It takes time for managers and employees to figure out the rules in each group, and more time to change them. Team leaders can speed the development of trust and confidence in various ways:

- *Model new behaviors.* Modeling desired behavior is powerful even in relatively stable times, and it is especially potent

during impressionable periods in team formation. Team leaders who do not abide by the espoused rules of the road cannot
expect their team members to do so.

- *Manage performance.* Directly rewarding desired performance
  is the most effective technique team leaders have for clarifying
  and reinforcing what they expect from members. Basic principles of effective incentive programs apply here: find out what
  rewards (financial and otherwise) people want, and clearly
  link them with desired behaviors. It helps as well to reward
  people's contributions to team building and to doing things
  the right way.
- *Manage diversity.* For one plus one to equal three in a work
  team, differences between individuals have to be understood
  and mutually addressed. Depending how it is managed by
  leadership, diversity in styles can bring a team to great achievements or tear it apart. Openly discussing the variety of approaches and contributions that can be offered by team
  members clears the way for team members to accept differing
  perspectives and methods. Good dialogue, built around self-
  assessment of individuals and the team's desired modus
  operandi, generates understanding.

Some managers we have worked with convene monthly mini-
team-building programs to discuss diversity, learn what is and is not
working in the team, and address performance issues and opportunities. In addition to diversity in working styles, combinations
can produce diversity on another level. We have seen mergers that
broaden the mix of ethnicity, gender, religion, and sexual orientation of work team members. The rising number of international
deals creates cross-border diversity. Anticipating difficulties in managing a diverse workforce, one U.S.-based firm volunteered its own
"valuing diversity" program to its Japanese owners in an alliance.
The training program focused on prejudice and stereotypes and
had participants role-play situations that called for managing
majority-minority relations in work teams.

## Developing Effective Postcombination Teams

Team building has about as many permutations as there are varieties of teams and team leaders. We've heard leaders of combined
groups define team building as everything from taking the gang to

a Chicago Cubs baseball game to participating in a weeklong outdoor survival experience. Here is a simple definition of team building: *any planned intervention that enhances a team's effectiveness.* Team effectiveness, in turn, develops when members have clear identity, appropriate work processes, ample communication and feedback, and goals achieved that are concurrent with personal growth and development.

Formal team building (as opposed to a social event at Wrigley Field) accelerates individuals' melding into a team. It does so by helping a group identify and address inhibitors to team effectiveness as well as by raising and reinforcing enablers of team effectiveness. Team building provides structure and clarity to the team's work early in its development and attends to the group dynamics and personal needs of members as the group matures.

### A Prescription for Teamwork at Pfizer AHG

At Pfizer AHG, Marks and Marilyn Showers met with functional leaders upon their appointment to review a team-building framework. It positioned requirements for team effectiveness into six components:[4]

1. *Context and team charter.* What is the role of the team in the postcombination organization? What are its key relations with other teams? What is required and expected of the team?

2. *Goals.* What is the core content of the team's work? What are the measures of team success?

3. *Roles.* What is expected or required of team members, leaders, and subgroups?

4. *Procedures.* How are meetings structured and the team's agenda created and managed? How are decisions made and output managed?

5. *Interactions.* What behavior is expected or required of team members? What ground rules and operating principles will predominate?

6. *Team quality assurance.* How are the team's process and progress reviewed? How is feedback provided on team effectiveness?

The framework helped leaders prepare for and act on team development, in both formal and informal ways. Several used the framework to set the agenda for offsite meetings to kick off their newly formed teams. Soon after their formation, AHG teams came together to clarify their charters, goals, roles, and procedures, as well as to establish the operating principles and feedback mechanisms that would position their interactions and ensure quality team-work. The consultants customized activities in these areas to fit the styles and needs of each team and its leader. Some team leaders committed to follow-up meetings in six months to assess progress and address any newly emerging is-sues. Many leaders also adopted the framework into their daily routine when working with new team members. It prompted them to discuss and clarify with direct reports the work requirements and expectations regarding how work would be accomplished in the team. These informal exchanges built upon and reinforced the progress made at offsite meetings.

# Regrouping

All of the efforts to build high-performing teams, positive inter-group relationships, and a desired culture in the postcombination organization rest on the motivation and abilities of the workforce. Even when resulting in a new and better organization, the process of building one organization out of two takes a toll on people. The transition from old to new produces a loss that must be dealt with before people can fully move on. All societies have rituals to help people cope with and adapt to death and loss. So, too, organizations are beginning to accept this natural psychological phenom-enon and help their members let go of the old so they are fully prepared to move onto the new.

## Change Versus Transition

To appreciate the need for psychological regrouping in the post-combination phase, it helps to understand the difference between change and transition. Change is a path to a known state, with or-derly, incremental, and continuous steps. Starting the weekly staff meeting at 8:00 instead of 8:30 is an example of a change. It may cause some disruptiveness and require some adaptation, but its dis-crete nature allows people to know exactly what to expect and lets them get on with their work.

A transition, by comparison, is a path to an unknown state: something discontinuous that involves many simultaneous and interactive changes. The selection of "breakthrough" ways of think-ing, organizing, and doing business in a transformational combi-nation is an example of a transition. Transition poses a break from the past. It involves death and rebirth; existing practices and rou-tines must be abandoned and new ones discovered and developed.

Adapting to transition is much more psychologically taxing than is adapting to change. Even when it results in positive enhancement, transition implies loss of the status quo, which must be dealt with before people can fully move on.

How can managers help people regroup and move on after transition? Three complementary courses of action contribute. One helps employees let go of the old, through methods such as venting meetings designed for people to work through their experience of loss or other negative emotions built up during the transition. Another course aids people in moving forward by giving them practical support for succeeding in the new organization. This might take the form of a training program that substantively enhances people's skills and capabilities while symbolically indicating their leadership has some understanding of people's needs in the postcombination organization. The third course strengthens newly forming mental models regarding cause-and-effect relationships in the postcombination organization. An obvious method for doing this would be to review and, where necessary, revamp the rewards and incentives available to employees for behaving in desired ways.

## Venting

Hopefully, employees have been prepared for the problems and pitfalls that beset any combination and, to whatever extent possible, have taken in stride the bumps along the path that are inadvertently disturbing or disappointing. No one gets through this journey unscathed, though, and people may need help letting go of the baggage they've picked up during the course of a combination.

A venting meeting provides many benefits as a means for people to work through their loss and anger.[5] First, it validates the experiences of employees who are struggling with loss in their personal situation and have trouble coping with the death of their precombination organization. Venting helps them cope with obvious maladies, such as layoff survivor sickness, but also with more subtle losses such as giving up a fondly held culture or cherished mentor. Second, a venting meeting gives people pointers for how to deal with and move beyond an uncomfortable or unsettling experience. It can be a turning point at which people let go of anger, guilt, and blame and take personal responsibility for accepting the situation at hand. Third, bringing people together to share in the venting meeting establishes a bond among members of the group. This is a step in building a new community of people who have together mourned their loss and are now ready to move forward. Fourth, the venting meeting accelerates the pace at which people let go. The dramatic scene of watching others acknowledge that precombination life is over weakens enduring forces for the status quo.

Letting go of the old occurs in three steps: consciousness raising, reexperiencing, and mourning.[6] People move through these steps *whether or not* the organization recognizes this basic human need. Thus, well-designed venting meetings contain activities to help people along each of the three steps of letting go:

1. *Consciousness raising.* The venting meeting alerts employees to common patterns of organizational and individual reaction to transition. This shows that reactions to loss are to be expected following a transition. The goal is to help employees acknowledge intellectually what they are personally holding on to, and become aware of their reasons for doing so.
2. *Reexperiencing.* The reasons for and implications of holding on become truly understood only when they are expressed experientially. Talking through where they have been and what they are currently experiencing as a result of the transition helps employees bring their feelings to a conscious level. This is typically an emotional and highly charged process, in contrast to the more intellectual level at which initial consciousness raising occurs.
3. *Mourning.* The psychological process of letting go is completed through an active mourning of what is being left behind: old ways of seeing and doing things and the loss of what was once satisfying, meaningful, or simply familiar. This mourning is sometimes accompanied by remorse, a sense of the life that could have been but never will be. Yet it also instills a sense of renewal and rebirth, and acceptance of what lies ahead.

Venting is distinct from bitching. Bitching is blaming, while venting raises up, legitimizes, and works through feelings. Employees who become aware of, reexperience, and actively mourn their losses are better prepared to accept new realities and move forward. For a workforce that is burned out after the grueling transition, a venting meeting is a forum for healing and renewal. When conducted in a positive, open, and safe manner, it reenergizes people and refocuses them on their work.

Venting can occur in a variety of formats, ranging from special meetings dedicated exclusively to the venting process to sessions piggybacked onto other meetings. Naturally, venting can be emotionally charged, so expert facilitation is advisable. The facilitator creates an environment that employees regard as a safe milieu for expressing their deepest and truest feelings, but also one that provides the proper degree of confrontation required to elicit those feelings. The impressions brought back and discussed by attendees of the initial venting meetings strongly influence whether others regard the meetings as something to look forward to or something to be wary of.

## Training

People progress in their adaptation when they feel confident in their ability to perform their jobs well in the postcombination organization. Employees who do not have the skills or know-how to do their jobs well become demotivated or regress to precombination patterns of behavior. Yet, preparing people to learn new job skills or work with new systems often is overlooked in combination planning. Plus, factors that have little to do with the combination itself, such as the fact that many training programs have been substantially downsized or altogether eliminated during the corporate cost-cutting era of the past several years, further hinder adequate preparation.

### Training for the Postcombination Organization

The dearth of in-house training and development programs can actually be turned to advantage in showing tangible benefits of the combined company. In a financial services alliance, the human resource task force conducting combination planning followed their CSF of "invest in developing our people" and recommended that an internal training-and-development function be included as part of the new company's HR function. This was in stark contrast to practice in both parent companies, one of which outsourced all of its training and development while the other traditionally lent corporate trainers out to subsidiaries and joint ventures. The task force made a strong case for having a training-and-development group dedicated and accountable to the alliance.

Demonstrating the flexibility required for successful implementation, leadership concurred and appropriated funds to create a budget for the function.

As the alliance took shape, the newly appointed training-and-development director designed a curriculum offering two tracks of training programs. One offered training in new systems, procedures, and policies being introduced during implementation. This prepared people to use order entry, financial reporting, and IT systems. The second contributed general career-development and skills-enhancement programs to educate people on everything from newly emerging financial services products to computing skills. Together, the tracks helped people contend with practical changes in their work environment and showed them that their company was genuinely committed to developing its people.

## Incentive

What's in it for people to contribute to a productive combination? The promised long-term benefits of the combination may not be realized for some time to come. They seem a long way down the road for individuals contending with the confusion and uncertainty of the developing organization. In the meantime, employees keep their eyes open to direct and indirect cues as to which behaviors are being rewarded and which are discouraged in the emerging organization. What kind of people are getting the best assignments? To whom are the most important responsibilities being given? Who is being called into the executives' offices to give input on key decisions? What's happening to people who are abiding by the espoused new culture and those who clearly are not?

Part of the work of refreezing desired norms in a combination is to design an incentive system suited to risk taking and growth. We have witnessed too many mergers and alliances where senior executives have called for growth and then relied on a compensation system that emphasizes base pay and punishes those who strive for stretch targets. This was certainly an issue in the alliance between Ameritech and GEIS, where the former's incentives emphasized "playing it safe" and the latter's pushed people to "go for the gusto."

Several companies we've worked with have designed multiple compensation systems for various business units and staff functions. In so doing, they have scrapped job grading systems based on points and given unit managers a pool of money to dispense as they see fit, under some general guidelines. In one case, acquired engineers in a high-tech combination actually had their base pay rates decreased but were given a handsome package of options keyed to product delivery and performance. This encouraged many who otherwise held out hopes of scoring big in another start-up to stick around and see their products to market. In another case, human resource managers in a real estate combination developed a kind of flex-pay program whereby sales people could put a greater or lesser proportion of their pay into cash, fringe benefits, stock options, and a pool of so-called risk capital to be paid out as bonuses.

Whatever compensation fits the strategy behind the combination, rewards must be timely. Waiting for the annual performance evaluation cycle to kick in is probably too late. Some short-term performance evaluation and reward systems help monitor and shape behavior as the organization moves from the old to the new. Otherwise, the norms and practices that were rewarded in the precombination organization—and are still being measured and reinforced through the precombination performance evaluation system—will prevail and people will have little incentive to contribute to transition activities or adopt new behaviors. Increasingly, firms are establishing special short-term reviews and rewards. After the merger of two professional services companies, one-time-only three-month and six-month performance reviews were conducted. Employees were told at the onset of the combination that their payouts from these reviews would be based on a formula integrating the extent to which they abided by key operating principles as well as their progress on regular performance targets.

## When Is a Merger Over?

At seminars and workshops, we are frequently asked, "How do you know when a merger is over?" There is no clear marker indicating when the postcombination phase ends. Sometimes a senior executive pronounces, "I'm tired of hearing about the merger already!" In other cases, a combination "ends" when the next deal is made and people start all over again at the precombination phase. Perhaps the most fulfilling indicator that a productive combination is ended is when people look up from their desks, machines, computers, or papers and sense that things around them have changed for the better. As individuals, they have received some gain for all the pain they feared or actually experienced; as team members, they are part of a group that is performing to expectations and embracing new methods; and as part of a new organization, they are proud of its culture and confident of its ability to perform in the marketplace today and in the future. Employees see that putting one plus one together has led to an organization greater than the sum of its parts. As the next chapter reports, successful combinations that build productive value take on a commitment to learning throughout the combination process—to improve current practice and preparation for the next one!

# Part Five

# Reaping the Rewards of Productive Combination

## Chapter Eleven

# Tracking and Learning from the Combination

Putting organizations together to create something more than the sum of their parts depends upon learning: how to translate theoretical synergies into real gains, how to recognize and deal with unintended consequences spawned by well-intended actions, how to capitalize on various approaches to managing a combination, how best to help people respond to stressful situations, and how to deal personally with change and ambiguity. Of course, some of the learning comes from trial-and-error. But effective learning requires front-end insight and a theory of the case, ongoing examination of progress and problems, and a context that is supportive of learning by doing.[1]

In typical combinations, the political climate prompts people to hide or ignore issues and miscues; people cover up the results of their actions out of fear that they may result in a long-lasting blemish on their record. *In successful combinations,* by comparison, missteps are treated as inevitable and as opportunities for learning. In these cases, not learning from a mistake is frowned upon. This developmental orientation toward changes comes from the early actions of leaders, in prepping managers for the rough road and modeling the process of learning from one's own actions. It also takes commitment of financial and human resources to promote learning, and the discipline to pull back from the combination process to observe dynamics, draw valid conclusions from them, and respond accordingly.

## Knowing What Is Going On

Joining forces effectively benefits not just from skilled management but also from *informed* management. Combinations have the potential to affect employee morale and productivity, work processes and quality, group and intergroup relationships, customer service and satisfaction, and practically every other aspect of organizational life. Even so, relatively few companies formally assess how the combination is going or solicit systematic feedback from managers and employees. Successful navigation through a complex organizational transition requires a constant flow of operational and behavioral data: information about how the business is performing and how people are acting and feeling. This information helps managers monitor the impact of the combination and the effectiveness of the process. It also directs attention and resources to the issues that matter most in eventual success.

Of course, most managers think they know what is going well and what isn't.[2] But when they consult exclusively with their peers and direct reports, what they hear is often censored and self-serving. This gives them a distorted picture of progress and false assurance that problems will pass so long as they stay the present course. Months later, the picture is clearer: transition trauma hits the bottom line, and executives have no recourse but to move into damage control.

Even in organizations having a good communications climate in normal conditions, a combination upsets regular methods of intelligence gathering and two-way information exchange.[3] People put on their poker faces and keep their cards close to the vest. Trust has yet to develop in the new organization, and people do not know the consequences of speaking up. Does the messenger get shot? Will a critical comment come back to haunt you when pending staffing decisions are made? Will a new boss and new peers feel betrayed by an employee's honest reports about problems in her emerging work team?

The critical mass of uncertainty and anxiety in the combination impairs perception and judgment. Although a moderate amount of stress increases people's vigilance in gathering information, a high level leads many to simplify and distort what they hear. Wishful hearing abounds. Even among the best listeners, there can be information overload. Receptive executives get an abundance of bad news from the ranks. Staying alert to all of the ways the combination is affecting their operations, customers, employees, and reputations, while concurrently attempting to run a business, taxes executives' cognitive capacities. As a result, important information is often overlooked or misinterpreted.

## Benefits of Combination Tracking

Several organizations we've worked with have reaped assorted benefits from a formal program to track the progress of a combination:[4]

- *Determining if the combination is proceeding according to plan or veering off course.* A formal tracking program provides decision makers with feedback on how the combination is affecting people and the business. In one case, interviews revealed that unclear work charters, timetables, and financial targets were preventing task forces from coming to decisions about the design of combining units. When briefed on the problems, however, the CEO met with each task force to clarify their situation.

- *Identifying hot spots before they flare out of control.* In one manufacturer, the secrecy of precombination negotiations created an air of distrust between employees and management. An attitude survey, conducted a few months following the firm's acquisition, showed morale eroding among production workers. Attributing this to "postmerger stress," management initially downplayed the data. However, when follow-up interviews showed that employees felt neglected by management and were agitating for union representation, senior management moved swiftly to open communication channels and respond to aggrieved employees.

- *Ensuring a good flow of upward communication.* Bad news seldom rises to the top of an organization. An effective tracking program gives employees the chance to communicate to upper management and provides a mechanism for top echelons to hear from those closest to the action. Often managers are dismayed to learn of the discrepancy between actions and words. In one case, for example, management of two combining salesforces ballyhooed the benefits of each partner's cross-selling the other's products. Salespeople were eager but had outdated sales literature, no demos, and no idea what to charge customers or when deliveries could be made. Busy with all the paperwork involved in processing employee transfers, setting up office space, and servicing existing orders, sales managers pushed these complaints aside. Once senior management learned of these problems through focus group interviews, however, they said "screw the bureaucracy," and sales aids soon flowed to the branches.

- *Highlighting needs for midcourse corrections.* Tracking lets executives assess the impact of change and make important midcourse corrections. An East Coast publishing firm had hoped within one year to consolidate the operations of two fiercely competitive midwestern firms recently acquired. Tracking showed that bad blood between the two acquirees could not be overcome without a "bloodletting." Needing executive talent from both companies, the responsible parent company executive decided to keep the two subsidiaries separate for a time. Revised plans called for gradual integration over a three-year period.

- *Demonstrating interest in the human side of change.* A tracking program also has tremendous symbolic value: it is a tangible reminder to employees that their leaders care about them and their opinions. Asking people how the combination has affected them, their coworkers, and their ability to perform demonstrates that management is interested in the human side of change.

- *Involving more people in the combination process.* A tracking program is a cost-efficient way to involve large numbers of employees in the combination process. Entire workforces or select samples can participate in surveys and interviews. In the Chemical Bank–Manufacturers Hanover merger, leadership commissioned a survey process that lasted throughout combination planning and implementation. Each quarter, a sample of employees received questionnaires focusing on key issues at that point in the combination process. Results were tabulated for the overall organization and key business units and found their way onto the top management agenda.

- *Sending a message about the postcombination culture.* How the combination is managed starts to define the new organizational culture. A formal tracking program signals the importance of two-way communications and conveys management's genuine interest in people's problems and perspectives. By comparison, the absence of any formal feedback channels can imply that management doesn't give a damn about what people think or feel.

## What to Look for

Combination tracking diagnoses both what is going on and how people feel about things. Tracking assesses progress in the combination process, such as the extent to which schedules and budgets are on target; ultimately, it contributes to answering the question of whether the combination is meeting its strategic objectives and financial and operational goals. Tracking also measures the impact of the transition on current morale and expectations for the emerging organization. Effective tracking programs zero in on the specific dynamics in each phase of a combination.

Early in the combination process, tracking tests for the extent to which people understand the purpose and promise of the combination and are affected by it:

- Is the rationale underlying the deal understood?
- Is the vision clear? attainable? energizing?
- Are the CSFs clear?
- What business benefits are anticipated in the combination?
- What personal benefits are anticipated in the combination?
- What signs of the merger syndrome are people experiencing?
- How are morale and productivity being affected?
- What messages is leadership sending?
- Do management's actions align with their words?
- Do people feel well informed about the combination process and progress?
- Does the full management team seem in sync regarding the combination?
- Are managers at all levels taking steps to minimize negative reactions and build positive feelings?
- What early impressions are being formed of the partners' ways of doing things?
- Are cultures clashing?

Then in the combination phase, tracking focuses on the quality of planning and decision making:

- Are the CSFs being adhered to?
- Are operating principles being followed?
- Are participants being pushed for the best possible solutions?
- Are new and better ways of doing things being considered, or are the old ways being carried forward?
- Are task force members getting the information and other resources they need?
- Are politics and favoritism influencing the decision-making process?
- Are task forces coordinating well with one another?
- Do people outside the process feel well informed?
- Do managers have sufficient information to give their people a clear picture of where, when, why, and how changes will be occurring?
- Are staffing decisions based on valid criteria?
- Is a truly better organization emerging?

Finally, as implementation proceeds in the postcombination phase, tracking assesses the extent to which people are prepared to make their contribution to the postcombination organization:

- Do people understand their new roles and responsibilities?
- Are reporting relationships clear?
- Do people have the information they need or know where to go to get it?
- Do people understand new policies and procedures?
- To what extent are new systems running efficiently and effectively?
- Do people have the equipment and resources they need?
- What is valued and rewarded in the new organization?
- Have the CSFs truly been followed in implementation?
- Are schedules on target, and are changes being effectively implemented?
- What are the business benefits of the postcombination organization?
- What are the personal benefits of the postcombination organization?
- Are managers being given the resources and support needed to reorganize their departments and rebuild capability?
- Is a one-company mind-set being developed, or are cultures clashing?

- Is teamwork being developed in work groups?
- Is teamwork emerging across work groups?
- Has a new and better organization been built, or are the pre-combination ways being carried forward?
- What new or unanticipated issues are emerging?

## Gathering Helpful Data

For information to be helpful in managing a combination, it has to be valid, timely, and focused on the critical issues that relate to eventual success. Transition leaders have to honestly assess the extent to which they can collect valid data from managers and employees. Information gathering that generates fallacious data is a waste of time and, importantly, misdirects focus from critical areas requiring attention. Moreover, the volume of data available in a combination is enormous and can overwhelm even the most capable of leaders.

The extent to which people are candid in responding to tracking questions very much depends on the prevailing levels of trust within and between the combining organizations. Keep in mind that even in precombination cultures characterized by high trust and open communications, a combination thrusts people into a mode of insecurity. Therefore, many executives rely on outsiders to conduct tracking programs, especially in the early months of a combination. Employees are more likely to speak candidly to an outsider than to an internal professional, especially if that internal person comes from the other side. If resources are available to conduct tracking internally—that is, if internal staff has the skill and the time—then a prudent approach is to have external consultants initiate the tracking process and build its credibility by ensuring that confidentiality is protected and that results are used. Once employees see that there are no personal repercussions for speaking up and that the input is indeed influencing combination management, then responsibility for running the tracking process can be turned over to internal staff.

One potentially sticky situation is when an external resource has been working with one of the partners prior to the combination and is asked to assist in combination tracking. People from the other side may hesitate at opening up to someone who is perceived as a spy or, at the least, having a bias toward the other organization. We know of one consultant, an extremely able practitioner, who had been coaching a CEO in the high-technology industry for three years. After making a major acquisition, the CEO sent him into the target firm to assess early impressions of the combination. He simply was ineffectual in overcoming target management's fears and suspicions about his intent and allegiance. Given the value of collecting and using valid data in a combination, executives are well advised to be as conservative as possible in ensuring that a climate of trust permeates the tracking process. The high-technology CEO ultimately brought in a truly independent consultant to assist in the combination.

A variety of methods can be used to collect data about a combination. Certainly there are distinct advantages to, for example, interviews versus employee surveys (depth versus breadth of opinion) and focus groups versus informal conversations (more structure versus spontaneity). Good tracking programs rely on multiple methods of data gathering:

- *Attitude surveys.* An entire workforce can be surveyed, or, alternatively, particular groups can be targeted or a cross section of the organization sampled. For a survey effort to be successful, employee participation should be voluntary (people cannot be forced to share their true beliefs) and anonymity must be ensured. This means keeping individual surveys strictly confidential.
- *Interviews.* Confidential interviews allow employees to expand on their opinions, offer detailed explanations, and provide examples. Interviews should be relatively unstructured when general information is desired or guided by a set of questions when specific data are needed. Interviews take time, usually at least an hour to conduct and an equal amount of time to analyze and consolidate results. Thus, care needs to be taken to select interviewees who truly represent the sentiments of the broader workforce. When collecting companywide data, it is useful to sample a mix of employees who are both supporters and critics of the combination; who come from multiple levels; and who represent various departments, divisions, and locations. It also helps that interviewees be reasonably articulate and forthright, people who speak up whether they are in favor of the combination or critical of it.
- *Focus groups.* These are interviews conducted with groups of employees. They save time by getting anywhere from two to

ten people to respond to questions about the combination. They also let participants build upon one another's responses. In a climate of low trust, people may clam up in focus groups. The facilitator must be skilled to elicit true feelings and, as well, to prevent focus groups from degenerating into bitch sessions.

- *Observation and informal conversation.* Managers can also assess the state of their combination by observing and informally chatting with supervisors and employees. Management by walking around, conversations in hallways, and after-work bull sessions all provide occasions for gathering data about a combination. Managers also can keep an eye out for combination-related graffiti, cartoons, underground newsletters, e-mailings, and such. They provide a good indicator of true sentiment.

- *Records.* Many corporate reports and records contain combination-relevant data. Records of turnover, absenteeism, grievances, accidents, and the like are good metrics of morale in the combination. Tracking customer orders, productivity levels, quality control, waste, and the like before, during, and after a combination can be useful in evaluating progress and spotting problems.

- *Exit interviews.* Interviews conducted with people leaving (during or soon after a combination) can be used to find out what, if any, aspects of the transition influenced decisions to seek employment elsewhere. If a repetitive pattern is found, action can be taken to address the causes of voluntary turnover.

- *Industry benchmarks.* Sometimes a good measure of a combination's progress comes from comparing it to others in the same industry. American Century and Benham executives prided themselves on successfully merging their recordkeeping systems in fifteen months, which is commendable considering that managers in another mutual fund combination spent four years attempting to integrate their shareholder services before giving up.

There will always be some resistance to combination tracking. In the precombination phase, managers fret that nothing positive has happened yet, so employees will only cite the downside if asked their opinion of the combination. During the combination phase, they object on the grounds that the time taken to collect, analyze, feed back, and work with data detracts from attending to business opportunities. In the postcombination phase, managers claim that it is too soon to assess employee attitudes, saying that their organization and people have not yet settled into a normal routine. These arguments have some validity. But managers' resistance clearly may be motivated by fear of being assessed or by recollections of previous poorly managed employee data-collection activities. It is important, then, that a developmental tone be set in guiding the tracking and that it be conducted in a manner that engages managers and their teams in truly understanding and using the results. The data are being collected to understand and focus on key issues influencing combination success, not to be used as a scorecard sizing up individual managers.

## Tracking Customers

Customers are another source of helpful data in a combination. Productive gains in a combination can be thwarted when customers do not understand the rationale or benefits of the combination and leave. Competitors take advantage of any perceptions of uncertainty, instability, or problems in quality or delivery in order to woo customers. As testimony to the disappointing results of typical combinations, many customers routinely line up alternate sources when they learn that a supplier is engaged in a combination.

Consultant Mark Feldman tells the story of a combination between two large high-technology companies in the Silicon Valley whose customers were among the biggest names in the business.[5] Three months into the postcombination organization, one of their largest customers, IBM, sent notice that it was cutting its orders in half and going to secondary sources of supply. Why? IBM said that, in the three months that had passed since the deal became legal, not one person had thought to call and talk about what would happen to the account in the postcombination organization. The account was worth millions and IBM shut down half of it, not because of any problem in supply or quality but because of a lack of attention.

Contrast this experience with that of an industrial products firm that carefully managed customers throughout the combination process. Executives expected that customers, just like employees, would weigh first impressions of the combined operation heavily and be apt to draw hasty conclusions regarding what it would be like to work with the postcombination organization. Immediately upon the combination announcement, sales representatives in the combining companies received communication guidelines and instructions to contact all of their customers. Senior executives telephoned or visited key accounts to review the rationale for the combination and to provide assurance that the customers' needs would be considered every step of the way. With a positive story to tell (featuring ways customers could benefit from new technology, a broader product mix, and reduced costs in the combined organization), executives got their message across to customers.

The firm also used the combination planning phase to solicit and utilize feedback from customers. Key contacts were invited to join a "preferred customer council." At monthly meetings, senior sales executives presented updates on combination planning and solicited input on matters pertaining to products and customer service. Other customers received a toll-free telephone number to offer their views or ask questions. It proved especially valuable when several customers called to question false reports being spread by a competitor about the elimination of some key product lines in the combined company. Having timely information from customers allowed sales executives to respond quickly and stave off any major damage.

A senior marketing executive from the industrial products firm put a positive spin on the merger's impact on customers: "This is great—it gives us a reason to contact our customers and an opportunity to sell them on why we are the ones to keep their business with."

## Learning . . . for Now and for the Future

A merger, acquisition, or alliance is a ripe opportunity for organizational learning—the ability to gain insight from experience. When learning-efficient organizations engage in a combination, they comprehend what works, what doesn't, and why. These organizations examine their overall strategy in relation to what is learned and incorporate new learning into their current and future combination activities.[6]

The reality today is that most organizations—and their people—will be involved in more than one combination. In one company we worked with, initial tracking revealed a strong fear among executives that their CEO would make another deal before the current acquisition was digested. Increasingly, organizations are interested in building an internal competence in combination management, to better manage both the current combination and future ones.

In the short run, this means quickly diffusing insights gained during implementation so that many can benefit from the lessons of a few. Obviously, reflection and interpretation provide feedback to planners as they move through the combination process and to executives and managers as they implement changes. Lessons learned by one manager or group, however, can be extracted and disseminated to others in the organization. This is especially helpful when implementation is staggered through the organization; managers in areas yet to experience changes can benefit from the hard lessons learned elsewhere. Some organizations sponsor formal learning forums; others create informal opportunities for managers to get together, mingle, and share their experiences. Both formats are extremely helpful, but they require a tone that recognizes that all combinations experience missteps, and that it is better to learn from them rather than push them under the rug.

Organizations with the most effective combination programs have gotten there by learning from past mistakes as well as successes. The California-based HMO PacifiCare made thirteen acquisitions of small and mid-size organizations between 1993 and 1996. After each acquisition, the executive team members asked themselves, "What have we learned, and what would we do differently?" One of the first actions taken when PacifiCare acquired a major competitor, FHP, Inc., was to pull out their list of lessons learned. Yet the PacifiCare executives did not follow the learnings with blind obedience. Rather, they recognized this $9 billion, four-million member acquisition was in a different league from their previous combinations and took the time to consider which lessons should and should not be applied to the FHP case. This is in stark contrast to the many organizations that develop a lockstep approach to combination management and do not question strict adherence to it until after a disastrous combination failure.

Anticipating a wave of acquisitions and alliances in their industry, leadership of a consumer products organization wanted to learn how to enhance its combination management approach. At a debriefing session, executives candidly assessed what worked and what didn't in a recently completed acquisition. Exhibit 11.1 reports

# Exhibit 11.1. Lessons Learned from a Successful Combination.

**Things we did right:**

Appointed a dedicated transition manager

Formed an Integration Team

Speedy decisions (thus shorter disruption period)

Appointment of Management Team by deal closing date

Decision to expand Management Team during transition

Aggressive employee communications program

External consultant working with Management Team and key staff

Managing Team driving structural integration (enhanced accountability and commitment)

People selection and outplacement process

Attention to details of major announcements, like headquarters location

Launch of postcombination vision and mission statement on one year anniversary of deal closing

**Things we could have done better:**

The Integration Team was under-resourced (not enough people)

Speedy decisions led to less analysis and some bad decisions

Committee approach to politically charged decisions like headquarters location

Better manage employee expectations (winners acting in a dominating way, losers acting in a passive way)

Not enough hands-on leadership presence

Underestimated the impact of cultural differences

Defining our expectations of staff groups and business regions to fully integrate business

Had no plan for educating ourselves on each other's products

Senior managers from lead company did not do as well as expected in overcoming culture clash

Pay more attention to field sales force

Pay more attention to undisturbed sites (although they were not directly changed, they resisted cooperating with changes in other areas)

Not be so naive as to believe what the investment bankers told us about sales synergies in the first year; underestimated disruption to business

**Therefore, we would do the following differently:**

Establish a larger Integration Team

Manage expectations from Day 1 and give clearer directions to senior management from lead company

Make site decisions by management and not by committee

Push more aggressively for some balance between the partners in all functions

"Select the best people while achieving the best balance"

Provide cultural integration training to broader organization, not just Management Team some of the lessons learned in this combination of two former competitors. By all accounts, it succeeded in financial and strategic terms. Yet, these executives identified several things they would do differently. The team did not beat itself up, however, recognizing that everything looks clear with hindsight and that some lessons simply have to be learned the hard way in the combination game.

The observations from this case illustrate just how challenging combination management is. One major learning was that even well-intentioned actions in a combination can backfire and result in caustic consequences. For example, the principle of choosing the best person for the job regardless of precombination affiliation guided the staff-selection process. Picking people no matter where they came from, however, resulted in some operational units' being made up entirely of people from only one partner. This was especially problematic in units completely staffed with people from the target company. They had been accustomed to a hands-off leadership style in their precombination organization and had no "internal guides" to help them navigate the maze of new procedures and practices in the postcombination organization; nor could they contend with the relatively high involvement style of their new president. The acquired executives had trouble gaining access to the informal social and communication networks of the new organization and encountered problems in simply getting the job done through normal channels. Conversely, no one from the acquired partner received positions in a few key staff departments at the new company's headquarters, resulting in a lack of awareness of and sensitivity to the issues acquired executives contended with in the field. The lesson learned for the next combination: "Select the best people while achieving the best balance."

Other learnings from this case underscore the tenacity of combination-related activity. Some of the operational areas in the lead company were untouched by the combination. Leadership assumed they did not need to attend to people in these functions; instead, they focused all their attention on those in areas being integrated. This proved to be a problem, as managers from the unaffected areas acted in a domineering manner when dealing with acquired executives and strongly resisted cooperating with implemented changes made in other parts of the organization. The behavior of these lead company managers added to culture clash and other tensions between the parties. In the next combination, senior executives vowed to have all managers attend transition management sensitization seminars whether or not their functions are directly affected by combination changes.

This particular lesson reflects the difficulty of putting two complex organizations together so as to generate some productive gain. Here, executives burdened by the dual demands of running a business while combining operations logically thought that they did not have to attend to areas of their company that seemingly were unaffected by the combination. To their surprise, friction between the "unaffected" managers and those directly impacted by the combination created significant problems. Yet, it also demonstrated the power of productive combination to enhance organizational life. Historically in the precombination organization, conflicts between operating groups were left unattended, allowed to fester, and then treated as untouchable rather than confronted directly and promptly. As part of what it gained from the combination, this organization embraced the process of identifying issues and addressing them promptly. The leaders of the supposedly unaffected function were quickly taken to task and required by their president to rebuild strained relations with combination partners. This drastic departure from the precombination way of doing things was as powerful as any executive speech or company policy in reinforcing the new postcombination culture in the eyes of the overall workforce.

This is the essence of productive combination: acknowledging the challenge of putting two complex organizations together, learning from the missteps while mining the opportunities, and building some productive gain that is not present in the precombination organizations to create both short-term benefits and longer-term organizational effectiveness.

## Chapter Twelve

# Joining Forces— Best Practices

Those who lead, assist, study, or simply write about combinations use many metaphors and genres to characterize the goings-on: the old west (shoot-outs); the high seas (piracy); chivalry (knights and damsels); warfare (raids and rescues); medicine (surgery); family (parent and child, sibling rivalry); and of course courtship, love, and marriage.[1] One way or another, they all speak to why combinations occur and how they play out. James Doughan, CEO of Abitibi-Consolidated, described the integration process this way to his senior team: "Managing a merger is a lot like killing a moose. The hunt is fun. But then, you have the dirty, smelly work of gutting, cleaning, and preparing the carcass."

As colorful and apt as these images may be in a specific case, what we often see in combination is "creative destruction"—the workings of capitalism as so well described by Joseph Schumpeter. Individual careers and corporate identities can indeed be destroyed in combinations, and corporate cultures and functions "gutted" during integration. At the same time, something new and of value can be created. Combinations produce new opportunities for people and businesses, yield new ideas and ways of doing things, and create organizations with new identities and cultures. When one plus one equals three, capitalism is working at its best.

## People Matter

Make no mistake: people matter in combinations and can make or break the results of a combination of firms. Certainly success depends on sensible strategies and financial acumen. But it also depends on people-minded management of the transition process and on winning over employees' hearts and minds to a new way of doing business. Frankly, much of the pain in a combination is created in people's minds, references to barbarism and battles notwithstanding. Still, as many executives in the midst of integration lament, perception is reality. A combination breeds uncertainty, unrealistic expectations, misperceptions, stereotypes, and anxieties, all of which are exacerbated by legal restraints, executive inattention, exhausting workloads, and crisis-management practices that result in constricted and pro forma communications.

People have legitimate questions and concerns at each stage of a combination:

|  | *Precombination* | *Combination* | *Postcombination* |
| --- | --- | --- | --- |
| Issue: | Insecurity | Uncertainty | Adaptation |
| Concerns: | What will happen to me? | What's going on around me? | Am I ready to perform? |
|  | How do I cope? | Who's looking out for me? | How do I succeed here? |
|  | Who are they? | Who's in control? | Is the new better than the old? |

As early speculation and rumors climax in the formal announcement of a merger, acquisition, or alliance, people wonder what will happen to themselves and their jobs, coworkers, leaders, and company identity. They worry that their track record will count for nothing to new bosses and that they'll have to prove themselves all over again. Most employees don't know much about their partner organization, and even less about their specific counterparts. Fearing a loss of control over their fate, they search (often futilely) for information that helps them make sense of and cope with their situation.

As companies move into the integration phase, uncertainty further envelops people. Many have characterized this phase as "mushroom" management: people are kept in the dark, covered with manure, and then canned! Even when management has good intentions about partnering, most people do not know who, if anybody, is representing them in deliberations or what will come out of the combination process. They question what their prospects are and whether they will even have a job. With few details forth-coming from official sources, employees have to base their views on rumors, uninformed speculation, worst-case scenarios, and what they heard from who they talked to last.

Contrary to the promises of stress-management pamphlets and change-management programs, not everybody survives and thrives in corporate upheaval; many feel like victims and do not let go of insecurity and anger once they learn of their status in a combination. Even if people retain the same position or a similar one, their work situation may change substantially. Now they must contend with new leaders, team members, work systems, or day-to-day procedures. They have to grope to gather information, master new work methods, and build new networks to perform their jobs. Many times, employees do not even know what is expected of them or how their success will be measured. Ultimately, they ask themselves whether anything new and better has come of combination; has the pain resulted in any true gain?

These human dynamics occur in even the most successful and value-creating combinations. A combination founded on a sound strategy and financials still depends on people to conceive, plan, and implement actions to produce synergies. Asking people to be part of a new and better organization implies, at some level, giving up the old. Even when there's little objective change in their situation, people often subjectively perceive shifts in accustomed norms and in their own frame of mind. Thus it is a requirement that the merger, acquisition, or alliance be managed such that the pain is acknowledged and addressed, while the gain is identified and realized.

## Joining Forces: Five Dimensions

People can never receive answers to all their questions in a combination; they can never get enough support to assuage all their anxiety. Given a critical mass of unknowns, an insatiable appetite for answers, and an overarching atmosphere of cynicism about corporate leadership, the best that senior management can do is make a solid case for the combination, plan it carefully, put the companies together sensibly, and reach out to people to get them involved and give them support. People's faith in leadership and confidence in the future grow when they see the combination being well managed. Their self-confidence is boosted, too, as their ability to cope with stress and adapt to change increases and as they are involved in building the new: generating ideas, working proactively with counterparts and customers, and living out the values and behavior of the desired culture.

What does it take to manage a combination effectively? Our experience and advice coalesce in five key areas in which to concentrate executive attention and resources over the course of a combination (Exhibit 12):

1. *Strategy.* Manage the combination with constant attention to its strategic goals.
2. *Organization.* Build a new and better organization.
3. *People.* Attend to the human element.
4. *Culture.* Use the combination to build a desired culture.
5. *Transition management.* Develop an effective transition structure and plan.

## Precombination Management

Actions taken—and not taken—in the precombination phase set a direction whereby a merger, acquisition, or alliance heads down a successful path or veers off toward failure. In this phase, management sets its growth objectives and business strategy and determines what kind of firm it wants to partner with, how, and why. It conducts a search, selects a partner, and negotiates a deal. To enhance the likelihood of a successful combination, management uses this period to prepare to join forces, strategically and psychologically.

### Strategy

Successful combinations begin with self-scrutiny and analyses that yield a conclusion that a company can realize strategic goals more realistically, rapidly, and/or cost-effectively through a combination rather than by acting on its own. This creates the basic rationale for scouting the marketplace with the intention of merging, acquiring, forming a joint venture, or making an alliance with another company. Fleshed out further, it also informs search criteria and is applied in screening candidates. As a partner is identified, strategy comes to life in preparing a business case for how the two parties will create value and in thoroughly analyzing potential costs and risks in putting the two together.

**Exhibit 12.1. Managing the Five Dimensions of a Combination.**

| | Precombination | Combination | Postcombination |
|---|---|---|---|
| **Strategy:** | Clarify strategy, rationale, and search criteria | Develop and follow vision and CSFs | Maintain executive oversight |
| **Organization:** | Conduct thorough screening and due diligence | Study opportunities to build a new and better organization | Align organizations, policies, practices, and groups |
| **People:** | Prepare people psychologically | Get the right people in place and onsite | Regroup individuals and build teams |
| **Culture:** | Respect the precombination cultures | Manage culture clash and culture building | Reinforce the desired culture |
| **Transition management:** | Know where you want to go . . . and what it takes to get there | Create and staff a transition structure to execute an integration program | Learn from this combination so as to better manage future ones |

### *Organization*

Companies have to organize themselves to buy and sell. On both sides, this means putting together a team that includes not only corporate staff and the CEO but also the executives who ultimately have to lead the combination. In addition to its obvious part in determining strategic and financial fit, thorough screening explores a partner's motivation for doing a deal, its culture, and the makeup of its people. Diligent due diligence, in turn, digs deep to understand if the values of the potential partners are compatible, if the bench strength exists to manage the combination while running the core business, if all parties are on the same wavelength on synergies and what it takes to combine, and if there is enough trust and chemistry to propel the combined operation into becoming more than the sum of its parts. Such diligence counters momentum and the rush to close, giving the parties a chance to get better acquainted—and when warranted, to back out gracefully.

### *People*

Good strategies do not necessarily produce good combinations. People have to be prepared psychologically for joining forces. Psychological preparation educates people about the mind-sets of winners and losers and readies them to meet and work with their counterparts. Seminars on the merger syndrome, guidelines on effective communication, and frank people-to-people discussions help employees to contend with the natural and expected concerns that arise early on and increase once integration starts.

### *Culture*

Combinations often upset traditional ways of doing things and can threaten prevailing beliefs and values on one or both sides of a deal. The precombination phase provides managers with time to learn more about their partners' cultures, begin to counter stereotypes and misperceptions, raise and discuss genuine differences, and look for and solidify similarities. Even when one side more or less dominates a combination, the lead partner can show respect for the other's culture and explain why they choose to implement their own ways. We recommend, in any case, that the two sides carefully consider cultural differences when setting integration timetables.

### Transition Management

Unfortunately, many organizations waste the period between the announcement of a sale and its legal close. During this time, executives can begin to identify the optimal points of integration between firms, define a desired cultural end state, and prepare for the grueling work of forming transition teams to identify synergies and implement change. They also need to think through how to allocate executive time and talent to the combination. Meanwhile, preparations have to be made to ramp up communications (internally and externally), conduct training and sensitization workshops, and develop and implement retention and layoff policies.

## Combination Management

At the core of the combination is the integration program, designed to translate the opportunities of the combination into actual gains for the partner organizations. Management of the combination phase encompasses the same five dimensions.

### Strategy

A clear and agreed-to definition of synergies guides planning and decision making in successful combinations. This end state for the combination confronts wishful thinking, denial, and tendencies toward empire building and flank protection that derail combinations in which integration decisions are based on political agendas. It directs some of the energy that typically goes into politicking toward collaborative planning instead. The desired direction is expressed in an elaborated vision of where the combined organization is headed and clearly defined critical success factors that must be achieved along the way.

### Organization

An alignment of strategy and structure is integral to the success of a combination. This is what makes analysis of organizational fit so essential in defining how, where, and when to integrate the two companies. Managers from both sides assemble into fact-finding and transition management teams. Their charge is to exchange knowledge, build rapport, and plan for integration. Carefully launching transition teams, determining and adhering to operating principles, and facilitating and monitoring their work all result in decisions that support the desired organizational end state and achieve desired synergies, as well as offset the tendencies toward personal empire building, domination, and ineffective group dynamics that plague typical transition teams.

### People

Building the best possible organization rests on how well leadership identifies and retains talent from a partner in a merger or acquisition (or incorporates it into an alliance). This is accomplished through a staffing process that elucidates strategically sensitive selection criteria and provides opportunities for managers from one side to get to know people from the other. Doing so challenges executives to make staffing decisions based on meritocracy and with an eye on building a new business. Meanwhile, as complex decisions are being made regarding structure and staffing, managers attend to the merger syndrome, in themselves and in their people. Outreach efforts, ranging from formal communications to informal chats, remind people of both the commercial and personal possibilities of the combination.

### Culture

Making one plus one equal three generally implies that partners either draw from the best of both or use the combination to transform the work culture. As for cultural fit, the ideal is to have at least moderate distinctiveness between partners, provided the differences are a source of learning rather than rivalry. As the two sides prepare to integrate, it helps if the partners gain an appreciation of one another's traditions and mores and collaboratively decide which characteristics from their old cultures are worth retaining and which are incongruent with the new situation. Frequently, cultural characteristics not present in either partner may need to be developed as part of building a new and better organization.

### Transition management

Transition teams are often based in a larger transition structure that dedicates executive time and talent to overseeing integration and implementation of any changes. Pulling from both partners' best and brightest contributors in order to staff transition management roles sends a symbolic message that it matters how the combination is put together. Substantively, a transition structure directs the abilities of top performers into creative decision making to mine the opportunities in a combination. Behaviors modeled by executives and rules of the road followed in combination planning exert a substantial influence on the norms that are to prevail in the emerging postcombination organization.

## Postcombination Management

After months of gathering data, sifting and sorting it, and making integration decisions, people feel the pressure building to get on with implementation. Even though organization building begins, the foundations for a productive combination are not set in place unless conscientious and dedicated efforts are made to shore up desired changes.

### Strategy

Once functions are combined, some companies treat strategy as a seasonal activity—something you do in spring and review in the fall. A wiser course is to revisit strategy monthly (at least for a year or two) in light of the strengths and weaknesses found as combined businesses operate together. Furthermore, market conditions, opportunities, and challenges may have changed since the deal was done, necessitating concurrent changes in the overall strategy and structure of the combined business. Thus, as part of their business reviews or in sessions dedicated to this task, functional executives need to monitor results and identify areas that merit rethinking or rapid attention. Meanwhile, the senior management team should scrutinize progress vis-à-vis the CSFs and allocate resources as needed to move the combined business forward.

### Organization

The complexities of combining previously separate organizations require careful knitting. Transition teams may suggest where to put the stitches, but it is up to executives and their teams to bind things together. This requires full upward, downward, and lateral communication and cross-unit coordination. Successful integrators build time and checkpoints into implementation plans to ensure that departments and work units, policies and practices, and supervisors and subordinates align, and that, taken as a whole, the new organization reinforces the strategic purposes of the combination.

*People*

In companies that achieve success in their combination, winners are crowned appreciatively, losers let go of graciously, and survivors handled gracefully. People receive the space, support, and time needed to adapt to the transition, and they get help in letting go of the old, dealing with change, and moving on to the new. In this process, managers understand postcombination mind-sets and help their direct reports sort out what's happening around then. In turn, team leaders take proactive steps to build their teams through the stages of development and accelerate the melding of individual contributors through formal team-building interventions.

*Culture*

Once new teams and structures are in place, they need to be anchored in a new company philosophy and culture. Otherwise, the new will crumble and people will lose faith in and never identify with the combined business. Successful managers begin the work of culture building early on, knowing that their words and actions influence the attitudes, expectations, and behaviors emerging in the combined company. They build new cultures by design, rather than let them emerge inadvertently or by default. Senior executives, functional leaders, corporate staff specialists, and middle managers coordinate actions across multiple leverage points to reinforce and refreeze desired ways of doing things. Reward and information systems are revised to ensure that they contribute to the desired cultural end state.

*Transition management*

Increasingly, multiple mergers, acquisitions, and alliances overlap one another. Experienced leaders build an internal competence in combination management. They do this by embracing a learning orientation toward their efforts, engaging key executives and managers so as to learn what has and has not worked in the current combination and what lessons may be applicable to future ones.

## Learning from Combinations

There is no lockstep approach or one-size-fits-all methodology to building productive capacity in a combination. Even organizations that do an exemplary job of learning from their own combinations realize that they cannot apply the lessons to another one uncritically. Accordingly, they learn how to ask the right questions as they undertake new deals. For example, rather than generically assess attitudes and experiences among employees and managers, experienced combiners focus their tracking activities on the issues that matter most in each phase of a combination (Exhibit 12.2).

In the precombination phase, the key question senior leadership needs to ask regarding employees is "Do people see the productive value in a combination and understand its business and personal benefits?" The answer is found in the extent to which people understand the deal's rationale (its purpose, strategic and operating objectives, and sources of synergy); the answer also comes by assessing people's concerns about the downside and how they anticipate being affected by it. As planning and decision making proceed, the investigation shifts to, "Is a better organization emerging?" Here, the answer comes from assessing the quality of fact finding and decision making—the criteria being used, the dynamics in transition teams, the synergies that hold up to scrutiny— and by determining if a work culture is emerging by design or by default. Finally, in the postcombination phase, tracking reflects people's readiness to get to work: "Do employees have what they need to perform their work at desired levels?" This focuses on postcombination mind-sets, the extent to which people have the tools, information, technology, support, and resources required to do their jobs, and whether or not people find a well-aligned organization emerging after the combination.

## Conclusion

Although every combination is unique, lessons from past combinations alert and prepare executives, managers, and employees to approach their current merger, acquisition, or alliance more productively. This means:

- Understanding how difficult combinations are to manage, and thinking through their impact on organizations, people, cultures, business performance, and customers
- Recognizing and readying the resources required to manage the combination well
- Knowing what it takes to create synergy, and translating that into definitions of a desired culture, critical success factors,

**Exhibit 12.2. Learning from Each Phase in a Combination.**

|  | *Precombination* | *Combination* | *Postcombination* |
|---|---|---|---|
| **The issues:** | The extent to which people understand the purpose and promise of the combination | The quality of planning and decision making | The extent to which people are prepared to contribute to the new organization |
|  | The ways in which people anticipate being affected by the combination | The creation of a new organization by design or by default | The extent to which individuals, teams, departments, and functions are aligned |
| **The question:** | Are the benefits understood? | Is a better organization emerging? | Do people have what they need to get focused on work and perform at desired levels? |

operating principles, organization designs, and human resource management

When applied with an appropriate mix of creativity, leadership,
hard work, attention to detail, and good fellowship, this knowledge
enables companies to capitalize on synergies and make their combination work. One plus one can equal three when the process of
joining organizations has them identify and achieve their real synergies, attend to human and cultural realities, learn from actions
and make midcourse corrections, work toward partnership, and
build a core competence in combination management. It is much
easier to simply slam organizations together or have one side dominate the other; but those outcomes are considerably less rewarding to shareholders, customers, and employees. Achieving a
productive combination is a peak experience in the careers of executives, managers, and employees. Moreover, value-creating combinations not only leave the combined organization in a better
competitive position; they can also help rebuild employee spirit,
trust, and motivation.

The organizations that are successful and creative in today's
mergers, acquisitions, and alliances are the ones that will excel in
tomorrow's combinations. Indeed, given the rate at which organizations are joining forces, it is our belief that the ability to plan, ex-
ecute, and learn from a combination will itself become a core
competency that separates winners from losers in the years ahead.

# Endnotes

## Preface

1. Fulmer, R. "Meeting the Merger Integration Challenge with Management Development." *Journal of Management Development,* 1986, *5*(4), 7–16.
2. Kanter, R. M. "Transcending Business Boundaries: 12,000 World Managers View Change." *Harvard Business Review,* May–June 1991, 1511–66.
3. Personal communication from Robert Lynch, June 1996.
4. Ernst, D., and French, T. D. "Corporate Alliances: After the Honeymoon." *Wall Street Journal,* May 13, 1996, p. 22.

## Chapter One

1. Zweig, P. L. "The Case Against Mergers." *Business Week,* Oct. 30, 1995, pp. 122–130.
2. Feldman, M. L. "Disaster Prevention After a Merger." *Mergers & Acquisitions,* 1995, *30*(1), 31–36.
3. Cartwright, S., and Cooper, C. L. "Of Mergers, Marriage, and Divorce: The Issues of Staff Retention." *Journal of Managerial Psychology,* 1993, *8*(6), 7–10.
4. Bergquist, W., Betwee, J., and Meuel, D. *Building Strategic Relationships: How to Extend Your Organization's Reach Through Partnerships, Alliances, and Joint Ventures.* San Francisco: Jossey-Bass, 1995.
5. About 15 percent of mergers and acquisitions in the United States achieve their financial objectives, as measured by share value, return on investment, and postcombination profitability (American Management Association. *Course in Mergers and Acquisitions.* New York: American Management Association, 1997). Up to 75 percent of European mergers end in failure (Harper, J., and Cormeraie, S. "Mergers, Marriages, and After: How Can Training Help?" *Journal of European Industrial Training,* 1995, *19*(1), 24–29). A 1995 study of large combinations—deals valued at $500 million or more—showed that one-half destroyed shareholder value, 30 percent had minimal impact, and just 17 percent created shareholder returns (Zweig,

1995). Separate studies by McKinsey and Company and Coopers and Lybrand report that 70 percent of strategic alliances fail or fall short of expectations (Kanter, R. M. "Becoming PALs: Pooling, Allying, and Linking Across Companies." *Academy of Management Executive,* 1989, *3*(3), 183–193). Partners rate one-half of international alliances as outright failures, and two-thirds of cross-border alliances run into serious trouble within the first two years (Bleeke, J., and Ernst, D. "The Way to Win in Cross-Border Alliances." *Harvard Business Review,* Nov.–Dec. 1991, p. 127).

6. For studies of postcombination financial results, see Davidson, K. M. "Why Acquisitions May Not Be the Best Route to Innovation." *Journal of Business Strategy,* 1991, *12*(3), 50–52; Elsass, P. M., and Veiga, J. F. "Acculturation in Acquired Organizations: A Force-Field Perspective." *Human Relations,* 1994, *47*(4), 431–453; Hitt, M. A., Hoskisson, R. E., Ireland, R. D., and Harrison, J. S. "Effects of Acquisitions on R&D Inputs and Outputs." *Academy of Management Journal,* 1991, *34*(4), 693–706; and Lubatkin, M. H. "Mergers and the Performance of the Acquiring Firm." *Academy of Management Review,* 1983, *8*(2), 218–225.

7. Lewin, K. "Frontiers in Group Dynamics." *Human Relations,* 1947, *1*(1), 5–41.

8. Levinson, H. "Easing the Pain of Personal Loss." *Harvard Business Review,* 1972, *50,* 80–88.

9. Marks, M. L. *From Turmoil to Triumph: New Life After Mergers, Acquisitions, and Downsizings.* San Francisco: New Lexington Press, 1994.

**Chapter Two**

1. Zangwill, W. I. "Models for Successful Mergers." *Wall Street Journal,* Dec. 18, 1995, p. A19.

2. Bergquist, Betwee, and Meuel (1995).

3. Uchitelle, L., and Kleinfeld, N. R. "On the Battlefields of Business, Millions of Casualties." *New York Times,* Mar. 3, 1995, p. 1. Copyright © 1996 by The New York Times Company. Reprinted by permission.

4. Hunt, J. "Managing the Successful Acquisition: A People Question." *London Business School Journal,* Summer 1988, pp. 2–15.

5. Harper, J., and Cormeraie, S. "Mergers, Marriages, and After: How Can Training Help?" *Journal of European Industrial Training,* 1995, *19*(1), 24–29.

6. Marks, M. L., and Mirvis, P. H. "Merger Syndrome: Stress and Uncertainty." *Mergers & Acquisitions,* 1985, *20*(2), 50–55; Mirvis, P. H., and Marks, M. L. "Merger Syndrome: Management by Crisis." *Mergers & Acquisitions,* 1985, *20*(3), 70–76.

7. Janis, I. L. *Victims of Groupthink.* Boston: Houghton Mifflin, 1972.

8. Brockner, J. "The Effects of Work Layoff on Survivors: Research, Theory, and Practice." In B. M. Staw and L. L. Cummings (eds.), *Research in Organizational Behavior.* Vol. 10. Greenwich, Conn.: JAI Press, 1989.

9. Brockner (1989).

10. Quinn, J. B. *Intelligent Enterprise.* New York: Free Press, 1992.

11. McCreight and Co. *Ensuring Success with Mergers and Acquisitions.* New Canaan, Conn.: McCreight and Co., 1996.

12. Reynolds, L. "America's Work Ethic: Lost in Turbulent Times?" *Management Review,* Oct. 1992, pp. 20–25.

13. Feldman, M. "Disaster Prevention Plans After a Merger." *Mergers & Acquisitions,* 1995, *30*(1), 31–36.

14. In a survey of 177 combining companies, one-third reported increased workers' compensation costs over a fifteen-month period; one in five had increases of 50–100 percent. Head count declined 13 percent on average in 37 percent of the companies (William M. Mercer, Inc. "A Study of Worker Compensation Costs in Companies." Unpublished report. 1992).

15. Cartwright, S., and Cooper, C. L. "Organizational Marriage: 'Hard' Versus 'Soft' Issues?" *Personnel Review,* 1995, *24*(3), 32–42.

16. Kanter, D. L., and Mirvis, P. M. *The Cynical Americans.* San Francisco: Jossey-Bass, 1989.

17. Uchitelle and Kleinfeld (1996), p. 1.

18. Marks, M. L., and Mirvis, P. H. "Situational and Personal Factors Influencing Employee Response to Corporate Merger." Paper presented at the ninety-first annual convention of the American Psychological Association, Anaheim, Calif., 1983; Marks, M. L. "Organizational and Individual Response to Corporate Acquisition Impact." Dissertation, University of Michigan, 1981. (*Dissertation Abstracts International,* 42:9B, University Microfilms No. 82-4708).

## Chapter Three

1. Boucher, W. I. *The Process of Conglomerate Merger.* Washington, D.C.: Bureau of Competition, Federal Trade Commission, 1980.

2. Sirower, M. L. *The Synergy Trap.* New York: Free Press, 1997.

3. Conference Board. *Change Management: Strategic Alliances.* Report no. 1090-94. New York: Conference Board, 1994.

4. Lynch, R. P. *Business Alliance Guide.* New York: Wiley, 1993.

5. McCreight and Co. (1996).

6. *Diversification: A Survey of European Chief Executives.* New York: Booz, Allen, and Hamilton, 1985.

7. Anslinger, P. L., and Copeland, T. E. "Growth Through Acquisitions: A Fresh Look." *Harvard Business Review,* Jan.–Feb. 1996.

8. Jemison, D. B., and Sitkin, S. B. "Acquisitions: The Process Can Be a Problem." *Harvard Business Review,* 1986, *64*(2), 107–116.
9. Baker, H. K., Miller, T. O., and Ramsperger, B. J. "An Inside Look at Corporate Mergers and Acquisitions." *MSU Business Topics,* Winter 1981.
10. *Organizational Issues in Mergers and Acquisitions.* New York: Delta Consulting Group, 1995.

## Chapter Four

1. Handy, J. "How to Face Being Taken Over." *Harvard Business Review,* 1969, *47*(6), 109–111.
2. Kübler-Ross, E. *On Death and Dying.* New York: Macmillan, 1969.
3. Lewis, J. D. *Partnerships for Profit: Structuring and Managing Strategic Alliances.* New York: Free Press, 1990.
4. Conference Board. *Strategic Alliances: Guidelines for Successful Management.* Report no. 1028. New York: Conference Board, 1996.
5. Lynch, R. P. *Business Alliance Guide.* New York: Wiley, 1993.
6. Lazarus, R. S., and Folkman, S. *Stress, Appraisal, and Coping.* New York: Springer-Verlag, 1985.

## Chapter Five

1. Boucher, W. I. *The Process of Conglomerate Merger.* Washington, D.C.: Bureau of Competition, Federal Trade Commission, 1980.
2. Zweig (1995).
3. Harrigan, K. R. *Managing for Joint Venture Success.* Lexington, Mass.: Lexington Books, 1986.
4. Lavin, D. "Robert Eaton Thinks 'Vision' is Overrated and He's Not Alone." *Wall Street Journal,* Oct. 4, 1993, p. 1.
5. Collins, J. C., and Porras, J. I. *Built to Last.* New York: HarperBusiness, 1994.
6. Kanter (1989), pp. 183–193.
7. Marks, M. L. "The CEO's Mea Culpa." *Across the Board,* June 1995, pp. 36–40.

## Chapter Six

1. Jemison, D. B. *Process Constraints on Strategic Capability Transfer During Acquisition Integration.* Stanford, Calif.: Graduate School of Business, Stanford University, 1986.
2. Marks, M. L., and Mirvis, P. H. "Rebuilding After the Merger: Dealing with Survivor Sickness." *Organizational Dynamics,* Autumn 1992, pp. 8–33.
3. Hunt, J. W., Lees, S., Grumbar, J. J., and Vivian, P. D. *Acquisitions: The Human Factor.* London: London Business School Press, 1970.

4. Katzenbach, J. R., and Smith, D. K. *The Wisdom of Teams.* Cambridge, Mass.: Harvard Business School Press, 1992.
5. Blake, R. R., and Mouton, J. S. "How to Achieve Integration on the Human Side of Mergers," *Organizational Dynamics,* 1985, *13,* 41–56.

**Chapter Seven**
1. Bridges, W. *Managing Transitions.* Reading, Mass.: Addison-Wesley, 1991.
2. D'Aprix, R. *Communicating for Change.* San Francisco: Jossey-Bass, 1996.
3. Marks and Mirvis (1983); Marks, M. L. "Organizational and Individual Response to Corporate Acquisition Impact." *Dissertation Abstracts International,* 42:9B (University Microfilms, No. 82-4708).
4. Brockner, J. "Managing the Effects of Layoffs on Survivors." *California Management Review, 34*(2), 1992, 9–28.
5. *Organizational Frame Bending.* New York: Delta Consulting Group, 1988.

**Chapter Eight**
1. British Institute of Management. "The Management of Acquisitions and Mergers." Discussion paper no. 8. London: Economics Department, British Institute of Management, 1986.
2. Bolman, L. G., and Deal, T. E. "What Makes a Team Work?" *Organizational Dynamics,* Autumn 1992, 34–44.
3. Schein, E. *Organizational Culture and Leadership: A Dynamic View.* San Francisco: Jossey-Bass, 1985.
4. Sales, A. S., and Mirvis, P. H. "When Cultures Collide: Issues in Acquisitions." In J. R. Kimberly and R. B. Quinn (eds.), *Managing Organizational Transitions.* Burr Ridge, Ill.: Irwin, 1984.
5. Berry, J. W. "Acculturation as Varieties of Adaptation." In A. M. Padilla (ed.), *Acculturation: Theory, Models and Some Findings.* Boulder, Colo.: Westview Press, 1980.
6. Elsass, P. M., and Veiga, J. F. "Acculturation in Acquired Organizations: A Force-Field Perspective." *Human Relations,* 1994, *47*(4), 431–453.
7. *Making Mergers Work in the Financial Services Industry.* Cambridge, Mass.: Management Analysis Center, 1984.
8. Harper, J., and Cormeraie, S. "Mergers, Marriages, and After: How Can Training Help?" *Journal of European Industrial Training,* 1995, *19*(1), 24–29.

**Chapter Nine**
1. Schein (1985).
2. Senge, P. *The Fifth Discipline.* New York: Doubleday, 1990.

3.  Sales and Mirvis (1984).
4.  Marks and Mirvis (1983); Marks (1981).
5.  *Changing Organizational Culture.* New York: Delta Consulting Group, 1996.

## Chapter Ten

1.  House, J. S. *Work Stress and Social Support.* Reading, Mass.: Addison-Wesley, 1981.
2.  The concepts in this section are reported in more depth in Marks and Mirvis, "Rebuilding After the Merger" (1992), pp. 18–32.
3.  Harrison, R. "Role Negotiation: A Tough-Minded Approach to Team Development." In W. W. Burke and H. H. Hornstein (eds.), *The Social Technology of Organizational Development.* La Jolla, Calif.: University Associates, 1972.
4.  "Team Building Framework," New York, Delta Consulting Group, 1991; Nadler, D. A. *Designing Effective Work Teams.* New York: Delta Consulting Group, 1985.
5.  For a fuller discussion of venting meetings, see Marks (1994).
6.  Tannenbaum, R., and Hanna, R. W. "Holding On, Letting Go, and Moving On: Understanding a Neglected Perspective on Change." In R. Tannenbaum, N. Margulies, F. Massarik, and Associates (eds.), *Human Systems Development: New Perspectives on People and Organizations.* San Francisco: Jossey-Bass, 1985.

## Chapter Eleven

1.  Michael, D. *On Learning to Plan—And Planning to Learn.* San Francisco: Jossey-Bass, 1973.
2.  Argyris, C. *Learning in Action.* San Francisco: Jossey-Bass, 1993.
3.  Marks, M. L., and Mirvis, P. H. "Track the Impact of Mergers and Acquisitions." *Personnel Journal,* 1992, *71*(4), 70–79.
4.  Mirvis, P. H., and Marks, M. L. *Managing the Merger: Making It Work.* Upper Saddle River, N.J.: Prentice Hall, 1994.
5.  Feldman, M. "Disaster Prevention Plans After a Merger." *Mergers & Acquisitions,* 1995, *30*(1), 31–36.
6.  Marks, M. L., and Shaw, R. B. "Sustaining Change: Creating the Resilient Organization." In D. A. Nadler, R. B. Shaw, A. E. Walton, and Associates (eds.), *Discontinuous Change.* San Francisco: Jossey-Bass, 1995.

## Chapter Twelve

1.  Hirsch, P. M., and Andrews, J.A.Y. "Ambushes, Shootouts, and Knights of the Roundtable: The Language of Corporate Takeovers." In L. Pondy (ed.), *Organizational Symbolism.* Greenwich, Conn.: JAI Press, 1983.

# Index

Chase Manhattan, 124
Chemical Bank, 15–16, 72–73, 99, 112, 123–124, 156, 157, 183, 219, 221, 231, 260
China, 7, 206
Chrysler Corporation, 113
Ciba-Geigy, 7, 69–70, 115, 117
Cisco Systems, 50–51
Clayton Antitrust Act, 25
Clinton administration, 26
Collins, J. C., 114
Columbia University, 57
Combination: conceptual and practical underpinnings of, 19–23; and creation of value, 17–18; elusiveness in, 3–23; forms of, 9–12; gain versus pain in, 18–19; history of, 24–28; mismanagement of, 44–51; outcomes of, 12–17; phases of, 28–44; and productivity, 5–6; reasons for, 6–9
Combination phase: and culture clash, 187–210; and leadership, 111–136; problems in, 33–35; and stress management, 166–186; and transition structure, 137–165
Combination preparation: psychological area of, 82–108; strategic and operational areas of, 55–81. *See also* Precombination phase
Combination rationale: access to technology and other resources as, 7–8; consolidation as, 9; globalization as, 7; innovation and learning as, 8–9; operational flexibility as, 8; product and service diversification as, 6; resource sharing as, 9; risk sharing as, 7; vertical integration as, 6–7
Combination tracking: attention to customers in, 266–267; benefits of, 259–261; focus of, 261–263; gathering of helpful data in, 263–266; and informed management, 258–259; lessons learned in, 269; and organizational learning, 267–271. *See also* New organization

Commitment: from leadership, 90–91; and stress, 167–177
ComputerVision (CV), 124, 125, 138
Condit, P., 128
Conglomerate mergers, 25
Consciousness-raising workshops, 88–90
Consolidation, 9
Continuous change, 50
Cooper, C. L., 11
Cooperative competition, 4
Core values, 210
Corning Incorporated, 63
Corporate combination. *See* Combination
Corporate cultures: characteristics of, 193–194; in combinations, 187–190; and core values, 210; easing clash of, 195–196; integration of, 204–205; and international combinations, 205–209; levels of acculturation in, 200–205; managing change of, 194–195; of partner, 196–200; respect for, 196; stages of clash in, 190–191; and synergies, 202–205; winning and losing in, 191–193
Corporate raiders, 26
Corporate staff hegemony, 33
Critical success factors (CSFs), 116–117
Crocker Bank, 102
Cross-functional relations, 217–218
Culture building: ceremonies for, 208–209; by default, 226–227; by design, 227; on individual level, 224–227; leverage for, 227–230; training for, 232; at working level, 230–232
Culture clash. *See* Corporate cultures

**D**

D'Aprix, R., 174
Deal, T. E., 289
Deloitte and Touche (D&T), 8
Delta Airlines, 71
Dennison, 178, 179